PICKING UP THE PIECES

Picking Up the Pieces

*Can Evangelicals Adapt to
Contemporary Culture?*

David Hilborn

Hodder & Stoughton
LONDON   SYDNEY   AUCKLAND

Scripture quotations are taken from the HOLY BIBLE,
NEW INTERNATIONAL VERSION
Copyright © 1973, 1978, 1984 by International Bible Society
Used by permission of Hodder & Stoughton Ltd,
a member of the Hodder Headline Plc Group.
All rights reserved.
'NIV' is a registered trademark of International Bible Society.
UK trademark number 1448790.

First published in Great Britain in 1997

The right of David Hilborn to be identified as the Author of
the Work has been asserted by him in accordance with the
Copyright, Designs and Patents Act 1988.

1 3 5 7 9 10 8 6 4 2

British Library Cataloguing in Publication Data

A CIP catalogue record for this title is available
from the British Library

ISBN 0 340 67899 2

Typeset by Palimpsest Book Production Limited,
Polmont, Stirlingshire
Printed and bound in Great Britain by
Clays Ltd, St Ives plc

Hodder and Stoughton
A division of Hodder Headline PLC
338 Euston Road
London NW1 3BH

This book is dedicated to Mia, Matthew and Alice

CONTENTS

ACKNOWLEDGMENTS

It is said that, when recording their epic single 'Bohemian Rhapsody', the rock band Queen used so many overdubs that the master tape became translucent and almost snapped in two. The very ambition and scope which made the song distinctive were also the greatest threats to its completion. If Queen fans will forgive the comparison, there have been times when I have felt the same way about this book. It is daunting enough to take on a subject as vast and diverse as postmodernity; it is at least as daunting to write about something as complex as evangelicalism. Attempting to relate one to the other has stretched me far more than I could ever have anticipated, and there have been times when I wondered whether the whole thing might break up under the strain. That the project has been completed in the midst of a demanding London ministry is down to a number of people.

First and foremost, thanks are due to my wife, Mia. Not only has she supported me emotionally and domestically through the writing of this book; as my co-pastor at the City Temple, she has worked diligently to ensure the smooth running of the church while I have buried myself deep in the study. Thanks are also due to the elders and members of 'CT', who not only gave me the time and space to write, but prayed so faithfully for me as I did so.

My appetite for interdisciplinary study was whetted during research for my doctorate at Nottingham University. My supervisors there, Professor Anthony C. Thiselton and Dr Vimala Herman, were both inspirational figures with whom I had many helpful discussions about postmodernity. By its nature, this book is far more general and journalistic than my thesis. Nonetheless, I could not even have contemplated writing it if I had not done that Ph.D. first.

I am deeply grateful to Rob Warner for inviting me to undertake this task, and to Elspeth Taylor and Annabel Robson for being such sympathetic editors. Alison Entwistle and Simon Fairnington kindly read various drafts and suggested helpful amendments. The development of this book also owes an immense amount to those I interviewed for it, many of whose comments are quoted in the pages which follow. There were a lot of busy people in this group, and I have benefited enormously from their ideas and their time. The places and dates of the interviews were as follows: Jenny Baker (Youth For Christ, Victoria, London, 20th December 1996); Fran Beckett (Shaftesbury Society, Morden, 20th January 1997); Clive Calver (Swanwick Conference Centre, Derbyshire, 16th February 1997); Gerald Coates (Esher, Surrey, 6th December 1996); Graham Cray (Ridley Hall, Cambridge, 15th November 1996); Graham Dale (Evangelical Alliance, Kennington, London, 29th October 1996); John Drane (the City Temple, 13th December 1996); Brian Draper (Northwood, 12th December 1996); Alan Evans (Holme, 10th December 1996); Roger Forster (Beckenham, 7th November 1996); Rob Frost (Premier Radio, 20th October 1996); Tom Houston (Oxford, 2nd September 1996); David Jackman (Cornhill Training Course, Plantation House, City of London, 14th November 1996); R. T. Kendall (Westminster Chapel, 15th November 1996); Graham Kendrick (Bournemouth International Conference Centre, 11th November 1996); Nick Mercer (Pinner, 11th September 1996); Lesslie Newbigin (Herne Hill, London, 5th November 1996); Alan Rogers (Islington, London, 7th February 1997); Mike Starkey (the City Temple, 16th December 1996); Derek Tidball (London Bible College, Northwood, 14th November 1996); Dave

Tomlinson (Bedford Arms, Clapham, 7th November 1996); Rachel Viney (Independent Television Commission, Central London, 16th December 1996); Phil Wall (Salvation Army Mission Team HQ, Merton, 11th December 1996); Pete Ward (Oxford, 2nd December 1996); Martin Wroe (the City Temple, 20th December 1996). Background interviews were also conducted with Eddie Boon, Elaine Storkey and Jon Wensley; time did not permit transcription and direct quotation of their insights, but I hope to make more explicit use of them at a later date.

Of course, despite all the help I have had from others, I myself remain responsible for any errors of fact or interpretation.

David Hilborn
Pentecost 1997

FOREWORD

The communication of the gospel, as of any message, requires both an understanding of the message and an understanding of the mind of the one with whom we are seeking to communicate. Foreign missionaries have to learn the appropriate language and – if they do the job properly – will realise that in using that language they are implicitly accepting a whole range of assumptions embodied in it. They have to find the way between two dangers: by not properly understanding the culture of their hearers they may simply remain incomprehensible; but by seeking to enter deeply into that culture, they may let the message lose its sharp challenge and become too much at home in the culture. We have learned to call this the problem of contextualisation.

Evangelicals in modern Western culture have not been foreigners. They have been part of the culture. Or have they? In many respects they have (rightly) sought to challenge it. Yet, as David Hilborn shows, they have often been far more deeply embedded in and compromised by Western culture than they have realised. Like many other Christians, they have sought to speak the language of modern culture and have thereby sometimes become so domesticated within that culture that the sharp questions which the gospel puts to every human culture have been blunted. When St Paul said that the message of the cross is a scandal to Jews and folly to Gentiles he was saying something which remains true in respect of every human culture in which the gospel is preached.

But what is the culture in which we have *now* to communicate the gospel? Many analysts speak of the culture of contemporary Britain as 'postmodern', though others question the use of this term. 'Modernity' may be defined as that set of beliefs and practices which assumes that the methods of modern science provide us with the reliable public truth which can be the basis for public policy. 'Postmodernity' has been defined by one of its principal representatives as 'incredulity toward metanarratives'. Whereas modernity believed that there were truths which could be acknowledged by all as valid – a dependable account of the human story as a whole – postmodernity denies this and affirms diversity against claims for ultimate unity. It is possible, as some do, to regard this as simply the abandonment of the effort to think coherently about the world. It is also possible to regard it, as postmodernists do, as the proper and authentic way for us to relate to our environment. What is, I think, certain is that for a great many people – perhaps a majority – both modernity and postmodernity are elements co-existing in their ways of understanding the world.

David Hilborn's book is a very welcome guide through this complex and perplexing world. I am sure that for many evangelical readers, and for many others also, his careful analysis will illuminate the whole scene, help us recognise what is going on and show us the ways in which – no doubt with sincere pastoral and evangelistic intentions – we have allowed ourselves to be trapped in the assumptions both of modernity and postmodernity.

I have found this book helpful in opening my eyes to the hidden implications of much I had failed to notice in many areas of contemporary culture. I am sure that it will help Christian readers to examine their own thoughts and practices and to become more effective communicators of the gospel in this world so dominated by a constant rapid movement of ever-changing images. I hope this book will be widely read.

Bishop Lesslie Newbigin
June 1997

PART I

ASSESSING THE CHALLENGE

1

POSTMODERNISM IN EVANGELICAL PERSPECTIVE

Postmodernism: an Explosive Issue

I left home for good when I was twenty-four. I had been away to university and theological college, but the first place I could call my own was a council flat in Birmingham. My wife Mia and I moved there as part of our ordination training. I worked at a church in the city centre, while she served the surrounding estate. It was important for us to live in the community, but it was not easy. Our flat was on the third floor of a crumbling concrete block. There was a staircase, but no lift. Most of the time, it stank of stale urine. The rubbish chute was a good idea, but it was frequently jammed full. Burnt mattresses lay on the walkways as stray dogs scavenged for morsels of food. Often, the passageway lights were smashed in, and I feared for Mia walking home after dusk.

One day, a woman came to the front door with a petition. She asked us about the block, and then put a final question. If we could be re-housed in a new, low-rise flat, would we vote for the bulldozers to come in and demolish the lot? As it happened, we were due to leave soon after that, but apparently all but two of the residents voted for the destruction of their home.

In a way, they were making a postmodern statement . . .

But what, you may ask, is 'postmodern'? What does

it mean? One definition has been offered by the architectural critic Charles Jencks. Jencks traced the birth of postmodernism to St Louis, Missouri, at 3.32 p.m. on 15 July 1972.[1] This was the moment when the infamous Pruitt-Igoe housing scheme was finally blown up, having been vandalised, mutilated and defaced by its inhabitants. Despite the millions of dollars which were pumped in to keep its fourteen storeys functional, the cost of maintaining the broken lifts, shattered windows and peeling surfaces had proved too great. In the end, dynamite was the only solution.

In Britain, the name of Ronan Point has acquired a comparable status, referring as it did to a dreadful tower block condemned even earlier, in 1968. Fewer people have heard of my old flats in Birmingham, but that is only because, by the time they were demolished, so many like them had gone the same way. Jencks knew that Pruitt-Igoe was one failure among many, but he singled it out because it was constructed according to the most progressive ideals of the Congress of International Modern Architects, and because it won an award from the American Institute of Architects when it was designed in 1951. With its vertical 'streets in the air', its replacement of private yards and corner shops with communal spaces and amenities, and its 'purist' style, Jencks saw Pruitt-Igoe as having offered 'rational substitutes' for traditional patterns of community.[2] My flat was just a pale reflection of the same ideal.

Although his main focus was architecture, Jencks argued that the cool rationalism and uniformity of Pruitt-Igoe was a defining feature of the 'modern' approach in all branches of the arts and in many facets of social and economic life. The modern age, for Jencks, was above all 'an age trying to reinvent itself on purely rational grounds'. Its effects could be seen in all aspects of society, from 'rational schooling' and 'rational health' to the 'rational design of women's bloomers'.[3] It was the industrial age of mass production and mass municipal housing. Nonetheless, when rationalism alone proved unable to deliver, as in Pruitt-Igoe, this modern age began to break apart, and even to explode.

Postmodernism: a Big Issue for Evangelicals

But perhaps you are not convinced. If you are a Christian, maybe you are wondering what this strange word 'postmodernism' could possibly have to do with you. Not least if you are an *evangelical* Christian, you might well be questioning its relevance to the unchanging gospel of Christ. Perhaps you have barely heard of it. Perhaps you have come across it quite a bit, but are none the wiser. Perhaps, like the leading evangelical R. T. Kendall, whom I met in his office at Westminster Chapel, you think postmodernism is little more than 'a cliché'. Then again, perhaps you share the apocalyptic view of Graham Cray, Principal of Ridley Hall Theological College in Cambridge, who told me that 'if Christianity cannot be inculturated successfully within the postmodern context, there will be no Western church'.

As we shall see, the subject of postmodernism provokes different responses from Christians. Without doubt, though, it is very much with us. Even if it is only a cliché, it is a pervasive cliché. Even if it ends up amounting to little more than a lifestyle choice, it is likely to be around for some time to come. For evangelicals, as for everyone else, it needs to be dealt with. The trouble is, neat definitions of postmodernism are notoriously hard to produce.

The blurb for one of the many 'postmodern readers' now on sale claims that few concepts 'can have come charging out of the ivory tower of academia and into the public consciousness in the way that postmodernism has'.[4] This may be so, but the fact remains that even the experts have a tough time pinning postmodernism down. Walter Truett Anderson is one of its clearest exponents, but he still calls it a 'puzzling, uppity term'.[5] The Italian academic Umberto Eco is a world authority on it. He actually managed to write a best-selling postmodern novel, *The Name of the Rose*, which was turned into a successful film starring Sean Connery. Nonetheless, he has admitted that it often gets applied 'to anything the user . . . happens to like'.[6] The *Independent* newspaper summed things up cynically back in 1987 when it advised style-conscious readers: 'This word has no meaning. Use it as often as possible.'[7]

Such comments might lead you to doubt the importance of postmodernism. That, however, would be a mistake. Awkward as it is to distil, something is definitely going on here. It may resist pat one-line summaries, but its dominant themes do tend to emerge cumulatively – in the stories, dialogues and symbols of contemporary life. With this in mind, what follows is more than just theory. It is based on a good deal of 'field' research. It is the product not only of 'library' work, but also of interviews with twenty-five key figures in and around British evangelical Christianity. In addition, it includes 'case studies' on a number of issues and situations in which evangelical Christians have come up against postmodernism.

What this research will show is that, whether consciously or not, many evangelicals are *even now* beginning to engage with, and in some cases absorb, postmodern influences. In certain cases the interaction has been for the better; at times it has been for the worse; elsewhere, the results have been fairly neutral. Often it has happened for pragmatic reasons, and has gone largely unacknowledged. Even so, it will become clear that in several quarters, evangelicals are doing postmodern things in postmodern ways. For them, postmodernism is being caught as much as it is being taught.

I want to show that this 'missionary pragmatism' is not new, but is something which has served evangelicalism well throughout its history. That history, and the evangelical identity which has emerged from it, will be discussed more fully in Chapter 4. It is worth stressing from the outset, though, that evangelicals have long been distinguished by their desire to 'get on with it'. In a now classic definition, David Bebbington has summarised the core evangelical agenda as comprising personal conversion, biblical authority and the cross of Christ. Vitally, though, he also identifies as an evangelical essential the chief means by which those convictions are spread – namely *activism* or *pragmatism*.

Bebbington confirms that evangelicals are Christians who will get things done for God, whatever their cultural milieu.[8] More recently, the Oxford evangelical theologian Alister McGrath has shown how the conversionist imperative has made evangelicals typically pragmatic, and how this has often invited the scorn of more overtly intellectual Christian traditions.[9] Through it all, in the words of Os Guinness, 'pragmatism has become part of the evangelical soul'.[10]

I shall argue here that, despite its benefits, such evangelical pragmatism can obscure the need to reflect theologically on what is going on. Moreover, I want to stress that this could be particularly disastrous in a postmodern context. Why? Because the sheer pace and scope of change in the postmodern world is greater than in any previous age, and without due care and attention it could just as easily overwhelm evangelicals as buoy them along.

I am not the first evangelical to address the postmodern challenge, and I will not be the last. As we progress, it will become clear that a growing number of evangelical academics – many of them American – have begun to deal with this issue in some depth. All the same, there is a dearth of relevant material drawn from the 'coal face' of British church life, where jobbing pastors and laypeople are encountering postmodernism 'on the hoof'. As someone who straddles the worlds of academic theology and local ministry, I am keen that this gap should be filled. I am also aware that a recent, somewhat tentative attempt to do so has sparked a debate which needs to be carried forward.

The Post-Evangelical Question

In his 1995 book, *The Post-Evangelical*,[11] the former House Church leader Dave Tomlinson argued that for those evangelicals who truly want to engage with postmodern culture, the best route to take might be one which leads out of evangelicalism altogether. A major reason Tomlinson gives for this is that evangelicalism is terminally wedded to modernity – that is, to ways of thinking and acting which will soon cease to be relevant to the postmodern world. As he puts it, 'during the twentieth century evangelicalism has had . . . to experience and express its faith, and contend for the integrity and credibility of that faith, in the cultural environment of modernity. Post-evangelicals, on the other hand, are people who relate more naturally to the world of postmodernity.'[12]

I shall examine Tomlinson's argument more closely in Chapter 7, but it is worth noting here that in a follow-up debate at the evangelical Institute of Contemporary Christianity, a majority of those present supported his position.[13] Around the same time, the highly respected evangelical magazine *Third Way* ran a poll in which 25 per cent of its readers identified themselves as post-evangelical.[14] A recent questionnaire distributed to clergy by Christian Research added 'post-evangelical' as a new option in its section on Churchmanship. This was followed by intense discussion in certain parts of evangelical culture,[15] and even by an acknowledgment of post-evangelicalism from the platform of the 1996 National Assembly of Evangelicals.[16]

These events may not add up to a crisis for evangelicalism, but they do ask some timely questions of it. It will become plain as we proceed that I believe Tomlinson's analysis to be flawed by a very partial interpretation of what postmodernism and evangelicalism actually are. It will also emerge that I am far more convinced, and far more excited, by the vision of a 'postmodern evangelicalism' which remains authentically evangelical than by a post-evangelicalism which seems to be defined more by what it has rejected than by what it has embraced.

Having said this, and having interviewed Dave Tomlinson at some length for this book, I am sure that his thesis deserves attention. Furthermore, I trust that any criticism I make of it will be understood to come not from an 'ivory tower', but from a genuine commitment to dialogue and ongoing discussion.

I have no doubt that some aspects of postmodernism present exhilarating possibilities for faith and witness, but I am equally sure that other aspects of it should be resisted. As we consider the narratives, conversations and examples which form the substance of this book, we shall need to discern which description applies in each case. Before we do this, however, we must try more fully to define what postmodernism means, and what evangelicalism might mean in relation to it.

Postmodernism: a Snapshot

Postmodernism may well be the most important social and cultural development since the Industrial Revolution of the eighteenth century.[17] It is difficult to define precisely because it is characterised by doubt – and not least by doubt about that revolution. The industrial age was fuelled by reason, objective thought, empirical science and a confident faith in progress. The years between 1730 and 1800 saw the invention of William Kay's fly-shuttle loom, James Hargreaves's spinning jenny, Richard Arkwright's water-powered spinning frame and James Watt's steam engine; a national turnpike network was created, along with a countrywide system of canals. From these beginnings, there developed the heavy manufacturing industries of the nine-teenth century and the production lines of the twentieth.

These days, however, two devastating world wars have left a legacy of scepticism and suspicion. We now realise that factories turned out machineguns as well as fridge-freezers, that industrial processes led to death camps as well as hospitals. Scientific progress gave us mustard gas as well as penicillin, the atom bomb as well as the incubator.

All this has taken its toll. We now live in a 'post-industrial' age where cities and communities are driven less by corporate manufacture and more by the exchange of information.[18] Human life itself has become increasingly diffused and estranged: Margaret Thatcher may have been exaggerating when she said, 'There is no such thing as society, only individuals and their families,' but there was something there to exaggerate.

Against this backdrop, postmodernism is typically knowing and self-aware. Its loss of faith in objectivity has shifted attention on to the different angles from which things can be viewed. Artists no longer simply represent what is in front of them: in postmodern culture they make the act of representation itself the focus of their work. So poster shops sell multiple copies of Andy Warhol's screen prints of a photograph of Marilyn Monroe, and Marilyn herself seems strangely distant. The progress myth has made people dubious about originality and profundity. There is nothing new under the sun – but there is still fun, and even healing, to be had in parody, irony and play. The Meaning of Life is a Monty Python film; love is declared by quoting from Barbara Cartland.[19] If anything is universal, it is also often superficial: a Big Mac and a Coke can be bought almost anywhere on the planet, but so what? The world-wide web covers the earth, but in many ways serves only to emphasise different identities and interests. To some, we are united by the biosphere which we share and must preserve; others will drive their cars regardless of the ozone layer. Some are trying to recover a sense of local community; others would rather commune in cyberspace on a mailing list or bulletin board. Some hold that there is an opportunity to develop long-neglected spiritualities;

others are content with the more immediate buzz of sex, shopping or drugs.

But you may still be confused. You may appreciate that things have changed over the past few decades, sometimes quite dramatically. Yet is not the term 'modern' more normally used to describe the forces which have brought about such change, rather than the things which have been left in its wake? Why are sixties tower blocks 'modern' when, by today's standards, they seem distinctly old-fashioned? And why the new word? What can it possibly mean to talk of something being 'post' the modern – being 'after' or 'beyond' what is now?

Why *Post*modernism?

Moving on and moving out

Despite Jencks, it is important to understand that the 'post' in 'postmodernism' is more than purely chronological. It expresses, rather, a sense of *leaving something behind* – of moving away from something intellectually, culturally and emotionally, even though that something may stick around for some time. A useful metaphor for this is the metaphor of leaving home. When young people get a place of their own, as I did in my mid-twenties, it does not mean that their parents cease to exist! Nonetheless, they will often come to inhabit different 'worlds' – worlds which intersect, but which move in quite different orbits.[20]

Forty-five years ago the residents on my mother's newly built council estate crowded into her front room to watch the coronation of Queen Elizabeth II. My maternal grandparents were the only ones in the neighbourhood at that time who had a television. Today, 97 per cent of all British households own a TV, 77 per cent have a video recorder and ever-increasing numbers are subscribing to cable or satellite.[21]

My grandfather worked for a Fleet Street newspaper in the days when newspapers were still printed in Fleet Street – the days before automation and desktop publishing. When my mother left school and took her first job at fifteen, she bashed away on a heavy manual typewriter. Today, as she nears retirement, she wordprocesses documents gently on a quiet keyboard using the latest package from Microsoft. For her class and generation, going to work at fifteen was overwhelmingly the norm; now, almost 50 per cent of all school-leavers progress to some form of further education.[22] I myself am a beneficiary of this trend, having been the first on either side of my family to go to university. When Mum helped with the shopping as a young girl, she went to a small corner shop and paid by cash; now, she buys everything at a massive mall with a debit card, and the corner shop has closed.

When my parents divorced in the early seventies, the rate of marriage break-up was almost half what it is now.[23] When the Beatles broke up around the same time, they had revolutionised popular music; as I write, a band called Oasis dominates the charts with perfect evocations of Beatles songs, and a clutch of Oasis tribute bands tour the country while Oasis themselves complete their next album. At Mum's school, religious instruction was Scripture, and thoroughly Christian. At my school, Religious Education meant an equal study of all major world faiths, even though most of us were nominally Christian. When my son goes to school, it is quite possible that those designated Christian will be in the minority. When Mum learned geography, she was taught about an emergent Soviet bloc; when Matthew does so, he will be told about post-communist independent states like Bosnia, Croatia, Serbia, Latvia and Estonia. When I grew up, children's television consisted largely of cartoons, dubbed serials and old-fashioned tales told by adults sitting in chairs. Nowadays, Matthew watches manic presenters running around lurid sets in rapidly edited assaults on the senses.

I do not know what his generation will be called, but mine has acquired its own name . . .

Boomers, Busters and Xers

As servicemen returned home after the Second World War, the birth-rate soared and their children became known as 'the Baby Boom generation'. This is the generation which grew up through the sixties, listening to the Beatles and the Rolling Stones, watching more TV, pioneering the sexual revolution. It was a generation 'liberated' by the pill – able to regulate the size of its families. The upshot was a fall in the birth-rate which resulted in those born between about 1963 and 1979 being dubbed 'the Baby Busters'. The novelist Douglas Coupland has brilliantly captured the more cynical, knowing air of these eighteen- to thirty-four year-olds in his book *Generation X* – a title which has led to Busters also being dubbed 'Xers'. Basically, Xers are those who have grown up with postmodernity. In Coupland's parlance, they move into adulthood with a 'divorce assumption', taking short-term 'McJobs' while they try to solve their 'option paralysis'. They are sceptical about grand philosophy but open to individual spiritual experiences, and not least to communing with nature.[24]

As one generation succeeds another, old houses will be sold, and new people will move into them. Some will keep the decor much as it was; others will make significant alterations. In certain cases, though, the old dwellings will be demolished altogether, and something quite different will be put in their place.

In truth, opinions differ as to how much postmodernism is a demolition of modernism and how much it is merely a radical extension of it. The main point, however, is that old models and principles of construction are being replaced by new ones. In order to appreciate more fully how this has come about, we need to go back further than just one or two generations.

From Modernism to Postmodernism

Enlightenment background

The rationalism which Charles Jencks saw embodied in Pruitt-Igoe has its roots in the momentous cultural and intellectual development of the seventeenth and eighteenth centuries known as the Enlightenment. It is difficult to grasp what postmodernism is without realising that it is in many ways a departure from Enlightenment ways of thinking and acting. This leads us into the more technical realms of philosophy and history, and there are several fine specialist studies available for those who wish to pursue this matter in detail.[25] Our purposes will be served by a brief summary.

Although reason had a prominent role in the medieval and Renaissance thought of the preceding centuries, early Enlightenment philosophers like René Descartes (1596–1650), Benedictus Spinoza (1632–77) and Gottfried von Liebnitz (1646–1716) were distinguished by an increased reliance on it. Indeed, their rationalism was marked by a conviction that the external world is not only *accessible* to reason, but can be known by *reason alone*. For the mathematician Descartes, this meant, for example, that 'those seeking the strict way of truth should not trouble themselves about any object concerning which they cannot have a certainty equal to arithmetic or geometrical demonstration'.[26]

Although Descartes, for one, conducted his philosophy as a search for proofs of God's existence,[27] Enlightenment thought generally shifted away from appeals to objective divine revelation, and emphasised instead the logical deduction of truths *about* God. As most thoroughly worked out in the philosophy of Immanuel Kant (1724–1804), this shift reached the point where God was cast as a 'regulative idea' which could neither be proved nor disproved, but which was valuable as a theoretical basis for morality.[28]

Theologically, the most distinctive consequence of this Enlightenment thinking was Deism. Socially and politically, its key development was the separation of church and state which accompanied the American and French Revolutions of 1776 and 1789.

Deism is most closely associated with the English thinker John Locke (1632–1704) and the Frenchman Voltaire (1694–1778). It held that once the process of creation had been completed, God withdrew to let human beings put their divinely given reason to work in constructing religious faith and ethics. Importantly, too, it shifted the ground of spiritual authority from church institutions to individual subjects, and in doing so paved the way for the modern secular state.

Thomas Paine (1737–1809) was also a Deist, and did much to influence the American Revolution. Although the new United States was to be a nation 'under God', it would do without an established Church. Government would control matters of public concern such as tax, finance and education, while the Church would deal with the 'private' sphere of religion. Christian faith might deliver personal fulfilment, but it was the job of government to ensure social and material prosperity. A similar distinction emerged in post-revolutionary France and, later, in Marxist communism, which not only marginalised religion but often went one stage further and persecuted it.[29] This brings us to another symbolic date in the modern–postmodern shift.

Beyond statism

Shortly after I left that flat in Birmingham, Poland held its first free elections since the war. Twelve days later in Hungary, Imre Nagy, who had led the rebellion against

Russian occupation in 1956 and was later hanged for
it, was at last given a proper burial. Five months on,
the Berlin Wall came down. My friend Jane was there
to see it, visiting the East German church which had
played such an important role in bringing change about.
The next month Czechoslovakia underwent a 'Velvet
Revolution' as communism gave way to democracy. The
year was 1989.

The evangelical theologian Thomas Oden times the dura-
tion of the modern age very precisely from the storming of
the walls of the Bastille Prison in Paris in 1789 to the fall of
the Berlin Wall.[30] The intervening two hundred years were
marked, he says, not only by a faith in rationalism and
centralised secular government, but also by a conviction
that the state should be the prime engine of technological
advance and moral development. By contrast, the collapse
of communism exposed the limitations of the state and
revealed 'the smug fantasy of inevitable human progress'.[31]
It is surely significant, too, that the church was instrumental
in the transformation of Eastern Europe which took place at
this time.[32]

Beyond Colonialism

Another date which has been suggested for the 'crossover'
from a modern to a postmodern era is 1992.

In their fine study *Truth is Stranger than It Used to be*, the
Canadian theologians Middleton and Walsh suggest that the
decidedly mixed reaction to the five-hundredth anniversary
of Columbus's 'discovery' of America, which fell in that
year, indicated a 'profound cultural shift';[33] 'Why is it,' they
ask, 'that we did not hear this kind of critical questioning
of Columbus when we were in elementary school? What is
the significance of this questioning? Could it be that such
questioning is indicative of an epochal shift in cultural
sensibility?'[34]

Middleton and Walsh answer their own question when they affirm that 'the Columbus controversy signals the end of modernity'.[35] They give two reasons for this: first, that the classical form of the Columbus story embodied the 'modern' view of state-sponsored progress and exploration – of a technologically advanced society pushing back frontiers and 'civilising' those not yet enlightened. Second, that its rejection in 1992 highlighted a new 'postmodern' situation marked by an 'insistence on the hearing of alternative voices', a 'challenge to the centre of . . . society from the margins' and 'a critique of dominant cultural institutions'.[36]

John Drane is a Scottish Christian academic who has written with great insight about the challenges presented to the Church by the onset of postmodernism.[37] He teaches in the pioneering Centre for the Study of Christianity and Contemporary Society at Stirling University. He is also an Adjunct Professor at Fuller Seminary in California, one of America's leading evangelical academies. As we talked in my office, he reflected on his own experience of 1992, and echoed Middleton and Walsh's point about a line being crossed from the modern to the postmodern at that time: 'I was in Latin America, North America and Europe during that year,' he told me, 'and nobody knew how to celebrate it. That, for me, said it all. Whatever the last 500 years have stood for, we are uneasy about it. On balance, there are more things that we are ashamed of than we are happy about.' Most commentators on the shift from the modern to postmodern world would agree with Drane that it carries with it a general disillusionment with former certainties. Nonetheless, his clarity about dates is more arguable, as is that of Jencks and Oden. Indeed, the fact that they disagree among themselves, and that several further dates have been offered elsewhere,[38] suggests that postmodernism might be better viewed as a varied cultural phenomenon rather than a tight-knit 'school' of philosophy.

To draw this distinction more clearly, it will be useful

from this point on to differentiate between postmodern*ism* and postmodern*ity*, or 'the postmodern'.

Postmodern*ism*, Postmodern*ity* and 'the Postmodern'

Many writers seem happy to use the word 'postmodernism' both to denote the world as it is *and* to describe a more formal current of ideas and reflections on that world.[39] This is certainly how it was used by the historian Arnold Toynbee, who provided the most important early discussion of what has come to be known as postmodern culture.[40] So far, we have been using 'postmodernism' in the same broad manner. Others, however, have been keen to make a distinction between postmodern*ism* and postmodern*ity*, or 'the postmodern'. Joseph Natoli and Linda Hutcheon, for instance, reserve the term 'postmodern*ism*' for 'more limited cultural and aesthetic realms', while taking 'postmodern*ity*' to refer to a 'more general frame of reference'. In a similar vein, the Christian sociologist David Lyon defines 'postmodern*ism*' in relation to cultural phenomena like music, art, literature, film and philosophy, but applies 'postmodern*ity*' to a wider sphere of 'changes occurring at the global, social and political levels, simultaneously and symbiotically with cultural change'.[41]

This distinction makes sense because the earlier term 'modern*ism*' is sometimes used to describe a particular literary and artistic movement of the late nineteenth and early twentieth centuries. This movement is associated by Ihab Hasan with the stream-of-consciousness fiction of Marcel Proust, James Joyce and Virginia Woolf, the allusive poetry of Ezra Pound and T. S. Eliot, the abstract paintings of Piet Mondrian and the cubism of Pablo Picasso and Georges Braque.[42] In architecture, it is most usually linked to the geometric designs of Le Corbusier and Mies van der Rohe,[43] and is thought to have reached a dead end in high-rise developments like Pruitt-Igoe.

By contrast to all this, 'modern*ity*' usually covers the whole civilisation spawned by the Enlightenment – a civilisation which Lawrence Cahoone sees typified by capitalism, secularism, liberal democracy, rationalism and humanism.[44]

Writing from an evangelical perspective, Gene Veith reflects these distinctions when he condemns postmodern*ism* as an ideology basically hostile to gospel faith, while maintaining that Christians can live effectively with what he calls 'the postmodern' – that is, the more neutral context of current society.[45] Mike Starkey, an Anglican priest and writer on contemporary culture, took a similar view when we talked together: 'I'd see postmodernity as a climate of the times,' he said, 'and any attempt to wrestle creatively with it and come up with new formulations is a wholly positive thing. Such wrestling is absolutely vital, and ought to be inevitable. Some people, however, also go on and call for a postmodern*ist* version of Christianity, and I would have more questions and reservations about those who are pushing that agenda in the Church.'

Inevitably, the terminology is far from hard and fast: different writers use it in different ways. Nonetheless, from here on I shall maintain the broad division between postmodern*ism* as a set of ideas and representations of the contemporary world, and postmodern*ity* and 'the postmodern' as more general terms to describe that world as it is.

What, then, does postmodernity look like? I have already offered a snapshot, but it will be helpful now to focus more sharply on its main characteristics.

2

POSTMODERN THEMES AND CHRISTIAN CONSEQUENCES

Time and again they said it: 'fragmentation'. Time and again the church leaders I interviewed spoke of postmodernity as something broken, divergent, scattered. Time and again they made me think of my demolished Birmingham flat. Yet mostly they were coping. Mostly, they were picking up the pieces.[1] Mostly, they were coming to terms with the way we live now. Indeed as we shall see, some of them were positively thriving on it – gathering the fall-out from the postmodern explosion into new and intriguing patterns.

One of the first things which need to be understood about postmodernity is that it is neither the New Jerusalem nor the pit of Hell. It is neither all good nor all bad. From an evangelical point of view, some aspects of it can stimulate and encourage faith, while others could do real harm. In the first chapter we looked at the historical background of postmodernity. But to help us separate the wheat from the chaff in postmodern culture, we must also assess that culture *thematically*. We must see it as something distinguished by a number of dominant trends, philosophies and attitudes.

Several commentators have tried to encapsulate postmodernity in a list of key words or phrases.[2] We have already seen how fragmentation is used as a stock postmodern image. But for our purposes, it can be supplemented by eight further concepts:

> ambivalence
> difference
> perspectivism
> secondariness
> superficiality
> immediacy
> globalisation
> pragmatism

In this chapter, I shall examine these trends and consider just how they might affect the evangelical agenda going into the twenty-first century.

Ambivalence

Every year, my church denomination gathers for its General Assembly. New Moderators of Assembly are elected each time, and there is always a sense of expectation when the incoming person stands to deliver the annual address.

Of late, it has become fashionable for our Moderators to adopt a defining symbol of their faith, and to make it the church's symbol for their year in office. More obvious symbols would be the cross, the burning bush or the water of life, but in recent times different Moderators have given us God's rainbow, the wind of the Holy Spirit and the open door of Christ. All well and good, and all very biblical. In 1993, however, we were presented with something rather different. The symbol our Moderator left us with that year was the symbol of the question mark – '?'.

In the published text of his address,[3] the Moderator claims the question mark as 'the image that has sustained my ministry for over three decades, and my faith for longer'.[4] He adds: 'It would take only a very little god to give neat, precise answers to life's questions; uniform apples plucked from a low-branched doctrinal tree and ready-picked for easy consumption.'[5]

From this opening, the Moderator went on to contrast his position with that of those who look for certainty in their faith – those who want clear answers beyond their wondering and questioning:

> The spectre of certainty is frightening. We knew it in the Star Chamber and the inquisition. It burned books and built concentration camps in the Third Reich. It created a revolution in Iran, and, no matter who threw the match, caused an inferno in Waco. God preserve us from those who – in politics or theology – are sure they own the truth.[6]

If he did but know it, the Moderator was exemplifying what is, perhaps, the definitive feature of postmodernity. If postmodern philosophers are agreed on one thing, it is the need for scepticism towards grand, unitary explanations of the world. As we have seen, this scepticism was first seriously aroused by the 'solutions' of German fascism and Soviet communism and, given the horrors of Auschwitz and Stalin's purges, few could doubt that it has a place. It is rare, however, for postmodern suspicion to stop there. It frequently locks on to other targets, and one of the most common is the kind of religion which not only makes claims about absolute truth but also expects to convince others of that truth.

In 1991, Zygmunt Bauman published a seminal article in which he defined postmodernity as 'living with ambivalence'.[7] Ambivalence for Bauman means 'existence devoid of certainty'. It is about living what he calls a 'contingent' life – a life free from eternal truths. It means abandoning faith in the order and design of the world. In this state of ambivalence, 'truth' is shown up as a mere 'deception'. Far from giving meaning to life, it becomes simply a tool which people wield in order to oppress others. In Bauman's words, it is 'an aspect of a hierarchy . . . a bid for domination'. People living in ambivalence might show 'a preference for their own form of life', but in Bauman's eyes they must never try to impose that form of life on others. As he puts it, they must be 'immune to the temptation of cultural crusade'.

Bauman goes on to endorse the view that belief in absolute truth leads inevitably to humiliation – humiliation of the other, the different and the alien. Absolute truth is a form of imperialism, says Bauman, and should be replaced by non-judgmental 'tolerance' and 'solidarity'. Jean François Lyotard had expressed a similar sentiment in 1979 when he summed up the postmodern condition as 'incredulity towards metanarratives',[8] doubting any system of thought which – like evangelical theology – appears to resolve life's questions with one grand story which explains how things are.

None of this means that stories themselves are off the agenda. Far from it: Steinar Kvale has observed that in postmodernity 'a re-narrativisation of the culture takes place, emphasising communication and the impact of a message upon an audience'. It is just that the stories are now localised and parochial: they are not taken to refer to any all-encompassing reality. Rather, 'they are legitimated by the simple fact that they do what they do'.[9]

As Bible-based Christians centred on the person and work of Jesus, evangelicals are typically defined by their commitment to absolute truth. As conversionists and activists, they are characterised by their desire to convince others of this truth, as it is revealed in the grand narrative of divine salvation. In Alister McGrath's words, 'evangelicalism is insistent that Christian "truth" must . . . accurately and consistently render the truth of the identity and purposes of God'.[10]

Evangelicals would almost certainly share Bauman's scepticism towards totalitarian regimes, but would still proclaim Jesus as 'the truth' and God's Spirit as the One who will lead everyone who follows Jesus into 'all truth' (John 14:6; 16:13). Having said this, the way evangelicals *conceive* and *express* the truth of God in a postmodern world may have to take account of the fact that past 'crusades' *have* presented the gospel in a coercive or oppressive way, and that the models of truth adhered to before may not be the only ones available.

I shall investigate this issue more thoroughly in Chapter 14. Here, however, we need to recognise a distinction which is often taken as a marker of the modern–postmodern shift.

The dominant understanding of truth bequeathed by the Enlightenment is the so-called *correspondence* theory. This assumes a particular statement to be true if it relates to some 'fact' in the world. The correspondence view assumes there is a direct 'fit' between our description of reality and reality itself. It tends to treat language as a set of *propositions* – that is, a collection of scientifically verifiable assertions whose reference is in some way quantifiable and objectively demonstrable.

The correspondence theory works well for statements like 'Ice floats on water' or 'All living humans breathe', but as Stanley Grenz has pointed out, Enlightenment rationalists and their heirs rarely stop here. Rather, they 'extend the limits of the "reality" that they believe we can grasp to include not just the everyday objects around us but the entire realm of nature . . . They maintain that we can attain sure knowledge in all realms of human enquiry.'[11] This propositionalist, correspondence view of truth is prominent in the work of 'modern' evangelical theologians like Carl F. H. Henry and Francis Schaeffer, for whom it is the proper basis of doctrine and biblical interpretation.[12]

By contrast to all this, postmodernists tend to favour the alternative view suggested by the *coherence* theory of truth. This rejects the idea that truth exists objectively as a series of atomic 'facts', which it is the job of human beings to describe. Rather, they see truth as something constructed within a whole system of knowledge – a system which is not simply 'mirrored' by human thought and expression, but which partly *comprises* such thought and expression. According to the coherence theory, we cannot step outside reality to gain a 'spectators' gallery' view of it, precisely because we are *part* of it. This means that truth gets regarded much more *contextually*. Statements are treated less as abstract formulae and much more as part of discourses and narratives, which are themselves *socially* determined. Hence, as the Jewish linguist Yehoshua Bar-Hillel put it, while 'Ice floats on water' may function quite well as a proposition, other statements like 'It's raining' or 'I'm hungry' are far less universally objectifiable, and are much more dependent on local circumstances and perceptions. Furthermore, when it comes to expressions like 'I love you' or 'Ouch!', the correspondence theory begins to look rather limited.[13]

One of the key challenges facing evangelicals in the postmodern world is to find ways of expressing gospel truth which respect the coherence view and recognise its validity while avoiding the kind of thoroughgoing ambivalence advocated by Bauman. Indeed, this is a challenge which underlies much of what follows in this study.

Difference

Postmodernity is not just ambivalent about truth; it celebrates the differences of understanding which result from that ambivalence. It both assumes and promotes heterogeneity – the distinctions and diversities of culture, religion and belief.

For the philosopher Isaiah Berlin, recognising that there is no final, fixed explanation of the world compels us to embrace *pluralism*, which he defines as an acceptance of the 'many different ends which [people] may seek', and a positive regard for different races, creeds and traditions.[14] What is more, in an increasingly multicultural society where these different strands of human life intersect, Berlin's gentility may mutate into full-blown *syncretism* – a 'pick 'n' mix' approach to symbols, spiritualities and identities in which the original context and integrity of each is subordinated to present wants and needs. Richard Schweder offers a vivid illustration of this when he recounts a story told by the anthropologist Clifford Geertz. 'A visitor to Japan wandered into a department store in Tokyo at the time when the Japanese had begun to take great interest in the symbolism of the Christmas season. And what symbol did the visitor discover prominently on display in the Tokyo department store? Santa Claus nailed to a cross!'[15]

Evangelicals should have little problem with heterogeneity as such. They inhabit a created order which is far from uniform: in the words of the great priest-poet Gerard Manley Hopkins, they can appreciate the wonder of 'things being various'. They believe in a triune God who is three persons in one substance. They exist within many different denominations, cultures and language groups. They read numerous different translations of the Bible. In addition, they tend to value religious freedom, which usually extends well beyond their own communities to a whole variety of other religious groups. Indeed, Thomas Oden has even gone so far as to suggest that the Church is one of the few institutions which is prepared for the postmodern world, since it is intrinsically multicultural and multigenerational.[16]

The problem for Christians living with postmodern difference, as with postmodern ambivalence, comes when openness to diversity in some areas extends to a denial of ultimate truth in general – when, for example, one claims that the crucified Christ is the only Saviour of the world rather than an all-purpose religious icon. In the 'Deconstructive' theory of Jacques Derrida, *différence* has a very specific relation to the denial of absolutes. Derrida rejects what he calls 'logocentrism'. In his view, words and statements cannot be linked to fixed objects or ultimate realities like God. There is no transcendent *logos* which regulates the meaning of everything else – no 'Word' above our words. Instead, the meaning of expressions is to be found in the shifting 'spaces' between them and all other elements in the system of communication. They are defined as much by what they are not as by what they are; they cannot be 'pinned' on to an objective reality.[17]

All this creates obvious difficulties for evangelicals, whose biblicism, crucicentrism and conversionism makes them appear particularly 'absolutist' to many postmoderns.

Perspectivism

The postmodern stress on difference often manifests itself as an emphasis on the many perspectives from which things can be seen. A much repeated illustration of postmodernity is Walter Truett Anderson's story of three umpires having a drink after a baseball game. One says, 'There's balls and there's strikes and I call 'em the way they are.' The second responds, 'There's balls and there's strikes and I call 'em the way I see 'em.' And the third says 'There's balls and there's strikes, and they ain't *nothin'* until I call 'em!'[18]

The point is that whereas the first umpire is stuck in modernity, the second and third represent respectively moderate and radical versions of postmodern theory – versions in which truth is either substantially or wholly dependent on our perception and definition of it. As a club cricketer who has had more than his fair share of dodgy umpiring decisions, I can see the validity of versions two and three, but Anderson's little fable has more serious implications.

If you have ever tried to share your faith with someone who keeps diverting the focus of conversation from Christianity to other religions, or from orthodox to apocryphal accounts of Jesus, you will have come up against perspectivism in action. If you have ever seen a cubist painting, read a novel by William Faulkner or John Fowles, or watched a more recent film by Woody Allen, you will have witnessed it up close.

Technically, perspectivism is a philosophy which holds that the external world is not susceptible to a single, objective explanation. Rather, it is to be interpreted by adopting a range of viewpoints and belief systems, none of which is more valid than another.

Perspectivism is evident in many of the writings of Friedrich Nietzsche (1844–1900), whose philosophy does much to anticipate postmodern theory.[19] Nietzsche's denial of grand explanations led him famously to declare the death of God, and to exalt the authority of the human will. Perspectivism is even more clearly advocated in the work of Ortega y Gasset (1883–1955), for whom the only ultimate reality was each individual's life – an outlook he summed up in the sentence, 'I am I and my circumstances.'

In the cubist canvases of Pablo Picasso and Georges Braque, objects are depicted simultaneously from a number of different vantage points. Women's faces, violins and herrings seem distorted and fractured, but this is because the artists want to show that there is always more than one way of looking at things. More recently, the built-in ambiguities of art have become increasingly apparent. This review of an installation by the artistic group BANK is typical, as well as pertinent to our subject:

> They show three life-sized . . . wax effigies of Christ – one black, one female, one white. Their faces grimace in pain, blood pools at their feet and the wounds appear freshly slashed. The spine-chilling violence triggers ambivalent reactions. Is this a critique of the white male ideologies which permeate Christian mythology, or an attempt to reinvent this bankrupt image of human suffering for politically correct times, or a cynical comment on the redundance of angst in art?
>
> Confusing? You bet. Disturbing? Definitely. That's BANK for you.[20]

In Faulkner's book *As I Lay Dying*, the same funeral is reported in starkly different ways by different mourners. In Fowles's *The French Lieutenant's Woman*, the reader is offered alternative endings to underline the artifice of the story and the diverse interpretations which are open to authors and readers.

In films like *Annie Hall, Hannah and Her Sisters* and *Crimes and Misdemeanors,* Woody Allen develops his plot through the eyes of several different characters, who have quite contrasting ideas of what is happening around them.

The great abstract expressionist painter Willem De Kooning was once asked how far he had been influenced by the Old

Masters. His reply was instructive: 'I influence them,' he said, 'with my eyes!' His point was that even finished works are subject to 'change' as they are perceived by later generations. When De Kooning's words are related to the latest interactive computer technology, they do not seem so fanciful. The rock singer Peter Gabriel recently pioneered a CD-Rom called *Eve*, which allows users to re-mix the sounds and images from past videos of his songs into 'customised' combinations of their own.[21]

It is not always clear in these examples whether the perspectives still point beyond themselves to an elusive but stable reality (the second umpire's view), or whether the perspectives *are* the reality (as with the third umpire). Getting technical for a moment, this is where artistic 'high' modernism tends to part company with thoroughgoing postmodernism: modernist cubism, for instance, has more in common with umpire number two, whereas 'postmodernist' John Fowles and Peter Gabriel could be said to be closer to umpire number three. In either case, though, it is very evident that 'reality isn't what it used to be'.[22]

The effect of perspectivism can be seen in the Church and in theology as much as anywhere else. Lesslie Newbigin is a distinguished Christian leader who has written a great deal on the challenges faced by Christians in contemporary Western culture.[23] His views have been shaped by the experience of returning to Britain after many years as a missionary and bishop in India. As we talked in his front room, he recalled that what had most shocked him on coming home was 'that theological teachers had such a very feeble grip on the Christian faith. When in theological gatherings I talked about the gospel I was looked at with puzzlement and asked, "What do you mean by 'the gospel'?" The very concept had evaporated. There was only Paul's view and Luke's view and Matthew's view and so on.'

Newbigin's point is not hard to confirm: pick up a textbook on the historical Jesus these days and you are offered a plethora of biographical reconstructions, from Jewish holy man to desert mystic, from political revolutionary to pharisaic teacher, from Stoic philosopher to wild end-time prophet.[24] Often, it seems that it is the biographer's own personality and preoccupations which are being projected on to Jesus as much as anything else. But this is no longer necessarily perceived as a problem. You just take your pick: perspectivism reigns.

All this might seem quite contrary to evangelical faith, which seeks to present Jesus as a unitary, authentic reality. Then again, it would be hard to deny that his personality *is* complex and pluriform. There is the seeming paradox that he is at once fully divine and fully human; there is the sense, when he is transfigured before Peter, James and John, that he is somehow operating in two 'worlds' – in both heavenly and earthly realms (Mk. 9:2–13). To the Pharisees and Sadducees, he is an unorthodox but formidable rabbi (Matt. 22:16, 24; John. 3:2). To many 'common people', he is a healer and wonder-worker (Luke 19:37). To others, he is the Moses-like prophet foretold in Deuteronomy 18 (John 6:14). To Peter he is 'the Messiah, the Son of the living God' (Matt. 16:16).

Now, of course, evangelicals will want to say that none of these aspects of Jesus's character is mutually exclusive: they are all parts of the same, integrated whole – different facets of the same gemstone. At different times and in different situations it may be appropriate to emphasise one facet more than another, but in the end Jesus is One Lord.

Despite this, within postmodernity it may be necessary for Christians to acknowledge the diversity which exists *within* this unity rather more than they have done in the modern world. This point was emphasised vividly by Phil Wall, a gentle giant who works as a national evangelist for the Salvation Army, and whom I met at his office in Morden:

> Paradox is crucial in postmodernity, but classical evan-
> gelicalism struggles and wrestles with paradox. And
> maybe through postmodernity the sovereign God is
> opening us up and forcing us to get hold of the full

revelation of who he is. We have tended to do our theology along one or two lanes, but perhaps God is saying 'No! I'm a flippin' eighty-four-lane highway!'

Similarly, with St Paul, we may need to accept that even as we present the One Christ to the world, we must do so in a way which demonstrably respects the heterogeneity of people and culture:

> To the Jews I became like a Jew, to win the Jews. To those under the law I became like one under the law (though I myself am not under the law), so as to win those under the law. To those not having the law I became like one not having the law (although I am not free from God's law but am under Christ's law). To the weak I became weak, to win the weak. I have become all things to all men so that by all possible means I might save some.' (1 Cor. 9:20–2)

Secondariness

In Spring 1997 the Booker prizewinner Graham Swift was accused by a literary scholar of having borrowed many of the themes and structures of his novel *Last Orders* from Faulkner's *As I Lay Dying.* His defence – and that of the literary establishment in general – was basically 'So what?' T. S. Eliot was quoted: 'Good poets borrow; great poets steal.' Shakespeare nicked his plots from others, they said; *West Side Story* ripped off *Romeo and Juliet*; what was the big deal? Swift was not plagiarising; if anything, he was paying homage. And yet for all that art and culture have long been self-referential, it is difficult to escape the sense that in the postmodern world, such reflexivity has mushroomed.

George Steiner[25] has used the idea of 'secondariness' to evoke the characteristic world-weary smirk of postmodernity – the sense that there is nothing wholly original to say and that things can only be reproduced, cloned, borrowed or sent up. As one postmodern slogan puts it, 'Been there, done that, bought the t-shirt'. In Jean Baudrillard's terms, 'the map precedes the territory' – our *simulacra* or representations of the world do not just reflect but actually help to construct it: there is, in fact, no longer a 'world' above and beyond them.[26]

In Derrida's outlook, language itself is merely a series of 'traces', 'iterations' and 'citations' of what has gone before: linguistic signs refer ceaselessly to other linguistic signs. There is 'nothing outside the text' which is not itself somehow shaped by the text.[27] This takes us firmly into the realm of Anderson's third umpire – the one who believed there were balls and strikes only when he called them.

Postmodern theorists are often quite frank about the implications of all this for faith in God. For Baudrillard, it means that God disappears 'in the epiphany of his representations' – there is nothing 'behind' the symbols of the liturgy, the icon or the stained-glass window, and it is those symbols themselves which must be seen as the sum and limit of divinity.[28] The French cultural theorist Roland Barthes treated theological discourse on a level with all other discourse: for him, it was essentially self-referential – an endless 'thread' of language with no fixed 'hook' into God, reason or law.[29]

No doubt this will seem shocking and blasphemous to many – and ultimately, of course, it *is* a denial of God's transcendence. Reflecting on the fate of Generation X, Douglas Coupland has more recently written, 'I think there was a trade-off somewhere along the line. I think the price we paid for our golden life was an inability to fully believe in love; instead we gained an irony that scorched everything it touched. And I wonder if this irony is the price we paid for the loss of God.'[30]

Desperately sad though this is, Christians can at least go *some* way in admitting secondariness. For example, the idea that much of what we say and write is second-hand is hard to refute. If we all spoke in a completely original way, we would not be able to understand one another! Virtually every word we utter has been uttered by someone else before: there are numerous dictionaries to prove it. Granted, the way we combine words is more distinctive, but even then grammar regulates our patterns of speech to a considerable degree.

More pertinently for us, not only does the Teacher of Ecclesiastes declare, 'What has been done will be done again' (1:9): there are whole chunks of Scripture which basically reiterate what has already been said, from the repetition of God's commandments in Deuteronomy 5 to the recounting of Israel's history in the speeches of Acts (Acts 7:2–53; 13:16–22). The contexts and recipients change, but the message remains pretty much the same.

Now as long as we do not abandon the idea of an original, divine Word, 'secondariness' could be seen as a suitably humbling concept for Christians. It may help us to realise that our preaching, witnessing or writing never finally belongs to us: in a very real sense, it is a re-presentation of what we have been given by God in Christ and the Bible.

Superficiality

Superficiality here is not meant in the common, pejorative sense, but denotes quite literally a focus on the surface of things. For Roland Barthes this meant *jouissance* – a celebration of sensual pleasure devoid of the search for 'deep meanings'.[31] It also extends to *consumerism* and fashion, where style is exalted over substance and image becomes reality.[32]

In a recent TV advertisement for the Peugeot 405 car, a highly postmodern montage of random 'thoughts' includes a girl in a red dress being rescued from the path of an oncoming juggernaut. It is a deft reference to Steven Spielberg's harrowing holocaust film *Schindler's List*, in which a similarly clad girl is picked out against mono-chrome scenes of mass slaughter. The difference is that in

Schindler's List the girl dies. To Peugeot's advertising agent, the subliminal power of the image is more important that its original reference.

Less cynically, in 1996 Oasis singer Liam Gallagher spurred a revival of the 'desert boot' – a hitherto nerdish piece of footwear long thought to be the epitome of bad taste. Liam decided that nerdism was cool, and hordes of hip dudes followed suit.

One of the most frequently cited models of postmodernity is the pop star Madonna.[33] For her, a new identity seems barely a makeover away. One moment she is a Catholic virgin, the next a punk rocker; next she becomes Marilyn Monroe; next, a leather-clad sado-masochist; next, Eva Perón; next, who knows? In the warts-and-all tour documentary *In Bed With Madonna*, she even plunders the mannerisms of the charismatic prayer meeting, as she gathers her dancers to ask for a blessing on her sexually explicit show!

I am not a big Madonna fan, but I do like Marc Cohn. Even so, I am always thrown into a flat tailspin by a line from Cohn's best-selling single 'Walking in Memphis'. The song's narrator (who may or may not be Cohn himself – more postmodern ambiguity) tells of visiting the city of the title, and of being transformed by its heady mix of musical traditions. Having seen 'the ghost of Elvis down on Union Avenue', he visits a hall where a gospel singer called Muriel is belting out a classic spiritual. He is so moved that he sings along.

It is a classic postmodern moment. Cohn seems to admire gospel music for its passion and style, but is much more tentative about its content. Like Madonna, he is willing to 'put on' a Christian identity for a while, but the implication is that there will be another identity to don tomorrow. As Graham Cray has pointed out, 'A significant number of white rock artists have a Roman Catholic upbringing [Madonna is one] and an even greater proportion of black singers come from Pentecostal or Baptist homes. In many cases the language of faith has been turned into a style of music, detached from the content of the original vocabulary.'[34]

Once again, there are clear moral and doctrinal challenges here. Evangelical faith traditionally has us finding our identity in the person of Christ, who represents not an 'image' to be borrowed or experienced fleetingly, but a life to be lived in all its fullness for ever. Having said this, God himself 'took on' human flesh for a specific period, and is not averse to sensual pleasure, as long as it is incorporated within a wider framework of love and submission to his law (Gen. 2:24; S. of S. 1:1ff.) In a postmodern world, evangelicals have somehow to make the gospel 'ready to wear' while ensuring it does not in the process become a victim of passing fashion.

Immediacy

A sixth key feature of postmodern life is its tendency to compress history into the present moment – that is, contemporaneity, or what Kurt Richardson calls *detraditionalisation*.[35] The National Lottery encourages us to 'Forget it All for an Instants', while television contracts complex world events into five minutes of news 'on the hour, every hour'. We live in what Douglas Coupland has called an 'accelerated culture'[36] – one which favours the 'now' over the 'has-been', and which 'takes the waiting out of wanting'. Long-term planning is undermined by short-termism in everything from employment to economic policy.

In a recent poll commissioned by the publisher Collins Harvill, the British public's top ten sporting memories all dated from the previous sixteen years. As Mark Lawson inferred at the time, this suggests 'a general loss of history' – a shortening of memories, an elision of the past into the present.[37]

All this is problematic for a faith which has a keen sense of God's unfolding purpose in history, and which looks with hope to the future return of Christ. Having said this, it ought not to be forgotten that Jesus himself commended 'living for the day' (Matt. 6:34), and was perceived by those who cherished the Jewish traditions as a dangerous iconoclast (Matt. 15:2). In responding to postmodernity, evangelicals will somehow have to maintain the best elements of their historic identity while responding to people's ever more immediate needs.

Globalisation

As Walter Truett Anderson has put it, 'for the first time in history we have a truly global civilisation . . . of rapid information exchange and unprecedented mobility'.[38] This can be seen in the culture of the Internet, the multinational corporation and satellite broadcasting, but also, perhaps, in the ecosystem, and the drive towards superpower co-operation in the post-Cold War world.

Of all the key features of postmodernity, globalisation is the most obviously positive from an evangelical point of view, and it is no surprise that in the field of global communications, evangelicals have been religious pioneers. Fuelled, no doubt, by their commitment to Christ's Great Commission to make disciples of all nations (Matt. 28:16–20), evangelicals today own more cable and satellite TV stations, web sites and publishing houses than any other branch of the Church. Through the eighties and nineties the evangelist Billy Graham has made extensive use of satellite links, while the Global March for Jesus has linked Christians across scores of countries in quite monumental acts of witness.

By contrast, evangelicals have not matched this globalised conversionism with a comparably universal effort for bio-ethics or international peace – and in some cases they have shown positive scepticism towards organisations like the United Nations.[39]

Graham Cray summed this tension up well when we spoke in Cambridge: 'It's one of the cultural and sociological characteristics of evangelicalism,' he said, 'that we somehow combine the theologically conservative with the innovative in mission and forms of communication.' The crucial question here is whether this approach will continue to be adequate in a 'global village' where, increasingly, 'the medium is the message'. Is global technology really so neutral that it can be left out of the theological equation, or will it not be necessary to develop a radically new doctrinal discourse for the coming information age?

Pragmatism

I mentioned earlier that evangelicals have tended to be pragmatic and activist. In common parlance, a pragmatist is someone who prefers doing things to reflecting on them. More specifically, though, the formal philosophy known as 'pragmatism' has had a big influence on postmodern thinking.

Pragmatism is a largely American school of thought which has its origins in the work of Charles Sanders Peirce (1839–1914), William James (1842–1910) and John Dewey (1842–1910). Although there are important differences between them,[40] Peirce, James and Dewey were all committed to studying the *effect* of ideas as they were put into practice in real contexts. For Peirce, this meant that 'the whole function of thought is to produce habits of action'.[41] In James's book *Pragmatism*, 'ideas become true just so far as they help us to get into satisfactory relations with other parts of our experience'.[42] And for Dewey, knowledge is not a key to some transcendent wisdom, but a tool which helps people adjust to their environments.

With the emergence of postmodernism, these early pragmatists have enjoyed greater attention. The way they subordinated 'the big picture' to more immediate, local concerns fits in well with postmodern ambivalence and heterogeneity. Contemporary 'neo-pragmatists' like Richard Rorty and

Stanley Fish argue that truth is not about the 'essence' of things, but simply a consensus about how to describe them – an agreement between all those who are present 'in the room'. Our language does not describe some pre-linguistic reality; it constructs reality, and because of this, truth is fluid and changeable: it is about 'what works' rather than what is 'correct' or 'right'.[43]

Again, this aspect of postmodernity seems flat contrary to the gospel. As a bewildered R.T. Kendall told me, 'Once they abandon the idea of revealed truth, they've lost me.' Most, if not all, evangelicals would surely agree. And yet even if we maintain the idea that there is objective, divine truth to be found in creation and in Scripture, we must accept that the Bible's own account of how God made the world devolves a significant linguistic and social construction of reality to human beings. Indeed, the ability to *classify* and *codify* our world with language is one of the things which distinguishes us from other creatures:

> Now the Lord God had formed out of the ground all the beasts of the field and all the birds of the air. He brought them to the man to see what he would name them: and whatever the man called each living creature, that was its name. So the man gave names to all the livestock, the birds of the air and all the beasts of the field. (Gen. 2:19)

Rorty and Fish are at least right to point out that words are not simply 'mirrors' of reality: they do help to shape, as well as to reflect, our perception. Can you say, for instance, exactly at what point a dog ceases to be a wolf? Can you define the precise scientific distinction between, say, a puddle, a pool, a pond and a lake? Going back to an earlier example, does it really make any sense to argue that there are balls and strikes apart from the umpire's call, when the umpire's decision is the only one that really counts?

Putting the best gloss possible on pragmatism, we might

say that it reflects something of the freewill which God has given us – something of the responsibility he expects us to exercise in his world. At its worst, it threatens to reduce him to little more than a marketing device: if it works, preach it! As we shall see more clearly in the next chapter, with their zeal to 'do' the gospel rather than contemplate it, evangelicals might well find themselves in trouble with postmodernity even as they are in tune with it. We must be wary of letting our true convictions serve our outreach strategies, however much God may use our defective means to achieve his ends (cf. Rom. 6:1–2).

What these eight trends show is that while evangelicals may find some aspects of postmodernity congenial, there are many others which pose big difficulties. Living as an evangelical in the postmodern world takes a lot of wisdom, and this cannot be achieved simply by comparing postmodern theory with Christian philosophy and doctrine. In true pragmatist fashion, something more down-to-earth is needed.

So let me tell you some stories.

3

CASES IN POINT: THREE STORIES

The Software Rack

I am now a church minister in the City of London. My congregation can trace its roots back to 1640, when the Puritan divine Thomas Goodwin gathered a small group of devout Independent Christians at a house on Anchor Lane, just off Thames Street, in the parish of St Dunstan's in the East. The church he started is known as the City Temple.

A number of Goodwin's books and sermons survive from the ten years he spent at Anchor Lane. They were written on parchment with a quill pen, printed on an early version of a printing press and published as a folio edition by Thankful Owen and James Barron in 1681. As the current pastor of the City Temple, I too write books and sermons, but my equipment and methods are very different from Goodwin's. More and more these days, I rely on computers. At any given moment, my Windows operating system gives me access to a plethora of options for receiving information and producing text. I can log on to the Internet and, using a single telephone line, can download papers, bibliographies, images and conference proceedings from all over the world. I can browse and contribute to mailing lists on countless subjects. I can even dialogue 'live' with someone on another continent. On a single CD-Rom, I can study vast amounts of data – data which in hard copy would take up considerable shelf space. As I compose directly on to the screen, the options for manipulating what I write are legion. For Goodwin's printers, changing type faces and fonts was a painstaking process; I can do so with a click of my mouse. Where they had to decipher a handwritten manuscript, I simply hand my publisher a floppy disk.

Next door to my church there is a large evangelical Christian bookshop. Even for an evangelical bookseller, it operates a particularly strict quality control. Several Christian publishers are excluded because of their more liberal stance, and even some titles which claim an evangelical pedigree are barred on doctrinal grounds. The theological outlook is most definitely conservative. The same cannot be said, however, of its attitude to technology. In recent years, the shop has stocked an increasing amount of sacred computer software – more than I have seen in any other British bookstore. Jostling for attention on the display racks are dozens of electronic Scripture aids, tour guides, ecclesiastical organisers, games and accessories. The film star Charlton Heston capitalises on his leading roles in several biblical epics to endorse a multi-media 'Voyage through the New Testament'. An interactive Bible Teacher's Resource claims 'more than 3 million satisfied customers'.

Another CD promises an armchair tour of Israel under the title 'Holy Land Scene Dream'. 'Membership Plus' announces itself as a complete church-management programme 'for your growing congregation'. 'The Dead Sea Scrolls Revealed' offers not only fresh insights into the famous documents of its title, but also promises 'actual Dead Sea Qumran sand inside'. If you want something more pocket-sized, 'The King James Bible for use on Gameboy' might be for you. 'Bible Sleuth' describes itself as 'a fast paced mystery game that tests your wits, skill and Bible knowledge', as well as providing 'a healthy alternative to violent computer games'. Meanwhile, 'Spiritual Warfare for the Sega Genesis' throws down its gauntlet to the customer in bold terms: 'You're a soldier in the army of the Lord. Explore the inner regions of a modern city as you endeavour to collect the Full Armour of God.' Then, should you need to leave your PC to do something else for a time, you can rely on 'Heavenly Angels Screen Savers' – 'fifteen "angelic" theme screens with inspiring biblical scripture'.

The shop selling all this is hardly trying to project a postmodern view of the world. And yet there is a startling irony – itself very postmodern – in the fact that it seems happy to use the most overtly postmodern means to get a very modernistic message across. Gameboy represents a thoroughly contemporary and fairly superficial call on leisure time; the King James Bible is not only Holy Writ – it is one of the crowning glories of seventeenth-century literature. The marriage of the two is, at least, somewhat bizarre.

Acting out spiritual warfare on the Sega Genesis begs a similar question: given that computer games are mostly played by children, what kind of preparation is it for instances of genuine deliverance or exorcism? Furthermore, what does it say about the unique and distinctive nature of the fight with principalities and powers to depict it by aping the gory combat so often marketed as entertainment by secular software companies? Here, surely, it is not enough to acknowledge a nice postmodern irony and move on.

Giving away Dead Sea sand with an interactive CD-Rom is also highly ironic. In typical postmodern fashion, it underlines the distance of the user from the reality being depicted, even while offering a remarkable simulation of that reality. You may feel 'virtually' present with the Dead Sea Scrolls but, in the end, you are participating in an illusion. For an evangelically produced piece of software, the free sand is also strangely reminiscent of a medieval Roman Catholic relic!

The fact that it takes a Hollywood star to guide you around the Holy Land bears out postmodernism's concern for image and celebrity. It also seems to reverse the 'natural' order of origination and representation: as much as the Holy Land itself, the draw is the actor whose films depicted the

Holy Land on celluloid. Hollywood, of course, is right up there with McDonald's and Coca-Cola as a cipher of the globalising tendency within postmodernity. Neither is it surprising that most of the software sold by the bookshop has its origin in the USA. Indeed, the Americanisation of world evangelicalism offers another significant example of the way in which the evangelical church itself reflects wider postmodern developments. It is seen also in the superbly marketed 'international ministries' of evangelists like Morris Cerullo, Benny Hinn and Kenneth Hagin, the mass beaming of American televangelism into the Two-Thirds World, and the spread of church growth teaching not only to Britain, but also latterly to Africa, Latin America and the Far East.[1] Reflecting on this phenomenon in his important book *Postmodernism, Reason and Religion*, Ernest Gellner makes a telling observation which also bears out some of the wider themes we have been discussing:

America's fabulous wealth and its relatively wide dispersal, the wide (though not of course complete) participation in the national cultural ideal, the egalitarianism and stress on mobility, and above all the absence of any real recollection or even any haunting smell of any *ancien régime* – all these traits make Americans, to this day, inclined to absolutise their own culture, and to equate it with the human condition as such, and hence unconsciously to treat other cultures as perversions of the rightful human condition. Individualism, egalitarianism, freedom, sustained innovation – these traits are, in the comparative context of world history, unusual, not to say eccentric; but to Americans they are part of the air they breathe, and most of them have never experienced any other moral atmosphere. The one indigenous American philosophy, Pragmatism, does in fact make experimental innovation into an inherent and eternal part of human cognition as such, thus showing a total blindness to its absence in most other cultures.[2]

The heavenly angels screen savers are another American import. They are theologically astute insofar as they play on the idea that angels are there even when you do not see them, and 'guard' your environment unobtrusively. Like much of the other merchandise on the rack, however, they come across as a rather strained and gauche attempt to 'redeem' technology which is more often used for ungodly purposes. Recently, I came home to find that someone had bought and installed for my son a screensaver featuring the anarchic and decidedly postmodern American cartoon character Bart Simpson. I suppose the angelic theme screens would have been more wholesome, but I also wonder whether it is necessary to festoon every nook and cranny of life with overtly Christian knick-knacks, just in case we forget that God is around. In fact, I do not simply wonder about this; I worry about it.

The shopping mall is a defining symbol of postmodernity, and consumerism a core postmodern creed.[3] As one wit put it: 'Tesco ergo sum' – I shop, therefore I am. The Christian software rack prompts us to consider the extent to which evangelicalism these days has become a great marketing opportunity, even as it has become a successful gospel movement. Dave Tomlinson surely has a point here. 'When a person becomes an evangelical,' he says, 'they are walking into a new world: they will soon discover an entire sub-culture of church services, events, festivals, concerts, conferences, magazines, books, merchandise, record companies, mission organisations, training schemes, holiday clubs and celebrities.'[4] What Tomlinson fails to see, however, is that this world is just as postmodern as the distinctly idealised version of postmodernity he endorses for himself and other post-evangelicals! Indeed, we shall see as we progress that postmodern life is both more banal and more negative than Tomlinson admits.

Now I do not want to be misunderstood here. I have already declared my attachment to computers, and there is clearly a place for Christian software. Perhaps if I had bought that church-management programme, I would by now have dealt with all my outstanding mail! Perhaps a person who cannot travel to Israel would appreciate the Charlton Heston CD. As Gene Veith says, it may be possible to honour God in a postmodern consumer economy. Nonetheless, we dare not go on to apply consumer values to *God himself*.[5] The software rack might offer useful aids to spiritual growth, but spiritual growth should never finally *depend* on getting the technology right.

Given that computers can be engrossing and even addictive, there is a real danger of making God fit *their* codes and demands, rather than the other way round. Neil Postman even goes so far as to suggest that the tendency of technology to emphasise process over content leads to spiritual malaise and an erosion of coherent thought. The resulting 'technopoly', he writes, may well deprive us of the 'social, political, historical, metaphysical, logical or spiritual basis for knowing what is beyond belief'.[6]

On one hand, the software rack confirms the typically pragmatic evangelical approach to mission and discipleship – one that is ready to use the latest methods to get the gospel over in the most effective way.[7] In this area, evangelicals are streets ahead of any major church tradition. Go into more traditional theological bookshops on Marylebone Road and Margaret Street and far less will be available. Then again, the assumption of many evangelicals that technology is entirely value-neutral can, at times, lead to a dilution and trivialisation of its message.

The Meeting

They were last off the train. We had prepared an almost military schedule for them, but they started as they meant to go on – casual, laid back, unruffled. For Steve, Richard, John, Rod and Mark this was the next date on a whistle-stop tour of Britain. It was April 1995, and they had come from Canada – from the Airport Vineyard Church in Toronto. They were riding a wave of charismatic evangelical renewal which was sweeping the world. The press had already dubbed it 'the Toronto Blessing', and it would go on to generate scores of books, TV reports and controversies.

We had given the visit of the Toronto team minimal publicity, but still 1,200 people turned up to receive from them. Most of those who came that night I have not seen since: they arrived, they got blessed, they went away again. A band led forty minutes of praise and worship, and then Steve spoke. He referred to a passage in Ezekiel 36, but he did not preach from it – at least not in the way I had been taught to preach at theological college. He did not expound the text verse by verse. He did not set it in its grammatico-historical context. He did not recover the writer's original intention. Instead, he told stories – stories of how the Blessing had come to Toronto, stories of how God had turned people's lives around, stories shared to illustrate how we, too, might be filled by the Holy Spirit in this fresh and exciting way. He drew symbolic and experiential parallels with Ezekiel, but he did not exegete Ezekiel. The crowd listened attentively, and then prepared for a time of ministry. The team moved among them, praying and laying hands on them. As they did so, they were very undemonstrative and matter-of-fact. As I prayed alongside him, John told me to keep my eyes open, the better to discern how God was dealing with folk.

Reactions varied. Some people stood quietly and thanked us for our attention. Some shook and swayed. Others acted out physically what seemed to be going on spiritually within them: they ran on the spot, fenced with invisible swords and laughed out loud. In certain cases, I could recall a Bible verse which seemed to relate to what I was seeing. In others, there was no obvious rational explanation, nor was I particularly encouraged to seek one. Once the meeting had formally closed, the team dealt with a few people who were in need of more aggressive deliverance ministry. On the whole, however, things had taken place in an ordered, low-key atmosphere.

Postmodernism was not mentioned once.

In a perceptive study, Michael Glodo has argued that postmodernity represents a shift from 'word-based' to 'image-and-experience-based' forms of understanding – in biblical terms, from *logos* to *eikon*.[8] That 'Toronto' meeting, and the 'wave of blessing' of which it was a part, drew severe criticism from many traditional evangelicals precisely because of its perceived preference for sensation and visuality over verbal explication and biblical proclamation.[9] In this regard, it is at least worth mentioning that, even from a non-Christian perspective, Ihab Hassan influentially cast the shift from modernity to postmodernity as a shift from emphasis on God the Father to an emphasis on God the Holy Ghost.[10]

It may well be that, though hardly recognised as such at the time, the Toronto Blessing could have represented a form of evangelical postmodern spirituality. Whether this is a good thing or not is a question to which we shall return, but it will suffice to stress here that whether something is or is not a part of postmodernity should not in itself be a reason either to damn it or to praise it. As I have said, postmodernity is basically a description of how society is developing. As with most broad social developments, some elements of it will be quite compatible with the gospel, some will be antipathetic, and others will be indifferent.

Here again, Tomlinson may have too selective a view of postmodern culture. Spiritually, he is happy to draw from it a more holistic and less purely rational view of humanity, a sense of journey, and positive ecological and anti-materialistic ethos.[11] But he is less willing to admit that, for better or worse, it may also have penetrated the charismatic evangelical world which he has left behind.

The Community Church

Alan Evans does not know much about postmodernity. In fact, as we talked over coffee in his study, he admitted that the first he had heard of it was when I phoned to ask him for a chat. Alan is an evangelical minister in Bradford, and like many evangelicals he is an activist rather than a theorist. He responds practically to the needs of his community, and leaves others to write about how those needs have changed. Yet as I listened to him talk, and as he showed me around the church project he has developed and led these past twenty years, I realised that in his own way he is as switched on as the trendiest theologian of culture.

Holme is an out-of-town council estate. It has a population of 17,000 and an unemployment rate three times the national average. Damaged by the eclipse of the Yorkshire textile trade, it could easily come over as a depressed victim of post-industrial decline. But Alan and his church tell another story – a story of tenacious hope and sensitive local engagement, a story of ordinary Christians dealing with massive social transformation in a pioneering way.

The Holme project consists of four closely linked initiatives: a faith centre for worship, a care centre for young and old, a training centre for adult education, and an advice centre for information and counselling. Its work is diversified yet integrated, devolved yet unified by a common Christian ethos. Its watchword is 'community'. There are other such projects elsewhere, but what especially caught my attention at Holme was Alan's vision for Sunday-morning worship. As things stand, it is already fairly informal. Coffee is served from 9.30 a.m. to those who arrive on the early bus. From 10.00 until 10.15 there is a preliminary session of singing and prayer. The service gets officially under way at 10.15, and after a quarter of an hour the children leave for all-age learning which offers them a choice of simultaneous activities from puppet shows to videos, word-searches and crosswords to team competitions.

'We've found that we need to present things in a snappier way,' said Alan. 'Especially with the children, the key is that nothing lasts very long.' On the other hand, he then remarked ironically that 'we've had to spend more time trying to achieve that'. Shortened attention spans demand greater variety, which in turn means more preparation, and a longer overall running time. Nonetheless, everything appears quite relaxed. Responsibilities are widely devolved, and Alan is far removed from the 'one-man band' model still embodied by many clergy of his generation. 'From one Sunday to the next,' he reflected, 'I have no idea what the music group are going to play. There is no service order. When I tell other ministers this, they find it difficult to comprehend.'

This is all relatively unusual, but not without parallel. What really intrigued me was the next stage in the church's plan:

> We are looking towards a longer, three-hour period on Sundays. We are aiming to offer people a range of activities, which will take place in different areas of the building at the same time. These will include quiet prayer, personal ministry, drinking coffee, talking or joining the main church worship. Apart from a central section in which everyone will be together, they will be able to choose from a 'menu' of other things.

Remember: when we met, Alan Evans had not read a single book or article on postmodernism.

For the educationalist Yvonne Craig the 'accelerated culture' of postmodernity is one in which attention spans reduce accordingly.[12] To Charles Jencks, it is a culture marked at best by an 'embarrassment of riches' offering new opportunities for the 'inventive combination' and 'synthesis' of different traditions and approaches.[13] As postmodern society becomes more heterogeneous, so Walter

James and Brian Russell have suggested that the Church 'should welcome and embrace the less authoritarian and more learner-centred styles of education that a postmodern spirit exacts'.[14] They add that such styles should naturally derive ideas 'from multiple sources [existing] alongside each other [and] interactively put to use by the people of God to explore their common inheritance'.[15]

For all his professed ignorance of postmodern theory, it seems to me that Alan Evans and Holme URC are living postmodernity out in practice. The children's activities 'speeded up' and 'multiplied' to keep their interest, the pluriform 'menu' of Sunday-morning activities planned to cater for different tastes and needs – these are almost textbook models for a postmodern church.

Also, despite his fostering of diversity, Evans's commitment to the ideal of local unity and community *within* that diversity – his interlinked projects and premises – could be seen as positively postmodern. It chimes in with Steinar Kvale's tracing within secular postmodern thought the desire for 'a return to the medieval village, with its tight-knit community and complex webs of buildings and places'.[16] And in theological terms, it echoes Stanley Grenz, whose creative attempt to 'revision' evangelical faith for a postmodern world includes the plea that 'we as evangelicals not view theology merely as a restatement of doctrine [but as] a practical discipline oriented primarily toward the believing community'.[17]

Holme URC is but one example of a constructive response to postmodernity. The Christian software sold next door to my church may raise more problems than it solves; the postmodern pluses and minuses of the Toronto Blessing may not yet be clear; but my visit to Holme convinced me that there was a book to be written which did more than take up arms against postmodernity or give it a cautious academic welcome. For Alan Evans, as for several of the other evangelicals we shall meet in the pages which follow, postmodernity is neither an enemy to be destroyed nor a wanton seductress to be resisted at all costs. It is, more immediately, something to be lived with and, where possible, assimilated. Of course there will be tensions and certain elements of it will have to be challenged – not least some more extreme forms of postmodernist ideology. Nonetheless, I hope to show that the postmodern world is too multi-faceted to be either dismissed sweepingly or embraced unthinkingly by evangelical Christians. We need a practical, mature, biblically informed view of it. So where better to turn than to Scripture itself?

4

BIBLE REFLECTION: ECCLESIASTES 3:5

We have seen how postmodernity has often been characterised by fragmentation, diversification and diffusion. But
we ought to ask, 'Are these things always so bad?' Granted,
when applied to notions of absolute truth they do seem to
strike at the heart of evangelical faith, centred as it is on a
unique Saviour and a divinely inspired Scripture. Even so,
at other points the postmodern dismantling of modernistic
assumptions could be seen as being as much a part of
God's providence as the abandonment and implied ruin of
the Tower of Babel in Genesis 11, the fall of Solomon's
temple in 2 Kings 25, or the destruction of Herod's temple
prophesied by Jesus (John 2:19; Mark 13:2) and fulfilled
in AD 70.

In my study, there is a wonderful book about early
Christian art. A whole chapter is devoted to the sacred
mosaics which were revived by the Eastern Church in the
fifth century, and which remained a prime Christian art-form
for the next thousand years or so. Mosaics go back at least
to ancient Greece, but their appropriation by the Church is
a reminder that not everything which gets fragmented *stays*
fragmented.

Mosaics rearrange what was once atomised and disparate
into a fresh pattern: the dis-integration is not an end, but
a new and creative beginning. Small stones and shards of
rock are painstakingly brought together to form a colourful
vision of life.

Mosaics remind us that breaking old structures down is sometimes as necessary as building new ones up. In fact, they show that it can be an indispensable *prerequisite* of reconstruction.

In Ecclesiastes 3:5, the Teacher reflects that there is 'a time to gather stones, and a time to scatter them'.

Some commentators see this as a sexual metaphor,[1] but the original meaning is probably more literal. It might denote the stones kept in a bag by traders for use in transactions. On the other hand, it could refer to the need to clear stones from a field so that it could be cultivated (cf. Isa. 5:2) and, in contrast, to the sabotage of a rival's field by casting stones into it (cf. 2 Kgs. 3:19, 25).[2] However, the Targum – a later Aramaic translation of the text – interprets it as describing the demolition of a house and subsequent preparations for rebuilding.

Unlike the destruction of Pruitt-Igoe or my old Birmingham council block, buildings which were knocked down in ancient Hebrew culture were often recycled. Some of their constituent stone was left scattered on the ground, but some was used again to erect new structures.[3] If we bear this in mind, 'scattering and gathering' can be seen to evoke a positive model of disordering and reordering, judgment and reconciliation, death and resurrection (cf. John 2:19–21).

At times postmodernity might appear hell-bent on destroying the whole 'household' of Christian faith (cf. 1 Pet. 2:4–10), not least because of its attack on key pillars like revelation, truth and authority. Gene Veith certainly sees this as a feature of what he calls 'secular postmodernism'. This, he says, 'sees fit not only to blow modernism to smithereens but to explode *all* stable forms, including Christianity'. He goes on pessimistically:

Instead of erecting some other structure out of the rubble, secular postmodernism concentrates on the explosion. The effort to help poor people by giving them a temple of modernism to live in did prove futile.

> While it may have been appropriate to dynamite mod-
> ernism, most postmodern theorists refuse to provide a
> more habitable alternative. The low-income inhabitants
> of the Pruitt-Igoe housing project no longer have to live
> in a sterile, inhuman structure. Under postmodern ways
> of thinking, they can be homeless.[4]

Even if one accepts Veith's basic critique, there is surely
another side to all this. If the pillars of the building have been
sunk deep into the foundations of sin-stained rationalism,
rather than into a bedrock of relationship with God and
neighbour, maybe it *is* best to accept their removal. As
Alister McGrath puts it, 'Why should evangelicals feel under
any pressure to conform to the highly questionable dictates
of the limits of fallen human reason? . . . fallen human
reason cannot fully comprehend the majesty of God.'[5]

Postmodernity in general, and secular postmodernism in
particular, may yet bring an uncomfortable fragmentation
and scattering of many things which evangelicals hold
dear. It may undermine our established forms of worship
and preaching; it may decompose our cherished modes of
witness and discipleship; it may shake up our ethics and
our political involvements; it may challenge the way we
do our theology and frame our doctrine. Several stones
may, indeed, have to remain dispersed on the ground.
But ultimately our model of demolition is the Hebrew
one – the Ecclesiastes model of scattering *and then* gathering. We put our trust in a God who works through
cultural change, but who has promised not to forsake us
in the process (Deut. 31:6) – a God who himself remains
our dwelling-place even when the very earth and moun-
tains fragment around us (Ps. 46). Given such a God, we
must trust that the essential raw material of Christian faith
will survive the shocks of postmodernity, to be gathered
up and re-presented once again, a vital new structure in
ancient stone.

In order to 'pick up the pieces' in the way I have

described, it will be helpful to consider in more detail the post-evangelical realignment proposed by Tomlinson. Before we can do that, however, we need to determine more clearly just what is meant by 'evangelicalism' itself.

5

EVANGELICALISM, MODERNITY AND POSTMODERNITY

Two More Stories

The Presentation

The conference hall went dark. After a few seconds, spotlights picked out a huge bank of video screens, which began to flash up disconnected images and slogans. Adverts familiar from TV; snippets of news; shopping malls; cars; soap operas; cartoons; theme parks; 'postmodernism knows no commitments'; 'that dress is so ten minutes ago'; everything is for sale'; 'overeducated and unemployed'; 'to be related is to be plugged in'; 'irony dulls the pain'; 'if you don't watch the violence, how will you become desensitised?'.

In the middle of it all, dwarfed by the technology around him, stood Brian Draper, resplendent in a parodic, seventies-style lime-green shirt. Voguishly monotonous yet eminently listenable, he commentated on the riot of colour and sound erupting around him. 'It's hard to believe in anything now except a protest group'; 'Consumer choice makes life a work of art'; 'skimming the surface'; 'multi-channel TV'; 'Next . . . next . . . next . . .'

And so it went on. Eventually, in good 'modern' fashion, everything was 'explained' in a more linear, rational way.

Talking heads appeared live and on film; the audience seemed less disconcerted. Still, more than anyone else, Draper had exemplified Marshall McLuhan's dictum about the medium being the message. This was a presentation on postmodernism, and he had executed his part of it in a truly postmodern way.

But what was all this in aid of, and where did it all take place? At a cultural studies seminar? In a contemporary art gallery? No. Remarkably enough, it formed part of a presentation by the London Bible College to the National Assembly of Evangelicals, in the Bournemouth Conference Centre on Monday, 11 November 1996. At the very heart of British evangelicalism, postmodern issues were being tackled in a genuinely sussed-out manner by apparently sussed-out people – and by one sussed-out person in particular. If you want to check it out for yourself, the video and booklet are available.[1]

I met Brian Draper at his flat in Northwood shortly after his *tour de force*. He was studying for a master's degree at LBC and on the brink of becoming Deputy Editor of *Third Way* – an evangelical magazine dedicated to the analysis of contemporary culture. In addition, he runs a monthly alternative worship service in Cranbrook, Kent, called 'Live on Planet Earth', more of which later.

Having been brought up as an evangelical through the seventies and eighties, Draper met opposition in his own church circle when he decided to study academic theology, and has since struggled to reconcile his intellectual journey with evangelical culture. Much of what he had encountered in that culture now struck him, he said, as 'shallow, narrow-minded and triumphalistic'. Echoing Dave Tomlinson, he went on to describe not only his own tensions, but those of several friends: 'We've been brought up in churches which tell us one thing about Christianity and living, but which our life-experience doesn't really reflect.'

During the Bournemouth presentation Draper had suggested with typical postmodern ambivalence that while

he was an evangelical in that context, he might be a
post-evangelical in others. When I took up this point, he
qualified things by saying, 'I believe that ultimately we as
Christians have something to hang on to which is true and I
would still hope to call myself an evangelical – *even though
I am often embarrassed to do so.*'

The School of Theology

'I have to say that I'm not impressed if I have to do that sort
of thing all the time to hold people's attention. The time it
takes to produce something like that! I dare say what we
saw took weeks and weeks, just for an hour. What's the
pastor to do? Is he going to have a staff of twenty people
who are going to come up with something like that every
week? And you've got to ask the question, "Does it edify?"
No! It entertains, and that's about it.'

R. T. Kendall was talking about the London Bible College
presentation, and its applicability to contemporary ministry.
He had been at Bournemouth as a member of the Evangelical
Alliance Council. He has led the Independent evangelical congregation at Westminster Chapel for over twenty
years. His predecessors include the great Bible expositors
Campbell Morgan and Martyn Lloyd Jones. As we talked, it
soon became obvious that despite what he had seen, he was
not in a hurry to give up the methods which have served him
so effectively during a distinguished career of preaching,
writing and conference speaking. Nor, as we have already
seen, was he very enamoured of postmodernism.

Later the same evening, R. T. led his School of Theology. A regular Friday-night fixture, this relies on a well-
established mode of presentation. For ninety minutes, he
stood in the vast open pulpit of the church and delivered
a talk on the vexed subject of predestination and freewill.
The audience sat and listened in the pews, most of them
following a pre-printed sheet of notes. Point by point, R. T.

took us through the arguments on both sides of the issue, assiduously referring us back to Scripture, and lightening things up every now and again with a joke or funny story. After he had finished, he took questions from the floor. At the close, he graciously asked me to come to the front and say a final prayer.

With his obvious love of the Bible and his systematic recall of Reformed doctrine, Kendall gave an impressive performance. Without doubt it was thoroughly modernistic, but as modernistic evangelicalism goes it was exemplary and absorbing. What is more, it is also popular. Every week around three hundred Christians – many tired from a week at work – turn up to the sessions. As R. T. had said earlier, 'It's the most successful thing I've ever done. And it's undiluted propositional truth! I do intersperse it with stories about how I came to see a particular point and what has happened in my life to make it more relevant.' But, he added, 'We're not talking about a ten- or twenty-minute sermon. We go on for an hour and a half! We're in our sixth year, and the course has just been published as a book. So don't tell me that propositional truth is no longer relevant!'

Two attempts to explain the gospel today. Both of them delivered by evangelicals in an evangelical setting, to an evangelical audience. Yet the methods, personalities, and conceptions in each case are different enough to suggest that before we can meaningfully determine the relevance of postmodernity to evangelicalism, we must try to grasp just what is expressed by the word 'evangelical'.

Evangelicalism and Modernity

Faced with the shift from modernity to postmodernity, Christians in general need to ask deep questions about their understanding and presentation of the faith. What makes this challenge especially urgent for *evangelical* Christians is the fact that to a large extent their tradition is a product of the modern age. Indeed, before we examine how evangelicals might go forward into the *post*modern world, we need to grasp where they have come from. This will put us in a better position to assess whether, as Dave Tomlinson implies, this heritage will disqualify them from engaging in a constructive way with postmodernity.

The 'pre-history' of evangelicalism

Reformation

Although the term 'evangelical' derives from the New Testament Greek word for preaching the gospel, it was first widely applied to the Lutheran wing of the Reformation in the early 1500s.[2] Martin Luther (1483–1546) had been an Augustinian monk and theologian, but was excommunicated by the Church of Rome in 1521 following a series of attacks on its doctrine and practice. From about 1512, when he took up a chair in biblical studies at the University of Wittenburg, Luther had begun to explore the Church's teaching on justification – that is, how human sins are forgiven. This led him away from the Roman emphasis on works of devotion and towards the idea that we are justified by faith alone, through the free grace of God. Although Luther's ideas on justification were not clearly published until later, they motivated him, in October 1517, to oppose the sale of indulgences for penance. The printing and distribution of his 'Ninety-Five Theses' on this issue are generally taken to mark the beginning of the 'Reformation' – so called because the mass movement which followed in Luther's wake sought to reform the organisation, theology and worship of the Church more specifically in accordance with the teaching of Scripture.[3]

Throughout the 1520s, this reformation became associated with the term 'evangelical', as Luther's followers began to use the word *evangelisch* to sum up their concerns. By the next decade, however, the church authorities had ensured that the more negative term 'Protestant' would be the main one by which the Reformers would be known. Consequently, 'evangelical' receded in prominence as the Reformation spread through the efforts of Martin Bucer (1491–1551), Philip Melancthon (1497–1560), John Calvin (1509–64) and others.

As we shall see, the designation 'evangelical' would not be broadly applied again to a movement within the Church for a further two hundred years – that is, until the dawn of modernity. Even so, as Alister McGrath points out, 'modern' evangelicalism still owes a great deal to the Reformation period: 'The Reformation remains a focus and defining point of reference for evangelicalism today, as it seeks to ensure that the central tenets of the Reformation – such as the doctrine of justification by faith alone and the Scripture principle – remain deeply embedded in the evangelical consciousness.'[4]

We should not assume, either, that just because the term 'evangelical' fell out of prominence between the later sixteenth and mid-eighteenth centuries, there were not important precedents during that period for what we call 'evangelicalism' today.

Puritanism

In England, the movement which became known as 'Puritanism' sought to extend Reformation thought – first into the Church of England, and then into society as a whole. Taking their cue from first-generation reformers like William Tyndale (1494–1536) and John Hooper (d.1555), Thomas Cartwright (1535–1603), John Field (1545–88), William Perkins (1558–1602) and others pressed for the Church of England to be 'purified' by the exclusion of any feature of church life which was not affirmed by Scripture. Much of the Puritans' dissent was focused on the Third Book of

Common Prayer of 1559, which to their mind had retained or reinstated a number of such unbiblical elements (e.g. liturgical vestments, kneeling at communion, etc.).

More radical Puritans like Henry Barrow (1550–93) and Robert Browne (1550–1633) broke from the Church of England altogether, while other so-called 'Separatists' emigrated to America as 'Pilgrim Fathers'.

Despite upholding Luther's stress on biblical authority and personal salvation, the Puritans leaned more towards Calvin in their theology – and not least in their approach to wider society. Whereas Luther had distinguished sharply between civil and church government, Calvin in practice ran them more closely together.[5] In England, the Puritan ideal of a 'Godly Society' found its strongest expression in the Commonwealth, which was installed under the Puritan Oliver Cromwell and which lasted from 1649 until 1660, when monarchy was restored under Charles II. Two years later Charles imposed the Prayer Book on all clergy. Those who did not conform were ejected, and the grander aspirations of Puritanism were mitigated by a more intimate, emotional form of Protestantism.

Pietism

By the mid-seventeenth century, the church which Luther founded in Germany had become dry and hidebound by formality. Many of its ministers occupied themselves more with esoteric debate than with the building up of their congregations. In addition, the religious undercurrents of the Thirty Years War (1618–48) had soured many people's attitudes to church life. Out of this unpromising situation came the movement now known as Pietism.[6]

In 1666 Philip Jakob Spener was called to the pastorate of Frankfurt am Main, whereupon he instigated a root-and-branch reform of church life. Not only did he start a *collegia pietas* or 'pious assembly' for the laity to study Scripture twice a week, he also wrote the influential preface

Pia Desideria (Pious Wishes), which analysed Germany's spiritual decline and offered clear solutions. As well as a return to biblical basics and greater lay participation, these included a shift of emphasis from academic theology to practical devotion, and from scholastic preaching to clear, edifying sermons.

Although Spener's ideas stirred controversy among the church authorities, they had a massive impact on ordinary Christians. His work was continued by August Hermann Francke, who extended the practical thrust of Pietism by establishing poor schools, orphanages, training colleges, publishing houses and hospitals.

In view of subsequent developments, it is also highly significant that Francke was spurred on to this work by a dramatic conversion experience in 1687. This in turn led to a lifelong passion for evangelism and mission. The university Francke established at Halle sent many missionaries overseas and also influenced the refugee community known as the Moravians, who, led by Nikolas von Zinzendorf, exported Pietism all over the world.

Momentously for evangelicalism, it was while sailing to Georgia in 1735 that a young Anglican cleric called John Wesley met a group of Moravians, and was so deeply affected by their faith and example that he began to explore the Pietistic way for himself.

The birth of modern evangelicalism: Wesley, Whitefield and revival

On 24 May 1738, Wesley's encounter with Pietism culminated in an experience which would prove to be foundational for British evangelicalism. His famous diary entry for that day runs as follows:

In the evening I went very unwillingly to a society

in Aldersgate Street, where one was reading Luther's preface to the *Epistle to the Romans*. About a quarter before nine, while he was describing the change which God works in the heart through faith in Christ, I felt my heart strangely warmed. I felt I did trust Christ, Christ alone for salvation; and an assurance was given me that he had taken away *my* sins, even *mine*, and saved *me* from the law of sin and death.[7]

It is pertinent that Wesley was listening to Luther on Romans when this happened, because it was Luther's emphasis on justification by faith which Wesley took up when he embarked with George Whitefield on an itinerant ministry which would lead directly to the so-called 'Evangelical Revival'.

Although Wesley himself developed an Arminian theology which stressed the freedom of every individual to accept or reject God's offer of salvation, evangelicalism was not defined along strict doctrinal lines. Indeed, Whitefield himself was a Calvinist – drawn more to an emphasis on the predestination and sovereign will of God in election. Likewise Jonathan Edwards, who around the same time nurtured a remarkable revival in North America, beginning with his own Massachusetts congregation and moving south into all the colonies. Indeed, on both sides of the Atlantic, those who had attempted to keep the Puritan flame alive in Independent and Baptist churches were given a remarkable boost by the new movement: between 1750 and 1800 their numbers more than doubled.[8] This was quite apart from the fourfold increase which occurred in Wesley's own new 'Methodist' communities between 1767 and 1830.[9]

In 1793, the *Evangelical Magazine* was founded as a non-denominational journal serving all those dedicated to spreading the gospel. As Bebbington has shown, right up to the present day evangelicalism remains identified more with this activist, conversionist agenda, and with the biblicist and crucicentric emphases which motivate it, than with any particular system of doctrine, liturgy or church government.[10] This breadth and diversity, stemming as it does from a combination of Reformation thought, Puritanism and warm-hearted Piety, needs to be borne in mind whenever evangelicalism is tagged to 'modernity' – and not least when it is associated with Enlightenment rationalism.

Evangelicalism and Enlightenment rationalism

'Enlightenment rationalism is the bedrock of evangelical culture.' The speaker was Nick Mercer, former Vice Principal of the London Bible College, now an Anglican priest. As we talked in his vicarage, he added, 'Without the Enlightenment there can arguably be no evangelicalism. The whole historico-grammatical method of evangelical exegesis is a product of the Enlightenment. Evangelicals often claim the Reformation as the rock from which they were hewn – but then evangelicals have always been good at rewriting history!'

The early British evangelical movement certainly drew on Enlightenment thinking;[11] Wesley himself even published a book on electricity.[12] Reports of discussions among evangelical leaders towards the end of the eighteenth century show many seeking to back up their arguments with reference to the empirical philosophy of Locke – that is, with a hard-headed 'weighing of the evidence'.[13] The Anglican evangelical Henry Venn and his protégé Charles Simeon were typical, presenting religion as a 'science' which should be based on an experimental search for 'first principles'.[14]

Even more striking, though, was the exaltation of reason which characterised the so-called 'Common Sense' theology of the Scottish Free Church leader Thomas Chalmers (1780–1847). Chalmers based much of his thinking on the work of Thomas Reid, whose *Inquiry into the Human Mind* (1764) had claimed that human beings perceive the real world not through abstract ideas *about* it but through intuition and direct experience *of* it. As reinforced by Chalmers's fellow Scot John Witherspoon, this approach influenced English Victorian evangelicalism as well – not least in the work of J. C. Ryle and E. A. Litton.[15] As Bebbington has observed, by this stage there was little doubt that evangelicals were 'integrating their faith with the rising philosophy of the later Enlightenment', and that 'they were in harmony with the spirit of the age'.[16]

Enlightenment rationalism and Common Sense have followed through into the more conservative parts of twentieth-century evangelicalism: they are clearly detectable in the writing of F. B. Meyer, the ethos of the Inter-Varsity Fellowship (now the Universities and Colleges Christian Fellowship), the preaching of Martyn Lloyd Jones and the early work of J. I. Packer. They are maintained today by organisations such as the Banner of Truth and Proclamation Trusts.

Having said all this, by far the most widespread and enduring impact of Scottish Common Sense philosophy has been on the United States rather than Britain. Indeed, it was only when John Witherspoon crossed the Atlantic to become Principal of Princeton Seminary in 1768 that Common Sense came really to dominate an evangelical constituency.[17] Indeed, it is significant that when surveying the influence of the Enlightenment on evangelicalism, Alister McGrath concentrates almost exclusively on the American rather than the British context.[18] In Britain, the truth is that the picture has always been more eclectic. For example, whereas significant numbers of evangelicals in the US extrapolated from Common Sense to the ultra-conservative, hyper-rationalistic creeds of Fundamentalism, Fundamentalist beliefs have always remained marginal here.[19]

True as it was, then, that large numbers of evangelicals adopted the thought-forms of the Enlightenment, this must be set alongside the fact that they also drew on a range of earlier, less overtly rationalistic influences. What is more, it needs also to be recognised that, since the eighteenth century, evangelicalism has been affected by a variety of *other* movements, some of which can be seen as a reaction to the so-called 'Age of Reason'.

Evangelicalism and Romanticism

For all that Tomlinson, Mercer and others might associate the modern era with Enlightenment rationalism, the fact is that the late eighteenth and early nineteenth centuries witnessed a major *revolt* against such thinking. This revolt took the form of Romanticism. What is more, significant branches of evangelical Christianity would go on to be deeply affected by the Romantic movement.

In Bernard Reardon's words, Romanticism 'deplored the [eighteenth century's] merely critical and analytical concept of reason as opposed to its own, which by contrast saw it as intuitive and synthetic'.[20] Against the reductive, mechanistic view of things which had dominated Enlightenment philosophy, Romantic thinkers like Johann Goethe (1749–1832), Friedrich Schiller (1759–1805), William Schlegel (1767–1853), and Samuel Taylor Coleridge (1772–1834) stressed a more holistic view of truth, insisting that scientific knowledge be put to a more unifying, humanitarian purpose.

Alongside his many other writings, Coleridge's poetry, together with that of William Wordsworth (1770–1850), William Blake (1757–1827), Lord Byron (1788–1824), Percy Bysshe Shelley (1792–1822), and John Keats (1795–1821), celebrated the natural order in a fervent, 'ecological' spirit.

Although the greatest Romantic influence on Christian thought came through the work of Friedrich Schleiermacher (1768–1834), who is widely considered to be the father of 'liberal' theology, it nonetheless also affected evangelicals in notable ways. The hymns of Charles Wesley, which formed a vital accompaniment to his brother John's ministry, anticipate the emphasis of the Romantic poets on emotion, sense and dynamic spiritual experience.[21] Later, during the 1820s, Coleridge himself developed a close friendship with the erratic but popular evangelical preacher Edward Irving. From 1822 Irving led the Church of Scotland congregation at Hatton Garden – a stone's throw away from my own church.

With Coleridge's encouragement, Irving strove for a new approach to Christian doctrine which would consciously depart from earlier Enlightenment emphases. In 1823 he wrote:

> We feel that questions touching the truths of revelation have been too long treated in a logical or scholastic method, which doth address itself to I know not what fraction of mind; and, not finding this used in Scripture, or successful in practice, we are disposed to try another method, and appeal our cause to every sympathy of the soul which it doth bear upon.[22]

By 1830, Irving was presiding over meetings at Hatton Garden which included speaking in tongues – the first recorded instance of this phenomenon in England. This had him expelled and led to his founding the Catholic Apostolic Church, over which he presided until his death in 1834. In his preaching and writing, Irving studiously promoted Schiller, Goethe and Wordsworth: his Romantic leanings were unmistakable.

A more widespread and long-lasting instance of Romantic evangelicalism was the so-called 'holiness movement' of the late nineteenth century.[23] At the centre of this movement was the Keswick Convention, which began in 1875, deeply affected evangelical spirituality well into the twentieth century, and still takes place today.

It was not only the Lake District setting which inspired

Keswick's Romantic flavour. Several of its leaders, including C. A. Fox and J. B. Figgis, were great admirers of Wordsworth – so much so that Bebbington has commented: 'It was as though Wordsworthian pantheism had become an additional article of the evangelical creed . . . The educated public was turning to Romantic sensibilities as an escape-route from the urban, industrial present, and the holiness movement was part of that process.'[24] In addition, under the guidance of Robert Pearsall Smith and Evan Hopkins, Keswick placed a typically Romantic emphasis on the force of the individual will as a means to sanctification.[25]

Now it is worth pointing out that this stress on individual volition and the other Romantic aspects of nineteenth-century evangelicalism – from its experiential character through its reverence for nature to its search for an integrative spirituality – could be said to have as much in common with a postmodernist as a 'modernist' ethos. Indeed, Richard Appignanesi and Chris Garratt have gone so far as to suggest that postmodernity may well open the way to a rediscovery of the Romantic tradition.[26]

Here, again, we can see the pitfalls of attaching evangelicalism to modernity in any way which implies that either phenomenon is singular and monolithic, or that the relationship between the two is straightforward. Here, again, we can see the problem of branding evangelicalism as 'rationalistic'. This problem is only compounded when we consider evangelicalism in the twentieth century.

Evangelicalism, Pentecostalism and Charismatic Renewal

Numerically at least, the most significant development within evangelicalism in the past hundred years has come from the Pentecostal and Charismatic Renewal movements.

Promoting a 'second blessing' experience of the Holy Spirit after conversion, and the use of spiritual gifts or 'charismata' such as tongues, prophecy and healing, Pentecostalism began under the Kansas ministry of Charles Fox Parnham (1873–1929) in 1901. It was then given considerable impetus by the so-called 'Azusa Street Revival' of 1906–8. Under the leadership of Joseph William Seymour (1870–1922), the Azusa Street Mission in Los Angeles, California, became the wellspring of a global movement which now numbers as many as 247 million or more people.[27]

Since the 1960s, Pentecostal influence has spread to various mainline churches through the so-called Charismatic Renewal movement, and also to a range of 'house' or 'new' church groupings such as Ichthus, led by Roger Forster, Pioneer, led by Gerald Coates, and Terry Virgo's New Frontiers network.[28]

If Pentecostal and Charismatic Christianity is 'modernistic', then, once more, it is modernistic in a way which must be distinguished from sheer Enlightenment rationalism. No doubt some branches of classical Pentecostalism draw their theology from Fundamentalist sources, but these sources have not dictated the more general recovery of charismatic ministry.[29]

One of the most telling contributions made by charismatics to recent British evangelicalism has been the remarkable growth of the Evangelical Alliance (EA). Under the leadership of the self-professed charismatic Clive Calver, the membership of EA increased fiftyfold to 53,000 individual members between 1983 and 1997, with similarly impressive growth occurring in church and agency membership.[30] This has in turn carried over into the establishment and development of EA-sponsored 'Spring Harvest' weeks, which from relatively modest beginnings in the late seventies now attract around 80,000 people every year.[31] Much of this expansion has been due to Calver's encouragement of the rapidly increasing charismatic and new church constituency.[32] What is more, the fact that this constituency has been so successfully integrated into what was a predominantly conservative evangelical body bears out a final, and for us crucial, feature of evangelical identity – namely pragmatism.

Evangelicalism, Pragmatism and Postmodernity

When I interviewed Clive Calver, he was preparing to leave the Evangelical Alliance for a new job in the USA. It was an appropriate time to reflect on a remarkable fourteen years. As he assessed the reasons for the growth of EA during his time at the helm, he was quite frank about his own pragmatic approach to things. He said:

> Evangelicals are basically magpies. We will acquire whatever's going. When I came to EA in 1983 and people were arguing about whether I was left-wing or right-wing, I said, 'Stuff the ideology!' I'm sick to death with ideology! I want actually to *achieve* something. I want to *do*, and not just to *aspire to.* Of course, I should add that as evangelicals we can only say that because we have a destination in mind.

For all its bluntness, Calver's approach has a strong evangelical pedigree. From its earliest beginnings, evangelicalism has been as much influenced by pragmatism as by rationalism. It was apparent in the punishing schedules of Wesley and Whitefield, and the expedient approach to church order adopted by the early Methodists. It also motivated the founding of activist interdenominational groups like the London Missionary Society and the British and Foreign Bible Society.[33]

Another important manifestation of evangelical pragmatism has been its commitment to social action. The great evangelical public reformer Lord Shaftesbury wrote in a diary entry for April 1850: 'Toil, toil, toil . . . nor should I lament could I say fruit, fruit, fruit.' Similarly, William Wilberforce's campaign against slavery, the involvement of

nonconformist evangelicals in the foundation of the trades
unions, and the many philanthropic campaigns headed by
evangelicals at the turn of the twentieth century, all bear
witness to this pragmatic drive. As the evangelical writer
Hannah More had put it back in 1808: 'Action is the life
of virtue, and the world is the theatre of action.'[34]

Although such socially applied pragmatism waned somewhat during the first half of the twentieth century,[35] the
relaxation of attitudes to sex, abortion and broadcasting
standards in the sixties, together with a genuine recom-
mitment to the poor and to international issues, has led to
a renaissance of evangelical social concern which Clive
Calver himself has linked with 'a firm desire [among evan-
gelicals] to recover the identity and emphasis of their
predecessors'.[36] The fruits of this can be seen in the vast
array of campaigning evangelical bodies formed in the last
thirty years or so: the Evangelical Alliance Relief Fund,
CARE for the Family, Keep Sunday Special, the AIDS
charity ACET and Evangelical Christians for Racial Justice,
to name but a few.

More recently, David Wells has traced the profound
effect of pragmatism on the evangelical 'church growth'
movement, which began in America but which has had a
significant influence on British evangelicalism in the last
twenty-five years.[37] At a broader level, James Davison
Hunter has shown in some detail how American evangelicals have pragmatically adapted their message to meet
the demands of the market and of a changing culture –
an adaptation which, as we shall see, can be discerned
increasingly within the British context.[38]

Despite its clear challenge to Enlightenment rationalism,
we noted in the last chapter that postmodernity tends to
be far less negative about pragmatism. Indeed, pragmatism
is in many ways essential to the spirit of the postmodern
age, since it, too, tends to sideline deep agonising about
metaphysical questions in favour of getting results in the
here and now.[39]

Clive Calver's emphasis on action over idealism could in this sense be seen as postmodern, as could the capacity of the EA to maintain considerable practical unity despite the wide diversity of doctrinal convictions held by its members.

Calver is fond of comparing this situation to that of Old Testament Israel. Using an analogy he attributed to the Scottish evangelical thinker Tom Houston, Calver told me: 'We are a tribal people. Some tribes are guilty of Enlightenment rationalism. But lots of other tribes are not. Part of the problem is that people assume a homogeneity among evangelicals which is simply not there. It needs to be clarified that evangelicalism is already very diverse.' This, of course, brings us back to our initial comparison between R. T. Kendall and Brian Draper.

In true biblical fashion, Calver himself has identified twelve major tribes within British evangelicalism: Anglican evangelicals, Pentecostals, ethnic churches, renewal groupings, separatists, Reformed evangelicals, majority evangelical denominations like the Baptist Union and the Salvation Army, minority evangelical groupings within mainline denominations, non-denominational evangelicals, 'New' churches, Independents and evangelical denominations.[40]

Given that we have already identified not only pragmatism but also heterogeneity as key features of postmodernity, Calver's analysis underlines that the status of evangelicalism in the postmodern world may be rather more complex than Dave Tomlinson has implied. In developing this point, it will be helpful to analyse the tribal analogy from a biblical perspective before going on to consider Tomlinson's argument in more detail.

6

BIBLE REFLECTION: GENESIS 49:13–19

Zebulun will live by the seashore
and become a haven for ships;
his border will extend towards Sidon.
Issachar is a scrawny donkey
lying down between two saddlebags.
When he sees how good is his resting place
and how pleasant is his land,
he will bend his shoulder to the burden
and submit to forced labour.
Dan will provide justice for his people
as one of the tribes of Israel.
Dan will be a serpent by the roadside,
a viper along the path,
that bites the horse's heels
so that its rider tumbles backwards . . .
Gad will be attacked by a band of raiders,
but he will attack them at their heels.

The different tribes which made up the nation of Israel all
had a common source. In Genesis 49, we see that they shared
the same 'father', Jacob, and were respectively descended
from his twelve sons. As with most families, however, the
offspring exhibited a wide variety of characteristics.

In this passage, Jacob pronounces blessings tailored to
each particular son, and these blessings in turn predict the
future fortunes of that son's line. Much could be said about

these blessings and predictions but, from our point of view, some interesting contrasts can be drawn concerning the way each tribe is destined to relate to its surrounding culture. These contrasts are especially stark in verses 13–19, where Jacob describes what will happen to the tribes of Zebulun, Issachar, Dan and Gad.

Although Jacob describes the future location of Zebulun as 'by the sea', the land allotted to this tribe in Joshua 19:10–16 did not reach the coast. Nonetheless, the preposition 'by' could be translated 'towards', and Zebulun's territory was certainly near enough to be enriched by seafaring trade. What is more, the walled city of Sidon was well known as a port (Josh. 11:8). Then as now, ports were cosmopolitan places, and maritime trade provided much opportunity for cultural exchange and assimilation. Despite this, there is no indication in the text that Zebulun would ever be fatally compromised by contact with foreign worldviews – nor did this prove to be the case in subsequent history. The Zebulunites distinguished themselves in battle with the nearby Canaanites and Midianites (Judg. 4:6, 10; 5:14, 18; 6:35), and although many of the tribe were deported in the days of the Assyrian empire (2 Kgs. 15:29; Isa. 9:1), its identity was preserved. Indeed, its members are included in Hezekiah's Passover feast (2 Chr. 30:10).

It would seem that Zebulun managed to engage with new cultural challenges in a positive way, without being overwhelmed by them. In New Testament terms, we might say with St Paul that it more or less succeeded in being 'in the world' but not 'of the world' (2 Cor. 10:3). In contemporary terms, Zebulun could be a model for those evangelical 'tribes' which seek to appropriate the positive aspects of postmodernity while resisting those elements in it which are set against the gospel.

Issachar presents something of a contrast to Zebulun, in that he/it is explicitly criticised by Jacob. The picture offered in verse 15 is the disparaging one of a docile, well-fed beast of burden settling for a comfortable but submissive life under a pagan regime. Unlike Zebulun, Issachar appears all too willing to assimilate with the surrounding culture at the expense of its own identity and heritage. The distinction is marked all the more by the fact that Issachar shared a common blessing and a common sanctuary with Zebulun (Deut. 33:18–19). Although under King David the 'men of Issachar' would acquire a reputation as culture vultures who 'understood the times', we cannot assume that this protected them against 'selling out' to the spirit of the age (1 Chr. 12:32).

Jacob's words can be taken as a warning about the dangers for the people of God of being too ready to absorb the norms of contemporary thought, fashion and politics. In Paul's terms, the tribe of Issachar is presented in this passage as the equivalent of those who are 'conformed to the pattern of this world' rather than 'transformed by the renewal of their mind' so that they can better obey God within their cultural context (Rom. 12:2). No doubt in the postmodern world there could well be evangelical 'tribes' who fall into this trap, and the implication here is that they would be all the less effective for doing so.

At face value, the tribe of Dan seems to have been destined for a very different future from that of either Zebulun or Issachar. It is described by Jacob as a tribe which is meant to *confront* its cultural milieu in a robust way, protecting the 'path' of righteousness from sinister invaders and usurpers (the horses and riders of verse 17). The picture seems to be more one of separation than assimilation. Dan was one of the smallest tribes, and seems from this text to have been charged with a fiercely independent mission. Not only would Dan have jealously to patrol its own territory: it would operate a strict rule of law among its own people and would plead their cause earnestly within the wider federation of Israel.

Despite these earnest obligations, however, Dan would later diverge wildly from the plan. Instead of separated piety, it fell into the most appalling idolatry, deception and wanton destruction (Judg. 18:1ff.) – all in the otherwise quite valid cause of seeking a new homeland. The lesson here is that apparently holy intentions and a seemingly holy image are no guarantee of true holiness – as various contemporary televangelists have shown, it is often those tribes with the most conservative pedigree who end up falling most deeply into cultural compromise. Dan's punishment is severe: it is excluded from the list of tribes which make up the Israel of Revelation 7:5–8. Perhaps there is a warning here for those evangelicals who repudiate 'the world' so much that they fail to understand it, and then in their ignorance naively fall prey to its charms.

As with Dan, Jacob charges Gad with a counter-cultural agenda. His lineage is to 'attack raiders at their heels' (verse 19). Unlike Dan, however, Gad seems pretty much to have stuck to the script. Situated as it was in the Transjordan area, the Gadite tribe encountered many border raids, but seems to have resisted them fairly effectively, and to have done the godly thing, even when the prevailing mood was to do otherwise (Judg. 10–12; 1 Sam. 13:7; I Chr. 12:1–38). Gad could be taken as a model for contemporary 'tribes' of God's people who have a very informed and acute sense of social sin, but whose nous enables them to reject that sin. The obvious parallel here is with Jesus's commendation of those who in the world are 'wise as serpents', even while remaining spiritually 'innocent as doves' (Matt. 10:16).

Reflecting on Scripture like this is a helpful way in to understanding the complexity of the evangelicalism–postmodernity issue. It could just be that in God's providence, different 'tribes' within the diverse evangelical constituency are destined to respond to the challenge of postmodern culture in different ways. Some, like Zebulun, will no doubt 'trade' a great deal with the culture, and pass the fruits of that trade on to others in a positive manner. Some, like Issachar, will align themselves so completely with the culture that they risk becoming enslaved to it, and thus do very little to advance the cause of the gospel. Others, like Dan, may rail against it, even while actually colluding with it. And still others will, like Gad, act as discerning critics of culture on behalf of the rest.

In the remainder of this book, we shall see that within the evangelical community as a whole something very like this pattern is already beginning to emerge. The difficulty comes in discerning which aspects of it apply to which movements and groupings. This problem is particularly pressing in the case of post-evangelicalism, and it is with this development that we must deal next.

7

EVANGELICALS, POST-EVANGELICALS AND POSTMODERNITY

The Church in the Pub

Clapham could be described as a postmodern place. It is one of the great bottlenecks of London life. Gentrified Victorian houses share streets with fading council flats. Ornate florists and exclusive interior-design shops ply their trade alongside greasy-spoon cafés, second-hand car dealers and short-lease discount stores. Cars crawl through it relentlessly on the South Circular road; Tube and rail lines converge on it manically; buses shudder in procession along its arteries. But in the middle of it all is a vast common – a bulwark of green against the urban tide. At one end of the common is a pub called the Alexandria. There, every Tuesday at nine o'clock, people go to church. The name of the church is Holy Joe's; its convener is Dave Tomlinson.

Holy Joe's is the latest stage in a journey which has taken Tomlinson from childhood in the Brethren church, through Charismatic Renewal and oversight of some fifty 'New' or Restoration churches, to advanced study at the London Bible College.[1] In his own terms, however, it also represents a conscious departure from the evangelicalism with which he was brought up and associated for so long.[2] Partly as a result of his academic explorations, and partly due to his disillusionment with mainstream evangelicalism, Tomlinson joined similarly jaded friends in the early nineties to form

Holy Joe's as a 'refuge' for those who had for various reasons left the institutional Church.

Perhaps fittingly, Holy Joe's gathers in the upper room. People get a drink from the bar and sit in an oval on a variety of soft and hard chairs. Some smoke cigarettes; Dave himself smokes a pipe. Some meetings take the form of a 'sacred space' – worship in a contemplative vein with candles and quiet music; on other nights there will be a Bible study or, as when I attended one night, a visiting speaker. Appropriately enough, the input on this occasion was provided by Dave's old supervisor from LBC – the self-professed 'continuing' evangelical Graham McFarlane. His theme was 'Faith, Doubt and Certainty'. He spoke sensitively about the need to rely less on rationalistic apologetics and dogma, and more on a relational model of knowing. He stressed that Jesus makes truth personal, rather than simply objective. He tried to meet people halfway. But he had a hard time. Folk listened courteously, but when he had finished the challenges came thick and fast. 'How can you be so sure Jesus said what he is reported to have said?' 'Why are you so insistent about the empty tomb when resurrection is about a spiritual encounter with God?' 'If faith in God is like falling in love and getting married, what about when things turn sour? What about divorce?' 'Why do you want to give us so many answers when Christianity is more like a journey – more to do with searching and questioning?' And so it went on.

To be fair, those who go to Holy Joe's express a range of theologies, some more orthodox than others. Nonetheless, what comes over powerfully is a great deal of hurt and alienation, most of which appears to derive from people's past experiences in evangelical churches. What also struck me was that, with a few exceptions, those attending are highly articulate, seemingly well educated and – dare I say it – either middle-class or from middle-class backgrounds.

Tomlinson handled the meeting very well, intervening only to coax the discussion in a more fruitful direction when it had got stuck on one point too long. His many years of pastoral experience were also evident in the way he listened to people and encouraged them afterwards.

The Post-Evangelical Case

Background

Holy Joe's is the main context from which Dave Tomlinson's book *The Post-Evangelical* emerged in mid-1995. Finding more and more 'refugees' from evangelicalism who had given up on church altogether, Tomlinson recalls experimenting with 'a quite different form of church, which might appeal to at least some of these people'.[3] Since those first steps were taken, he says, Holy Joe's has become 'a symbol of hope for people in many parts of the country, most of whom have never attended one of its meetings'.[4] Without doubt, his book has raised the profile of such disaffected evangelicals, as well as offering a 'credo' around which they can gather. This credo is quite loose and informal – indeed, Tomlinson insists that it is aimed at a popular, non-specialist audience.[5] Furthermore, he readily admits that its formulation owes something to his own and others' tiredness, boredom and 'irritation' with evangelical culture[6] – whether with 'the style of worship, the language, the attitudes towards the rest of the world or the political assumptions'.[7]

Above all, however, Tomlinson's argument is distinguished by one very decisive claim. This is the claim that evangelicalism is ill-suited to postmodernity, and that if they are to relate authentically to the postmodern world, evangelicals may well have to move out of evangelicalism and become what Tomlinson calls 'post-evangelicals'. Since this is an argument which has clearly caught on, and since it relates very directly to our own concerns here, it is worth examining in some detail.

In Tomlinson's own definition, post-evangelicals 'tend to be people who identify culturally more with postmodernity . . . than with modernity' and who recognise that this 'has a significant bearing on the way that they approach and understand the Christian faith'.[8] Resisting the jibe that to be post-evangelical is simply to be ex-evangelical, Tomlinson argues that the former will 'take as given many of the assumptions of evangelical faith, while at the same time moving beyond its perceived limitations'.[9] Elaborating on this point, Tomlinson argues that when sociologists distinguish the postmodern from the modern, it is usually 'taken for granted that in order for something to be postmodern it has to be building on, or be linked with, or be continuous with, that which is modern'.[10] Although this view may be challenged by more seismic ruptures between modernity and postmodernity like the collapse of Soviet communism, it allows Tomlinson to commend evangelicalism's love of the Bible and its ability to express Christian faith simply. All the same, he goes on to argue that *over*-simplification has in many quarters led to bibliolatry and unhealthy anti-intellectualism.[11]

A 'Grown-Up' Faith

Arising from all this, Tomlinson casts post-evangelicalism as a more 'mature' form of Christian faith than evangelicalism. Early on, he notes that 'evangelicalism is supremely good at introducing people to faith in Christ, but distinctly unhelpful when it comes to the matter of progressing into a more 'grown-up' experience of faith'.[12] Later, he co-opts M. Scott Peck's popular four-stage model of spiritual growth and argues that while many evangelicals remain stuck at the second or 'Conformist' stage, a lot of post-evangelicals 'are moving from stage II to stage III' – that is, from the Conformist to the Individualist stage, on their way to a fourth stage of 'Integration'.[13]

Part of the growing up process for Tomlinson is a recognition of theological diversity – an acceptance that divine truth is wider than evangelical truth and that an integrated faith will require 'fewer predigested opinions', fewer 'categorical conclusions' and more 'space to explore alternative ideas'.[14] It means, for example, ceasing to regard all theological liberals as 'bogeymen' and, where appropriate, adopting their insights gladly.[15] After all, says Tomlinson, 'Who decides where lines are drawn or who is the appointed keeper of the gate of evangelical tradition? . . . Probably the best thing we can do is remind ourselves of the old dictum that there will be no evangelicals in heaven . . . just people who love God.'[16]

A non-liberal alternative

Having advocated his more 'open' stance, Tomlinson is keen to stress that post-evangelicals are not just 'woolly liberals'. Unlike many who profess liberalism, they still cherish the evangelical characteristic of conversionism, and will often continue to value their own acceptance of Christ as Saviour. They typically maintain that Christianity is a religion based on historical realities, and are quite at ease with its supernatural dimension. What is more, in the majority of cases the Bible and creeds remain in some way normative for them.[17]

Indeed, as he emphasises these points, Tomlinson argues that post-evangelicals are distinguished from liberals and evangelicals *alike* by their preference for postmodernity over modernity. As Tomlinson puts it, 'To a large degree liberalism exists because of its acceptance of modern scientific knowledge as the final arbiter for determining truth . . . But evangelicalism effectively does just the same in that it chooses to fight the modernist challenge by using the framework and criteria provided by modernism.'[18] This brings us to the heart of Tomlinson's thesis.

The need for a postmodern Christianity

In doctrine

We have seen how Tomlinson leans heavily on the premise that evangelicalism has situated itself 'in the world of modernity', whereas post-evangelicals are emerging as 'those who relate more naturally to the world of post-modernity'.[19] We have also begun to suggest that the picture may be rather more complicated than this. Now we need to look at just what Tomlinson understands by 'postmodernity' and 'evangelicalism'.

Tomlinson defines postmodernity as follows:

> The postmodern world in which we live is a world . . . in which people now reject truth claims which are expressed in the form of dogma or absolutes. It is a world in which dignity is granted to emotions and intuition, and where people are accustomed to communicating through words linked to images and symbols rather than through plain words or simple statements. It is a world in which people have come to feel a close affinity with the environment, and where there is a strong sense of global unity. It is a world in which people are deeply suspicious of institutions, bureaucracies and hierarchies. And perhaps most of all, it is a world in which the spiritual dimension is once again talked about with great ease.[20]

From this starting-point, it soon becomes apparent that modernity, for Tomlinson, is not only the movement against which these trends have developed, but also the crucible in which evangelicalism was formed. Indeed, as far as he is concerned, evangelicalism is terminally wedded to the modern age and mindset. So, in its attachment to Enlightenment rationalism and absolute truth, it has cultivated a 'near obsession with doctrinal correctness',[21] an overly propositional theory of biblical inerrancy and an excessively 'black and white' approach to scriptural truth.[22] But, as I have shown, these expressions of Enlightenment rationalism are only one aspect of a much broader and more diverse evangelical heritage. By focusing so narrowly on this 'rationalist–Enlightenment' strand within evangelicalism, Tomlinson has to some extent set up an Aunt Sally. Admittedly, he concedes that many evangelical scholars have moved beyond inerrancy into an acceptance of biblical criticism and contemporary models of interpretation, but he still complains that this development has not filtered down to local churches.[23]

By contrast to all this, Tomlinson says that post-evangelicals 'find themselves instinctively drawn towards an understanding of truth which is more relative'.[24] Specifically, this means recognising the value of metaphorical,[25] symbolic,[26] dialectical[27] and narrative[28] language as means to expressing what they believe, in preference to the typically propositional language of evangelicalism. It also means recognising that there is no pristine 'view from nowhere', and that all accounts of truth are mediated through human perception and community.[29] If this means loosening one's grip on certainty, Tomlinson frankly admits that he 'would tend to agree with those who see the threat from certainty as greater than that posed by "anything goes"'.[30]

In morality

Not surprisingly, Tomlinson's new-found theology has implications for the post-evangelical view of morality. Tomlinson is keen to point out that several activities which were once thought of as unacceptable are now allowed in most evangelical circles – e.g. drinking, theatre and cinemagoing and taking the Sunday papers.[31] This, he says, shows that 'holiness' often gets confused with middle-class respectability.

Nowhere is this confusion of respectability and holiness

more apparent for Tomlinson than in evangelical attitudes towards marriage and the family. The fact that over half those getting married in England and Wales have lived together first, he argues, throws the need for formal marriage into severe doubt – not least because 'there are many couples co-habiting, many of them Christians, who are quite evidently as committed to their relationship as any formally married couple, in many cases more so'.[32] Similarly, where gender roles are concerned, post-evangelicals challenge the traditional pattern of male headship: 'For the most part,' says Tomlinson, 'they are heirs to a completely different, post-feminist culture. They assume sexual equality and take for granted the right of a woman to follow a career. They have no reservations about house-husbands.'[33]

Without doubt, though, it is Tomlinson's brief but provocative comments on the vexed question of homosexual partnerships which stand to alienate him most immediately from his former evangelical constituency. On the face of it, he only hints at the validity of such partnerships, but in the context of the rest of the book an endorsement of them does not seem far off: 'From a conservative point of view,' he writes, 'few things evoke such violent reactions as the suggestion that gay couples might legitimately live together within the same parameters as heterosexual couples, or even worse, act as parents.'[34] It seems unlikely that Tomlinson would have bothered to moot the possibility of 'gay marriage' in this way unless he felt a degree of sympathy towards the idea.

In spirituality

When it comes to emotion, intuition and the devotional life, Tomlinson contrasts a postmodern culture 'longing for the spirituality which [has] been squeezed out by [the] materialism and rationalism' of modernity[35] with the 'social claustrophobia' and 'flat-pack legalism' of the evangelical church.[36] Unlike many evangelicals, Tomlinson views the rise of the New Age movement not simply as a threat, but as an 'incredible opportunity' for Christians to reassess 'the foundations of our faith: the way we understand truth, the Bible, and even God'.[37]

Clearly, too, the concern of much New Age thinking for ecological issues is a challenge which Tomlinson feels post-evangelicals are better placed to deal with than evangelicals, plugged in as they are to 'a postmodern world . . . which understands itself through biological rather than mechanistic models; a world where people see themselves as belonging to the environment, rather than over or apart from it'.[38]

The problem of evangelical sub-culture

Of all Tomlinson's targets, the most prominent is the whole sub-culture which has grown up around evangelicalism. Given that postmodernism is suspicious of 'institutions, bureaucracies and hierarchies', Tomlinson suggests that post-evangelicals will reject many of the structural and organisational trappings which accompany evangelical faith.[39] They will also leave behind its distinctive 'social attitudes and behavioural expectations'.[40]

This issue of faith versus culture has become especially significant, says Tomlinson, because of the 'remarkable period of transformation' which British evangelicalism has undergone in recent years.[41] From being a marginal movement which rarely hit the headlines, Tomlinson agrees that since the early 1980s 'many evangelical churches [have grown] dramatically and new churches are being planted regularly. High profile personalities . . . are continually "coming out" about their faith, and the media pay increasing attention to evangelical and charismatic issues.'[42] Tomlinson puts this growth down largely to a 'new generation of evangelical leaders' spearheaded not least by Clive Calver, who from 1983 until 1997 led the Evangelical Alliance from relative obscurity to considerable prominence in the media and the institutions of state. This was achieved, argues Tomlinson, through Calver's astute recruitment of younger charismatic and New Church leaders who were for the most part 'theologically conservative' but also 'socially and politically aware', and 'eager to promote evangelical values within society'.[43] Aided by social projects like Tear Fund and CARE, mass festivals like Spring Harvest and international acts of witness like the March for Jesus, the movement grew to its current impressive proportions.

Given such success, Tomlinson admits that it might seem odd to voice major criticisms. Nonetheless, he insists that 'not everyone feels at home with all that is happening', and that 'there are questions to be asked'.[44] Many, he claims, experience what psychologists might call cognitive dissonance: they have difficulty 'reconciling what they see and experience in evangelicalism with their personal values, instinctive reactions and theological reflections'.[45] He goes on to comment that 'ironically, a significant cause of many people's discomfort in the present evangelical scene arises out of the climate of success itself'.

'It goes without saying,' he adds, 'that whenever any group or movement is buoyant or doing well, a dynamic is generated which makes dissent very difficult indeed, and many people feel this.' Tomlinson then draws a stinging analogy: 'It is the same old effect of the emperor with no clothes on – nobody dares speak up.'[46]

Specifically, Tomlinson charges that the whole super-structure which has accumulated around evangelicalism in the last twenty years or so is eclipsing serious debate – and not least a serious attempt to engage with postmodernity. He attributes this to the fact that such engagement might 'split the constituency and thereby undermine its united voice'.[47] While understanding this caution, Tomlinson stresses its long-term weakness:

My severe reservation is that . . . it holds the movement back from facing challenges which it must confront.

> Lots of us would be in sympathy with evangelical-
> ism if there were more open debate, if instead of
> being shielded from the disturbing discussions which
> lie just around the corner, people were facilitated in
> the task of rethinking and reinterpreting the Chris-
> tian faith.[48]

But are these really fair criticisms? Indeed, how well does Tomlinson's analysis of contemporary evangelicalism tally with what is happening on the ground? Is it true to say that evangelicals are as tightly bound to modernity as Tomlinson implies? Besides, is Tomlinson's version of postmodernity as representative as it should be? These are crucial questions, and I shall address them shortly. In looking to answer them, however, it will be helpful first to gauge the reactions of various prominent figures in and around evangelicalism to what Tomlinson has proposed.

The Post-Evangelical Debate

Evangelical responses

Perhaps not surprisingly, many in the 'continuing' evangelical constituency have reacted negatively to Tomlinson's argument. Writing in the evangelical monthly *Alpha*,[49] the Oxford theologian Alister McGrath dismissed *The Post-Evangelical* as 'one of the most superficial and inadequate treatments of the contemporary state of evangelicalism which I have read'.[50] McGrath went on to list several scholarly works by committed evangelicals, most of them American, which had tried to reinterpret evangelical faith in the light of postmodernity. These he took as a sign that 'evangelicalism is perfectly capable of meeting the challenges of postmodernity without lapsing into the confusion found in this profoundly unsatisfactory book'.[51]

Other leading evangelicals to whom I spoke were similarly critical. Clive Calver himself compared Dave Tomlinson's answers to 'those of a second-year theology student' and told me that 'they don't offer a coherent alternative' to evangelicalism. As we talked during a conference for evangelicals in the United Reformed Church, Calver conceded that 'the questions and doubts Dave raises are very valid and very authentic'. All the same, he was hurt that Tomlinson had felt compelled to leave the evangelical community in order to ask them: 'If someone had raised those questions from *inside* evangelicalism I'd be backing them up and saying that they're the right questions – that we need to be facing up to them and seeking to answer them.' Similarly, John Drane was as welcoming of the questions posed by *The Post-Evangelical* as he was sceptical about its solutions: 'Dave Tomlinson hasn't really worked out where his answers might come from' was his reflection on the debate spurred by the book. On much the same point, the livewire Salvation Army evangelist Phil Wall acknowledged across his desk in Merton that 'Dave Tomlinson has lifted up the cries of many people's hearts, but what he hasn't done is give us the answers.'

Gerald Coates leads the Pioneer network of new churches and worked alongside Dave Tomlinson for a period. He told me at his home in Surrey that he was particularly upset by the course his former colleague had taken: 'One of the problems with the book is that it is full of straw targets, with inferences that people like me believe things that we have never believed. I have never believed, for instance, that we approach life *solely* on the basis of Scripture.' Coates went on:

Dave's got a good turn of phrase, but when you put the book down you have to ask, 'What is he actually talking about?' Is he saying that we need new wineskins for the new cultural wine? If so, I

would say that we do. And I think churches – whether
in homes, schools or pubs – which adapt to culture
while remaining orthodox in faith and supernatural
in approach are just what we need. If that's what
Dave is saying, fine. But I don't think he's saying that. He's saying, for example, that it's OK for
homosexuals to sleep together, which is something else
altogether.

Other continuing evangelicals were more generous, if still
finally doubtful about the post-evangelical concept. Tom
Houston, based in Oxford as Minister at Large of the
Lausanne Covenant for World Evangelization, thought that
Tomlinson had offered a quite acute analysis of contemporary British evangelicalism, but still took Coates's line
that evangelicalism had within itself the capacity to adapt
and change so as to meet the demands of postmodernity.
'If I had been writing that book,' he told me, 'I would
have given it a very long title like "What Evangelicals
Have Always Been, and How It Applies Today"! From
his perspective in a mixed Holloway parish, Mike Starkey
was equally convinced that Tomlinson had been too quick
to drive a wedge between evangelicals and postmodern
culture, and suggested that this might have had more to
do with his own personal pilgrimage than with any general
principle. Although he had commended the book when it
came out as 'crucial reading for anyone calling themselves
Evangelical',[52] Starkey voiced to me a certain concern about
Tomlinson's motives:

He is writing off too much of what has gone before.
The image that always comes to mind when I look
at the book is of somebody who has crossed a lot
of bridges, and then wants to burn the bridges after
him to make sure that nobody else follows, because
he feels he's had bad experiences in the places he's
come from.

Despite all this, another group of those I interviewed were far more enthusiastic about what Tomlinson had written. It has to be said that most of these were younger evangelicals, and to some extent this reinforces the generational aspect of postmodernity discussed earlier.

Jenny and Jonny Baker work with Clive Calver's former organisation, Youth For Christ, and are both deeply concerned about the relation of Christian faith to contemporary culture. I spoke to Jenny at YFC's Victoria headquarters.

> At the time *The Post-Evangelical* came out, a lot of my husband's and my friends were going through problems with the Church. They still loved God, but felt frustrated with the structures. So when Jonny and I read the book there was a great deal of resonance. Somebody was articulating what we felt, and there was a sense of relief that others were feeling the same way.

Baker went on to observe that 'response to *The Post-Evangelical* has been a "love it or hate it" thing. People have either said, "This is brilliant!" or have reacted against it by saying, "We've got to get back to basics – we've got to tighten things down and write out again what we believe."' Recounting evangelical history, she then made a suggestive comparison: 'People like John Wesley got fed up with the Church as it was and went out and did their own thing, but later on that became mainstream. Though people in certain circles wouldn't touch him with a bargepole, I wonder whether Dave Tomlinson won't also be integrated similarly into the mainstream.'

Over at the Evangelical Alliance itself, I found similar comments being made by Graham Dale. Dale works for Whitefield Associates, a political lobby established by EA to get the evangelical voice heard more effectively in Parliament. A switched-on Scot in his early thirties,

Dale confessed to being 'annoyed' by certain parts of Tomlinson's book, but readily accepted that it had become 'a banner around which people have gathered'. He continued: 'It articulates what a lot of Christians feel, and to some extent it articulated what I feel. I've held on to my evangelicalism, but not without wrestling with it often – and that's why the subject of post-evangelicalism is quite close to my heart.' At a wider level, Dale reflected that Tomlinson's book had 'scratched the itches of those who are the children of postmodernity', while at the same time 'poking at the generation brought up on modernity'. 'That,' he added, 'is why people like Alister McGrath and Clive Calver have been critical of it.'

For all his qualms about Tomlinson's conclusions, thirty-something Phil Wall recalled how he had read *The Post-Evangelical* and 'enjoyed two-thirds of it'. 'I found myself saying, "Yes, yes, yes!" because anybody who has the honesty to look at the evangelical sub-culture has to hold their hand up and say, "OK – a lot of what Dave Tomlinson says is true." To deny that would be naive or blind.' Similar appreciation was expressed by Graham Cray as we talked at length in the Principal's office at Ridley Hall, Cambridge. Cray has long been active at the more radical edge of evangelicalism, having helped to organise the Greenbelt Arts Festival for many years and having sustained a consistently thoughtful Christian response to pop and rock music. Cray had endorsed *The Post-Evangelical* when it was first published, declaring that it had raised 'pastoral and theological issues which must be faced'.[53] He told me, 'The book has clearly touched a nerve. I am grateful for Dave's courage in actually doing it, because I think there is a danger within evangelicalism that if something is thought of as suspect or "unsound", it cannot be talked about.'

But what about the one who declared the emperor's nakedness in the first place? What does he make of the substantial reaction generated by *The Post-Evangelical*?

Tomlinson's Reflections

Not only does Holy Joe's meet in a pub: Dave Tomlinson suggested that we talk in one. The Bedford Arms is at the opposite end of Clapham Common to the Alexandria. As we chatted over a pint, I asked him what it felt like to be an iconoclast. 'I've actually only ever had one letter that was a negative letter,' he said, surprisingly. 'The letters I've had have otherwise been positive.' But surely he must have been aware of a more general evangelical backlash? 'Yes, the book has caused a greater stir than I anticipated, but that may be more an expression of my naiveté than anything else.' First and foremost, he said, 'I wrote the book as a pastoral response to people who I could see were clearly dropping out of evangelicalism, and in some cases out of Christianity altogether.' More specifically, he reflects that *The Post-Evangelical* has helped such people find an identity: 'I am really quite antagonistic about labels, but they do serve a purpose, and an awful lot of people have expressed what a relief it has been to feel that there's now a name for what they are.'

Something else Tomlinson did not anticipate was the range of ages and backgrounds represented by those who have warmed to his book. Despite all the generational distinctions which appear to correlate with modernity and postmodernity, Tomlinson recalled having had 'literally hundreds of letters from people, a large percentage of whom haven't come from my target audience'. This target audience he had identified as 'a youngish one – people in their thirties, whom I had perceived to be influenced largely by postmodern culture, whether they realised it or not'. Nonetheless, many favourable responses came 'from an older and probably more culturally conservative group who look like fairly solid members of evangelical churches and yet clearly carry beneath the surface a whole raft of doubts and questions which they've never felt able to talk about. And the overwhelming response has been "Thank

God someone has said it!" There's been relief that they
didn't have to pretend any more.'

Pastoral implications

Whatever else may be said of Tomlinson's argument,
serious-minded evangelicals must surely share his concern
for those who leave the evangelical constituency and appear
to abandon active churchgoing altogether. There is a lack
of full and accurate statistical data on the extent of this
problem,[54] and it must be said that, overall, evangelicals
have shown a greater net numerical gain in recent years
than any other major theological grouping in England.[55]
Still, this should not make us complacent. It will not do
blithely to assume that all such departees are apostates, or
to cover our embarrassment with a blanket misapplication
of Hebrews 6:4–6. Jesus's regard for the lost sheep should
be salutary here (Luke 15:4–7).

One evangelical who certainly appreciates this aspect of
Tomlinson's book is Nick Mercer. Mercer left his post
as Vice Principal at the London Bible College to take
up Anglican orders. He now ministers in a high-church
parish in Pinner, Middlesex. Liturgically he may have
embraced more catholic approaches, but he still speaks
at Spring Harvest and is highly knowledgeable about the
evangelical world. What is more, he has written and spoken
extensively on postmodernity and the gospel.[56] As we talked
in his vicarage, Mercer told me:

Dave Tomlinson reflected the fact that those of us
who've been around not only the evangelical world,
but also the world in general, are always meeting
ex-evangelicals. I don't mind so much meeting such
folk when they're now liberal Anglicans or woolly
Methodists or when they've returned to their Roman

Catholic roots, but many of them simply aren't *any-where*. They either say that they're not Christians, or they say they're Christians but they're not going to church. And you begin to realise that there are a lot of disenchanted people out there.

If Tomlinson's efforts prompt a more thorough investigation into this phenomenon, he will have done evangelicalism a service.

Having said all this, there is obviously much more to the post-evangelical debate – and most of it is highly conten-tious. Principal areas of dispute concern whether Tomlinson has adequately described evangelicalism, modernity and postmodernity; whether he mistakes proper *engagement* with postmodern culture for *absorption into* postmodern cul-ture; whether post-evangelicalism is not just warmed-over liberalism; whether it will unnecessarily divide evangelicals; and whether or not Tomlinson is simply seeking to legitimate his own personal pilgrimage by projecting it into a new 'movement'.

Whose Evangelicalism? Whose Postmodernity?

One of the sharpest criticisms made of Tomlinson in Alister McGrath's *Alpha* article was that he had misrepre-sented contemporary evangelicalism. Specifically, McGrath accused Tomlinson of failing to acknowledge that a sig-nificant number of 'continuing' evangelicals had *already* begun to grapple with the serious challenges posed by postmodernity. Now it ought to be noted straight away that those McGrath had in mind were overwhelmingly professional North American theologians – hardly typical of the sort of people who go to Holy Joe's, or of those ordinary British evangelicals who have written to Dave Tomlinson in their hundreds thanking him for saying the unsayable! Even so, McGrath saw fit to comment tartly that 'Tomlinson's book would have benefited had he been obliged to sit a course in evangelical thought since 1984.'[57] It is worth examining this criticism before moving on to offer a critique of our own.

The date in McGrath's put-down is significant. The year 1984 saw the publication of the Canadian theologians Brian J. Walsh and J. Richard Middleton's *The Transforming Vision: Shaping a Christian Worldview*. In that ground-breaking work, Middleton and Walsh urged evangelicals to rethink the way they did their theology and mission, and to do so specifically using the concept of 'worldview'. Worldviews, they argued, help to provide faith with answers to a set of ultimate, grounding questions. They provide a way into understanding fundamental human enquiries like 'Where are we?', 'Who are we?', 'What's wrong?' and 'What's the remedy?' Although these questions had long been seen as crucial by evangelicals, Middleton and Walsh's work was distinguished by its insistence that they be thought of as *cultural* questions as much as *theological* questions. In a postmodern age, they said, it was no longer appropriate to divorce such questions from their social context, as if the answers to them could be expressed in some sort of discarnate, trans-temporal language. Purely rationalistic books of doctrine and apologetics were no longer sufficient to 'prove' the case for Christianity: its credibility had to be established in relation to particular historical, sociological and philosophical frameworks.

In their later book *Truth is Stranger than It Used to be*, which McGrath also commended as 'excellent', Middleton and Walsh note that although their model proved highly controversial among evangelicals when first mooted, talk of worldviews, and acceptance of the need to relate theology to culture, is now virtually a given.[58] They go on to suggest that authentic evangelical faith in a postmodern world will be a faith which truly 'indwells' the biblical text rather than looking 'behind' it for the 'abstract, contextless, timeless' truths sought by much modernist evangelicalism. This faith will recognise that there is no point 'outside' tradition and culture from which Christians can view the gospel, and will accept that interpretation is 'intrinsically tradition-dependent'. Nonetheless, it will insist on seeing the Bible *itself* as formative of Christian community.[59] Not only this: a biblically shaped worldview may well be one which 'shatters what we take to be orthodoxy. And perhaps it is in orthodoxy-shattering biblical texts that we will find resources for a genuine postmodern orientation.'[60]

It has to be said that Middleton and Walsh's sheer passion for a radically scriptural worldview is not echoed in *The Post-Evangelical*. Neither is their profound account of how churches formed by Scripture must risk having their norms overthrown as the same Scripture speaks afresh into new cultural circumstances. Even so, there is no doubt that Tomlinson is on a similar track to theirs philosophically when he disavows the idea of a 'grandstand' view of truth distinct from history and tradition.[61] Granted, he takes this forward in a rather confused way. Too often, he cites a philosopher on a particular issue without making it clear how fully he agrees with that philosopher. Thus Rorty, Cupitt and Derrida are useful insofar as they highlight the difficulty of talking precisely about God.[62] Yet beyond noting this difficulty and making the obvious point that much religious language is metaphorical and paradoxical,[63] Tomlinson offers at best a tentative model for interpreting Scripture in a postmodern age. All the same, he at least agrees with Middleton and Walsh on how it *cannot* fruitfully be read – namely, in a rationalistic or purely propositional way.

Another area of scholarship McGrath accuses Tomlinson of neglecting is the new movement which Roger E. Olsen has called 'post-conservative evangelicalism'. Prominent in this movement are two more Canadian theologians, Stanley Grenz and Clark Pinnock, and a growing cast of evangelical thinkers attached to projects sponsored by Wheaton College, Illinois, and the Southern Baptist Theological Seminary.

In a series of books and articles,[64] Grenz has called for a 'revisioning' of evangelical theology in the postmodern context. Though he writes from an American perspective, Grenz confirms much of what Tomlinson has implied when he comments that evangelicals are living 'in the throes of an identity crisis'.[65] Indeed, if what Grenz argues is true, it would seem that this crisis is rather more advanced in America than it is in Britain. Still, the pattern of mounting disenchantment despite great public success is very similar. 'In recent years,' notes Grenz, evangelicals 'have witnessed unprecedented growth in church membership. Evangelical congregations mushroom, while mainline denominations struggle. Yet there are signs of growing dissatisfaction with traditional evangelical ways of doing church.'[66] Like Tomlinson, he says that this is apparent not least in the field of systematic theology, where the models of Enlightenment rationalism are perceived as no longer adequate.[67]

Specifically, Grenz is concerned by the extent to which evangelicals have absorbed modernist emphases on the individual as a unitary thinker, producer and consumer. At great length, he has sought to redress this individualism by proposing a 'theology of community' which offers a 'new understanding of the relationship between the personal life of faith' and the corporate body of the Church, with its interdependent networks of support and expertise.[68]

Admittedly, one struggles to find anything quite so constructive in Tomlinson's view of the Church – though this is hardly surprising given that he sees himself and Holy Joe's as offering 'first aid' to the damaged 'victims' of evangelicalism. Nonetheless, Grenz does anticipate Tomlinson's penchant for stories[69] when he adds that to be 'evangelical' in this new definition means 'to participate in a community characterized by a shared narrative concerning a personal encounter with God told in terms of shared theological categories derived from the Bible'.[70] Likewise, Grenz insists, with Tomlinson, that an authentic postmodern Christianity will still reserve a place for the old evangelical stress on conversion, even if this needs to be tempered by an increased awareness that spirituality is a 'corporate project' and that 'each believer needs the resources of the group in order to gain spiritual maturity'.[71]

When it comes to the authority of Scripture, Grenz again makes proposals which resonate with much of what Tomlinson says. Like Tomlinson, he questions the usefulness of the concept of inerrancy – not least on the grounds that it may itself be an unbiblical idea.[72] Granted, Grenz is considerably more subtle and nuanced, but his fundamental point that the inspiration, authority and interpretation of the Bible must be seen as deriving from the work of the Holy Spirit *through* the community which collated it, as well as from *above* and *beyond* that community, is basically what *The Post-Evangelical* is driving at when it calls for a 'communal' rather than a 'didactic' approach to Scripture.[73]

Grenz's discussion of the Bible acknowledges a considerable debt to Clark Pinnock.[74] Although Pinnock's book *The Scripture Principle*[75] ends up holding on to the word 'inerrancy', it does so by defining it in a largely functional way with respect to the compilation and use of the Bible by the church community.[76] Elsewhere, Pinnock has attempted to revise other cherished evangelical doctrines which he believes owe rather too much to modernist rationalism. One example, which Tomlinson also discusses,[77] is the doctrine of the atonement. Pinnock questions the traditional idea that God is impassable – that is, immune from pain or sorrow in the face of suffering. Where evangelicals have relied too much on a hard 'forensic' model of the cross in which God is a distant judge arranging Jesus's death as a 'penalty' for our sins, Pinnock argues for a heavenly Father who empathises 'tenderly' with his Son's agony on Calvary, and thereby establishes his solidarity with subsequent victims of pain and injustice.[78] Again, Tomlinson does not develop his view as thoroughly, but he suggests a similarly dynamic view of God's involvement in the drama of the crucifixion.[79]

Post-Evangelicalism as Postliberalism

Another way in which McGrath attempts to discredit Tomlinson is to charge him with having offered a naive rehash of 'postliberalism'. Postliberalism is a theological movement associated especially with the Yale Divinity School and Duke Divinity School. Its primary expression is found in George A. Lindbeck's *The Nature of Doctrine: Religion and Theology in a Postliberal Age*.[80] Those who have taken their cue from Lindbeck include Hans Frei, Stanley Hauerwas, Ronald Thiemann, George Hunsinger and William Placher.[81]

Like Tomlinson, postliberals diverge from the modernist evangelical assumption that religious doctrines correspond in a direct, objective way with reality. They also challenge the idea that religious experience is in some way universal or 'pre-linguistic', and that religious statements are merely secondary descriptions of this experience. Rather, they argue that religious experience takes shape only in and through the language and practice of a particular community, and is therefore not interchangeable with the religious experience of another community. Doctrine is thus not to be seen as a set of propositions, but as the 'story' of a specific group or tradition. The Bible is to be read as a set of narratives rather than a series of cosmic formulae. Much of their methodology is borrowed by Grenz, Pinnock and other postconservative evangelicals, but they push that methodology to more radical (and more relativist) conclusions. Their apologetics, for instance, can only ever be *ad hoc* because there are no absolute, eternal standards accessible to all people everywhere.

McGrath is right to state that Tomlinson appears only implicitly supportive of postliberalism. He is certainly equivocal about the possibility of absolute or objective truth[82] and, as we have seen, prefers a narrative approach to theology. He is less clear, however, on the authority of communities, or even what 'community' might mean in a church context.

McGrath chides Tomlinson for failing to acknowledge that postliberals and evangelicals are already talking creatively to one another in the United States, and draws attention to an account of their dialogue edited by the Wheaton theologians Timothy Phillips and Dennis Okholm under the title *The Nature of Confession*.[83] First, it must be said that this book was published *after* Tomlinson's, and that evangelical–postliberal dialogue is not nearly as advanced in Britain as in America. Second, it ought to be underlined that, like Grenz, Phillips and Okholm share Tomlinson's basic concern about evangelical identity. Despite acknowledging its success, they, too, talk of evangelicalism 'fragmenting' and 'collapsing'. They, too, criticise the way it confuses faith with culture.[84] They, too, lament the divide between the academy and the Church.[85] Admittedly, their critique comes from a more conservative viewpoint, but they and the other evangelicals who contribute to the dialogue – one of whom is McGrath himself – do genuinely seem to appreciate the attempt made by postliberals to move beyond the rationalism which dominated liberal and older evangelical theologies. Tomlinson may not mention postliberalism as such, but he does at least grope in the same general direction.

Reviewing the Debate

I would be the first to agree that Tomlinson's attempt to relate evangelicalism to postmodernity is hardly as thorough as the studies mentioned. Neither does it bear comparison with the work of another Wheaton scholar, Roger Lundin,[86] or with Mark Noll's masterful but rather more general book, *The Scandal of the Evangelical Mind*.[87] It is nowhere near as erudite as the related collections of essays edited by Phillips and Okholm on apologetics in a postmodern age,[88] or by the Southern Baptist theologian David Dockery on the 'challenge' of postmodernism to evangelicals.[89] But then it never claims to ape these studies.

The same point applies on the British front. McGrath compares Tomlinson's suggestion of a 'critical realist' faith unflatteringly to that offered in Tom Wright's monumental *New Testament and the People of God*.[90] He also sets Tomlinson's attempt to define a new Christian identity over against Anthony Thiselton's 'brilliant' and 'highly recommended' *Interpreting God and the Postmodern Self*.[91]

The problem here, as with McGrath's rifle-range of American references, is that he is not comparing like with like. As Tomlinson pointed out when he replied to McGrath a month later, these books are specialist, academic works whereas Tomlinson was writing for a much wider, more popular audience:

> Naturally, I recognise that there are numerous evangelical academics wrestling with the matter of postmodernism. I have read most of the books McGrath refers to and, on the whole, enjoyed them . . . As for the suggestion that I would benefit from being 'obliged to sit a course in evangelical thought since 1984' – I was recently awarded a Master's Degree at London Bible College where I was of the impression that I'd received excellent exposure to contemporary evangelical thinking. All in all, if my knowledge of evangelicalism is inadequate and dated – pity help the rest![92]

Tomlinson went on to remark that 'it is McGrath's knowledge of grassroots evangelicalism that is deficient. If he imagines that the sort of thinking expressed in the books he refers to is trickling down to "High Street Evangelical Church", he's sadly mistaken.'[93]

In a way, it is unfortunate that McGrath polarised things so starkly. As I discovered, several leading evangelicals do at least recognise the sincerity and seriousness of Tomlinson's project. Neither is it particularly helpful to bury his book under a mass of far more weighty material written for a very different purpose. I speak with some knowledge here, as I was Tony Thiselton's doctoral student for three years. He was a superb Ph.D. tutor, but he could hardly be described as a populist! His work is indeed brilliant, but it will never reach the audience which has bought *The Post-Evangelical* in such large numbers. As Tomlinson put it curtly when we met: 'I have read Thiselton, but who the heck else is going to?'

Tomlinson's own book is undoubtedly a rag-bag. Many of the ideas he endorses are undigested. But perhaps this is itself a symptom of the post-evangelical condition he describes. Perhaps his own confusion produced a confused text, but the confusion is still genuine, and ought to be taken seriously – not least since it has been expressed by someone who for nearly twenty years was a leading figure in evangelicalism. Graham Cray underlined this point when he told me, 'Because post-evangelicals are the hinge tradition between modernity and postmodernity, they are struggling: they don't know what to hold on to and what to give up.'

Often, the most influential books are not the best-written. McGrath himself compares *The Post-Evangelical* to John A. T. Robinson's *Honest to God*,[94] which when published in 1963 caused a much bigger stir, with its radical questioning of miracles, biblical authority and the deity of Christ. Robinson's book was just about the first work of theology I ever read, and I was struck even then by how bitty and second-hand it seemed. But it came at the right moment; it touched a nerve, sold phenomenally and spawned an often painful, but quite necessary, debate. In fact, it could even be said to have awakened evangelicals in Britain to the need for more committed theological engagement. Tomlinson's book has not sold as well, but it does merit a consideration which goes beyond McGrath's riposte. Admittedly, it is not always easy to grasp what Tomlinson is trying to say, but if one thing emerges loud and clear it is his desire to recast Christian faith in a postmodern mould. The key question which arises from this, however, is whether he has represented either postmodernity or evangelicalism in an adequate way. The answer, I believe, is that he has not.

Tomlinson and postmodernity

To a large extent, Tomlinson's definition of postmodernity accords with that which I offered in Chapters 1 and 2. Nonetheless, his version is rather more selective and upbeat than is really fair. He subtly equates belief in absolutes with 'dogma', but the one does not necessarily imply the other. It is quite possible to tell non-dogmatic stories which forgo propositional 'plain words or simple statements', or to emphasise images and symbols, and yet through them still express absolute beliefs. From Aesop's fables to Eastern Orthodox icons, from the Exodus narrative to early church mosaics, faith in absolutes is hardly disqualified by a non-dogmatic medium.

Likewise, postmodernity may well have strands of environmentalism, but as we have seen, it is also marked by a consumerism, hedonism and individualism which are hardly conducive to saving the planet. Furthermore, Tomlinson seems to mistake the morally ambiguous phenomenon of globalisation – which owes more to marketing and technology – for 'a strong sense of global unity'. This hardly does justice to the aggressive nationalism and inter-ethnic hatred which has swept across Eastern Europe and the former Yugoslavia in the 1990s. It fails to recognise that the equally strong counter-trend of postmodern pluralism and difference can give free rein to bigotry as well as liberation: it was the French National Front leader Jean Marie le Pen who said, 'I adore North Africans. But their place is in the Maghreb.'[95]

As Zygmunt Bauman has pointed out, postmodernity has its 'discontents' as well as its beneficiaries.[96] Not least among its drawbacks is the fact that by refusing to conceive of anything as universal, it is at best ambivalent about universal human rights. Indeed, the United Nations may well be weaker now than it was when it was first formed in 1948. Surfing the Internet and buying a Big Mac abroad may remind you that the world is becoming a global village, but these things will not guarantee world peace! At one point in his argument, Tomlinson does briefly quote Bauman on the 'dark side' of postmodernism,[97] but having done so moves on breezily to describe it as a 're-enchantment' of all that modernity tried hard to dis-enchant.[98] Thereafter he simply neglects to discuss the consciously anti-Christian sentiments expressed by leading postmodern thinkers like Barthes, Derrida and Baudrillard.

In much the same way, Tomlinson's endorsement of the increased 'spiritual dimension' in postmodernity fails to recognise that, in and of itself, 'spirituality' is quite neutral: from a Christian point of view, it can be either positive or negative. It can lead people equally to holistic love for Jesus or to mass suicide in deluded cults like the Branch Davidian, the Solar Temple or Heaven's Gate. The flamboyant rock legend Elton John recently told an interviewer, 'I am beginning to get some spirituality into my life', as if it could be plucked off a shelf like multi-vitamins or Lucozade. Indeed, the Old Testament theologian Dan Beeby once told me that just as the overworked word 'culture' led Herman Goering to reach for his revolver, so because of its catch-all vagueness, the use of 'spirituality' in the postmodern world tempted him to do the same!

Tomlinson legitimately describes postmodern society as one in which people are 'accustomed to communicating through words linked to images and symbols rather than through plain words or simple statements'.[99] He also presents it as a society in which 'the book age is giving way to the screen age'.[100] At a time of increased computer ownership and multiplying TV outlets it would be hard to dispute this, but Tomlinson offers little in the way of reflection upon it. As we shall see in the next chapter, the new 'visual age' may well prompt evangelicals to rediscover the non-verbal modes of worship and communication which reside in earlier Christian traditions. Nonetheless, it is at least worth noting Lawrence Osborn's reservations about this development. 'Images,' he warns, 'subvert our critical faculty by confronting us with what purports to be reality . . . With the advent of virtual reality, the manipulative potential of images is greater than ever. Anyone who . . . advocates their use in spirituality without proper safeguards is, at best, naive.'[101] This caveat bears out once again that Tomlinson may well have taken too partial and optimistic a view of postmodernity.

Another point at which Tomlinson leaves himself open to criticism is in his assertion that postmoderns tend to be 'deeply suspicious of institutions, bureaucracies and hierarchies'.[102] Insofar as this point refers to more formal social organisations, one wonders what implications it has for the Church. No doubt Holy Joe's is one postmodern model, but Tomlinson expresses the hope that most post-evangelicals will 'remain in their churches,'[103] and has himself undertaken training for ministry in the Church of England. This begs the question of how a post-evangelical might practically vent his or her 'suspicions' as a member of a mainline denomination – but this is a question Tomlinson does not answer in his book.

Assimilation v. engagement

The issue of conformity versus dissent also relates to the wider matter of cultural assimilation versus cultural engagement. Tomlinson argues that post-evangelicals will naturally question cultural norms, and yet in the same breath characterises them as those who have conformed to the cultural norms of postmodernity! In my conversations with leading evangelicals, this matter in particular produced a good deal of criticism. While several were ready to admit that evangelicals had allowed themselves to absorb too many modernist, middle-class assumptions, they were concerned that Tomlinson had for his part absorbed too many *postmodern* assumptions without properly critiquing them from a biblical point of view. In Graham Cray's terms, 'You get serious problems if you start to inculturate Christianity within postmodern *culture* at the same time as being insufficiently critical about postmodern *theory*, and I think that's what's happening in Dave's book.'

Others were more forthright on this issue. Clive Calver declared bluntly that Dave Tomlinson had become 'a late-twentieth-century Gnostic'. By this he meant that, like the Gnostics of early church history, he had become more attached to prevailing 'wisdom' than to the eternal Word of God: 'Dave Tomlinson is trying to get people to think in the mindset of contemporary culture. I want to challenge that mindset. Dave is not into cultural *engagement*; he's after cultural *absorption*. But adapting our methods of communication to the culture does not mean that we should compromise or change our message.' John Drane was also dubious – not least because of what he had learned about some aspects of Holy Joe's:

> What I would want to ask is, 'Are these people being challenged with following Jesus?' That's about taking up your cross, it's about hardship and service. I'm sure it's about loving yourself, but it's also about becoming more like Jesus. I don't see Jesus as an abstemious traditionalist evangelical, but equally I don't see Jesus as a cohabitor who spits on the floor as a complement to worship.[104]

These comments are especially significant given that Tomlinson championed Drane's work enthusiastically in *The Post-Evangelical*.[105]

Are post-evangelicals closet liberals?

'Selling out' to culture is one of the great criticisms which evangelicals have made of the theological movement known as liberalism. Tomlinson acknowledges this as a danger.[106] Indeed, he devotes a whole chapter of *The Post-Evangelical* to explaining how he and his companions differ from 'woolly liberals',[107] and to warning against its 'slippery slopes'. At times, however, I cannot help thinking that he doth protest too much!

Unlike Tomlinson, I come from a liberal Christian background and have been drawn towards evangelicalism not so much as an immature emotional reaction as by sheer theological conviction. I know liberal Christianity pretty well. I belong to a denomination whose fellowships described themselves in the English Church Census of 1989 as predominantly 'liberal'.[108] I was nurtured in a local church whose minister allied himself with liberalism. I was trained in a liberal theological college. I regularly interact – and argue with – liberal Christians. I think I recognise liberalism when I see it.

Admittedly, Tomlinson distances himself from the sort of liberal thinking which is so enslaved to Enlightenment rationalism that it simply refuses to accept the historicity of supernatural events in the gospels.[109] Granted, he wants to cling on to the importance of conversion in a way most liberals do not. Fair enough, he distinguishes an 'open' sort of liberalism, such as that promoted by John Habgood, from an 'illiberal' liberalism which appears to accept any version of truth apart from the orthodox, evangelical one.[110] Still, I think he fails to realise that liberalism is at least as adaptable and amorphous as evangelicalism. He overlooks the fact that there are many Christians who would still call themselves liberals while trying to adapt to postmodernity, yet who feel no need to go down the 'postliberal' route.

Leslie Houlden has observed that it is a mistake to treat 'liberal' as 'a label for a strongly homogeneous point of view'. Rather, he says, it may be best seen as 'a certain style or disposition in approaching religious belief, marked by a civilized readiness to consider arguments and evidence'.[111] Dave Tomlinson would certainly be a liberal if this were the only criterion. It is not, of course, but I am nonetheless reminded of a comment made by the sociologist Andrew Walker in his impressive study of the House Church movement, conducted while Tomlinson was still active within it. Walker compares Tomlinson to his more conservative former colleague Bryn Jones by saying that whereas Jones is a 'classical convergent thinker' who 'presses on regardless of opposition and set-backs, running a tight ship', Tomlinson is 'a divergent thinker' who is 'always rethinking his position, always seeing new angles and aspects of doctrines and practices, always learning and changing'.[112] At best this is a highly attractive quality, and it makes Tomlinson an excellent conversationalist. At worst, it betokens a lack of direction. Tomlinson is well aware of the liberal 'pitfalls' of out-and-out relativism.[113] He knows that one cannot keep asking questions without seeking some resolution. Yet his practical programme of 'communal reflection', 'uncompromised integrity' and heightened spiritual awareness is hardly very new, nor particularly clear.[114]

When it comes to more specific aspects of liberalism, certain similarities between it and post-evangelicalism beg further comparison. The New Age-inspired quest for 'spirituality' evident both at Holy Joe's and in Tomlinson's book has echoes of the great liberal F. D. E. Schleiermacher's search for a universal awareness of God derived from humanity's inner, aesthetic relation to reality. Schleiermacher's stress on religion as 'feeling and relationship',[115] and his willingness to shape theology around this rather than around the specific revelation of God in Christ and Scripture, also comes uncannily close to Tomlinson's ideal.[116]

Similarly, just as liberals tend to have an innate suspicion of dogma,[117] Tomlinson dismisses systematic doctrine as a 'pre-packed gospel' which is 'really just a stringing together of lots of little pieces which in their original context were presented as they stood, without being fitted into a coherent scheme'.[118] Furthermore, his oft-stated preference for local stories and 'modest episodes' draws him closer to the earthy parables of Jesus than to the more conceptual writing of St Paul – a preference which was very evident in the writings of nineteenth-century German liberals like Adolf von Harnack (1851–1930) and Albrecht Ritschl (1822–89).[119] Tomlinson also shares Ritschl's stress on the Church as a community linked inextricably with wider social networks and, like Ritschl, is far less concerned to describe the Church's distinctiveness from such networks.

On occasion, Tomlinson purports to distance himself from liberalism, but does so by setting post-evangelicals against what is, in effect, a stereotype of liberalism. He implies, for example, that liberals are sceptical about the transcendence of God, the uniqueness of Christ and the priority of personal salvation. Yet these points all featured prominently in the writings of later American liberals like Harry Emerson Fosdick, William A. Brown, Rufus Jones and Henry Sloane Coffin. For them, it was a generally critical attitude to Scripture which defined them as liberals, not a deviation from creedal orthodoxy. Likewise, Tomlinson contrasts a post-evangelical penchant for metaphorical and analogical models of meaning with a modernist liberal reliance on propositional truth. But so-called 'Chicago' liberals like David Tracy have been suggesting for a number of years that theology must proceed with an 'analogical imagination' and a 'conversational' model of interpretation.[120]

None of this is meant to 'out' Dave Tomlinson from some liberal closet. Nonetheless, Graham Cray did at least moot to me the possibility that 'Dave is becoming a liberal without knowing it, and rather an old-fashioned liberal at that.' David Jackman, who heads up the Cornhill Training course under the auspices of the conservative evangelical St Helen's Church, Bishopsgate, expressed even more severe reservations about where post-evangelicals might be headed. He told me:

My fear is that the 'post' in 'post-evangelicalism' actually means leaving evangelicalism. Dave Tomlinson
might deny that, but a liberal bishop recently said to
a friend of mine who asked him how liberals will
sustain their cause when so few were offering for
ministry, 'Oh, we'll do what we've always done –
we'll recruit from the evangelicals!' And sadly, this
is what happens. People do drift away. You hear a
number of liberalised bishops, for instance, saying that
they 'value their evangelical roots'!

Whether or not he becomes a bishop, it does seem that
Dave Tomlinson's proposals may not be quite as novel
as they appear to be. There are several precedents for
what he is proposing in liberal theologies written before
postmodernism ever became trendy. In the liberal United
Reformed Church where I grew up, I can well remember
discussing the ecological crisis in the seventies; I also
remember pushing the green agenda of the World Council
of Churches' Justice, Peace and the Integrity of Creation
Programme in the mid-eighties. When I trained for the
ministry over a decade ago, the post-feminism endorsed
by Tomlinson was taken as read: prayer language was
inclusivised and female ordinands left their husbands looking after the kids. The quest for alternative spiritualities
was well under way: people would come back from France
raving about the Taizé Community and from Iona extolling
the virtues of Celtic mysticism. 'Community' had become
a big buzzword, thanks to the liberation theologians of South
America.

At the risk of sounding like a 'been there, done that'
postmodern, when you have lived with liberalism as much
as I have the post-evangelical agenda does not seem so
exotic. For all Tomlinson's talk about 'paradigm shifts'
and the 'enormous' cultural divide between modernity and
postmodernity,[121] the theological response he makes to the
changing situation often prompts a feeling of *déjà vu*. What

has distinguished that response is that it has been packaged for a disillusioned evangelical constituency which is still wary of full-blown liberalism, but which has begun to express the doubts and fears which liberals take for granted. Without question, there are some evangelicals who need to explore what Tomlinson calls the 'grey' areas of Christian experience, and for them his book could offer a helpful beginning. On the other hand, there are many evangelicals in mainline or 'mixed' denominations who will be all too familiar with much of what Tomlinson is proposing, and who have ultimately been led to resist it. The reasons for such resistance are sometimes intellectual, but they are often also mission-driven and practical.

As I have shown, my own United Reformed Church is more attuned to postmodern themes than most. Yet it is one of the fastest-declining mainline denominations in Britain.[122] The reasons for this are many and varied, but they are partly summed up by the Moderator's symbol which I mentioned in Chapter 2 – the symbol of the questionmark. In the URC, we have plenty of questions, but we are far worse at giving answers – at least the sort of answers which might attract people into our churches! We cannot agree on what the gospel is, and we therefore cannot agree an agenda for evangelism. So evangelism gets redefined as 'mission', and mission is redefined as an uncontroversial agenda of good works. I am not saying that post-evangelicalism will necessarily fall into the same trap – but if it remains caught too deeply and too long in its current ambivalence, it will almost certainly do so.

Tomlinson's definition of evangelicalism

Viewing things from a 'mixed' denomination also makes me wonder whether Tomlinson is addressing the whole of evangelicalism, or just one specific part of it. His own journey began within strict Brethrenism and took in House

Churches which he left partly as a reaction to their perceived authoritarian ethos. This is a very specific journey – quite different from my own and many others' journeys, which have moved towards evangelicalism from a non-Christian or liberal base. Furthermore, although Tomlinson is now training to be an Anglican priest, he has hitherto operated outside the mainstream of church life. As a result, he may have overlooked the fact that many evangelicals in traditional churches have had to work out their salvation in the midst of much open debate, discussion and interchange with those of different views. Furthermore, he may have missed the point that, for many of us, this process has actually helped to inform and sharpen our evangelical convictions, even while we have continued to be evangelicals!

When Tomlinson attacks 'evangelicalism', it is unclear whether his target is simply the ethos of large events like Spring Harvest, or whether he means also to include radical evangelicals, liturgical evangelicals, conservative evangelicals, charismatic evangelicals, alternative worship evangelicals and so on.

When I discussed this point with John Drane and Gerald Coates, both felt that Tomlinson had indeed theologised much of his own personal history. Drane told me that, in *The Post-Evangelical*, Tomlinson seemed to have been 'escaping from certain really quite strange evangelical lifestyles, which are nothing to do with theology'. He added that 'if you don't share that kind of background, it might not mean a great deal'. To Coates, post-evangelicalism seemed to reflect Tomlinson's 'disillusionment' – first with Bryn Jones, then with Coates's own network of churches, and finally with an independent group of fellowships which Tomlinson had tried to form himself.

Even if this tells only part of the truth, it serves to underline how regrettable it would be if post-evangelicalism were to split the evangelical community. If this sounds alarmist, then it is a view which was voiced by a number of those I interviewed. Derek Tidball, who was Tomlinson's opponent in the Institute of Contemporary Christianity's debate on post-evangelicalism, and is Principal at the London Bible College, reflected, 'If we're not careful on this, we're going to do what evangelicals have been very good at down the years – namely, polarising. The boundaries could be drawn very clearly and we could fail to listen to and understand one another.' He elaborated:

> My fear is that we are going to end up with fur-ther division, which on the one hand pushes con-servative evangelicalism to become more reaction-ary, and post-evangelicalism to become more liberal. Post-evangelicals need desperately to hear what con-servative evangelicals have to say, but conservatives need to be listening a lot harder and more sympatheti-cally to some of what post-evangelicals are saying.

Clive Calver made a similar point:

> The problem with post-evangelicalism is that the oppo-nents of evangelicalism are just sitting on the sidelines laughing. They think this is wonderful stuff: it's the ammunition they've always looked for. Also, of course, more conservative, separated evangelicals are roaring with laughter as well, because it gives them all the more ammunition. Dave hasn't seen the implications of what he's doing. He hasn't thought through what the repercussions might be.

For Gerald Coates, 'There will always be something wrong with evangelicalism somewhere, but Dave generalises spe-cific problems, and I wonder about the value of doing that.'

Such mainline evangelical critics may be pleased to learn that Tomlinson does see possible lines of reconciliation. He told me, 'The driven, pragmatic aspect of evangelicalism does actually make change possible. I don't doubt that evangelicalism has got a future in the twenty-first century.

Alister McGrath thought I was writing its obituary. Far from it! I think evangelicalism has an enormous capacity to re-birth itself.'

In the conclusion to *The Post-Evangelical*, Dave Tomlinson admits that he has offered a 'rather crude' argument which 'begs many more questions than it answers'. He also expresses the hope that it 'will stimulate the rigorous debate that is needed, as people wrestle with the issues of living in a postmodern world, and try to understand its implications'.[123] In the chapters which follow, I shall apply Tomlinson's challenge to more specific areas of Christian faith and life – namely worship and preaching, witness and discipleship, personal and public morality, and theology and doctrine.

PART II

RESPONDING TO THE CHALLENGE

8

WORSHIP AND PREACHING

Dancing to a New Beat: the Rise of 'Alternative' Services

I never went to barn dances before I became a Christian. Since my conversion, I have been to many. Most especially, I have done the dosi-do and swung my partner as an *evangelical* Christian in an evangelical setting. My first ever student Christian Union bash was a barn dance. While other undergraduates were embarking on freshers'-week pub crawls, we evangelicals made figures of eight to the sound of violin, concertina and washboard. It was a perplexing experience – not because I wanted to get drunk instead, but because I could not understand what linked this strange, mock-rural ceremony so closely to the faith I held.

I still do not understand, but I still go to barn dances. A while back, we held one in my church. As I have said, it is an historic church on the western edge of the City of London. It is about as far away from a country barn as you could hope to get. But that did not seem to matter very much. People from a wide range of ages and cultural backgrounds came and, given its modest purpose, the event was a success. Folk had drawn together. They had met, eaten, talked and danced. The non-Christians were not too threatened, but one of our members had closed with a short talk on the love of God.

That evening, I was the last to leave the church. It had been a busy week, and I had to return to my office to complete the next morning's sermon. It was midnight before I finished. I set out on my normal route home through Farringdon to Clerkenwell. I had not walked back this late on a Saturday before, and I became conscious of something I had never previously noticed. During the week the City is a sober business centre, but this was the weekend, and things change at the weekend. Within a few hundred metres of one another, a series of clubs were pulsating with music very different from that I had heard earlier. It was not exactly my preference, but it was far closer to what I listen to on the radio. People in their twenties were spilling out on to the street. Some looked happy; others looked dazed. Several were clearly on drugs. It was not especially threatening, but it was disconcerting. I was not much older than many of those around me; I worked just around the corner. But in cultural terms the church environment from which I had come was light years away.

Some of the clubbers were still out on the street the next morning. I saw them as I drove in early to prepare for the Sunday service. That service would include a number of young people, a handful of whom go occasionally to clubs. But there was no real connection between the two worlds – no link between the church and its temporary neighbours from down the street.

Elsewhere, though, things are different . . .

The request came out of the blue. A phone call from the bursar at our old theological college. Could Mia help out with an 'alternative' worship service at the Greenbelt Christian Arts Festival? It was the summer of 1991.

I had been to Greenbelt as an undergraduate a few years before, and had enjoyed it very much. At that time, I had been longing to find a context in which my creative interests could mesh positively with my faith. I had been one of the few English students in my university CU. I had edited a poetry magazine and the review pages of the student newspaper; I had acted in plays and made features for the campus radio station. Yet all these things had seemed to take place in a distinct sphere: it was hard to make links between them and my evangelical student sub-culture. No doubt this was partly my own fault, but in any case Greenbelt had helped. It had been started in the mid-seventies, as a modest parallel to the great outdoor pop festivals of the preceding few years. By the time I made my first visit, it had grown large enough to occupy a huge field on the Knebworth estate. By 1991, it had expanded further, and had decamped to Northamptonshire.

Mia agreed to the bursar's request. It turned out that he attended an Anglican church which supported a pioneering organisation called Oxford Youth Works, which was experimenting with forms of church service geared to the younger generation. He told us to contact someone called Pete Ward. We did, and a few weeks later we found ourselves meeting with Pete and his team at the Festival, going over the details of what would be called 'Critical Mass'. By this time, Mia and I had been ordained as ministers in the United Reformed Church. It soon became clear why they wanted Mia! At that stage, the Church of England had not yet made its controversial decision to ordain women, and because Greenbelt was beyond Anglican jurisdiction, Pete and his co-workers decided to make a statement. As the name suggested (rather awkwardly for Low Church nonconformists like us), 'Critical Mass' would include communion – and Mia would preside.

The time came for worship to begin. Mia was by now behind the scenes, but I joined the congregation. I stepped into a darkened tent, illuminated only by random strobe lighting. There were no chairs. A crowd of people were dancing in a free, unmechanical way to a song I had heard once or twice before. Then, it had seemed repetitive and vaguely spiritual. Now, it acquired a fresh depth and meaning. The rhythm was still driving, incessant, accentuated by the loud sound system. But the words began to make more sense. Before, I had taken them to be one more romantic love lyric. Now, I realised that they were expressing a different kind of devotion – praising someone greater than the latest boyfriend or girlfriend.

The song spiralled on for ten or fifteen minutes, and I was beginning to wonder whether I had walked into the wrong tent. Just then, a familiar voice came over the speaker. I recognised the tones of the black American preacher and campaigner Jesse Jackson. At the same time came a burst of lighting which revealed Pete and his band, surrounded by screens on to which Jackson's words were projected:

> THIS IS NOT A PROGRAMME,
> THIS IS A WORSHIP SERVICE!

The band crashed into a number called 'Eternal Love', and we were away. The next hour or so ranked among the most exhilarating and disorienting Christian events I had ever attended. I knew about 'rave' and 'acid house' culture, but to see it even mildly reflected in a Christian setting was both exciting and overwhelming. At the time, I had just begun a Ph.D. about communication in worship. I had set out to look at how postmodern philosophies of language might relate to Reformed and evangelical church services. As I danced, I began to rethink my thesis. Parts of the Prayer Book were still recognisable, but the style was more colloquial:

> Everloving Lord, our hearts are open to you
> And you know all our desires.
> We can't hide from you.
> By your Holy Spirit,
> Come into us;
> Purify our motives and strengthen our minds . . .

> Please forgive us for all the things we've done which
>   we're ashamed of.
> Please help us to start again.

More notably, the prayers and responses came intercut with
the accompanying beat and melody. We progressed through
the liturgy in an episodic rather than a linear way. From
one moment to the next, a different medium was dominant:
music, light, text, image, spoken call, chanted response.
Then Mia appeared, as if from nowhere. Engulfed by the
carnival of adoration around her, she read the familiar words:
'Take eat, this is my body . . . Drink this all of you . . .'
Again, the band hit a deep, insistent groove:

> Christ has died,
> Christ is risen
> Christ will come again!

The mood calmed a little as we went to receive communion.
Then more music and more dancing. A blessing, and a
laid-back, understated dismissal:

> Thank you very much for coming to our service.
> We hope you enjoyed it.

On reflection, 'Critical Mass' was the first postmodern
service I ever attended. Its heterogeneity, immediacy and
sensuality set it apart starkly from the 'hymn sandwich' I
had grown up with, and which I had begun to inflict on
my own congregation as a minister. I mentioned this to
Pete Ward when we met again, five years on, at his base
in Oxford. Pete is now the Archbishop of Canterbury's
adviser for Youth Ministry. Still, despite his promotion, he
was disarmingly honest about the genesis of his approach
to worship. 'We were never consciously postmodern at all,'
he told me. 'I'd been leading worship for three or four years
before I'd even heard of the word! Our agenda was to be
contextual with young people. We were shaping worship
from *their* perspective. And that led to people in the *rest* of
the church saying "Oh, this is different – therefore it must
be postmodern."'

Pete's change of job might suggest that 'alternative' worship has gained a much higher profile in recent times – and indeed it has. It must be said, though, that this profile has not always been raised in the most positive way . . .

NOS: from Evangelicalism through Postmodernism to Scandal

In August 1995, the alternative worship scene provided tabloid journalists with the ultimate 'Randy Vicar' story. On Monday 21st of that month, a terse Church of England press release declared that 'an internationally renowned worship experiment in Sheffield appears to be gravely damaged after the uncovering of alleged improper sexual activity involving a former leader'.

The leader in question was Rev. Chris Brain – co-ordinator of the so-called 'Nine O'Clock Service', and without doubt one of the true pioneers of alternative worship. The 'alleged improper sexual activity' referred to in the press statement was based on a Sheffield Diocese estimate that Brain had manipulated fifty or more women involved in the community which had developed and sustained 'NOS'.[1] Later, Brain would tell the *Mail on Sunday:*

> To find that I am some kind of abuser of people I dearly love, in the areas I most passionately believe in, and thought I had worked so hard for, fills me with utter despair and I do not know what I can say. I am sorry for the consequences of what I have done. I can see what I could not see before and I am profoundly and desperately sorry.[2]

Back in 1988, I had visited Sheffield on an industrial mission course. One afternoon, we were taken round St Thomas's, Crookes. A staff member there told us of a radical new worship event which had begun on Sundays at 9 p.m. The time had been chosen specifically to reach young people who were used to the late hours of the club scene. It sounded intriguing, but I thought little more of it until that experience three years later at Greenbelt. Then, shortly afterwards, our church youth group went to a Nine O'Clock Service. They were certainly impressed by the film loops, the multi-track mixing, the computer-generated imagery and the sheer professionalism of it all. But they were also uneasy. There was a 'gothic heaviness' about it all, some said. The leaders were clothed in black, and much of the symbolism seemed deliberately foreboding.

It was around this time that NOS had begun to transform itself from a radical evangelical worship project into a more self-consciously postmodern movement – one which would turn for inspiration to a broader range of theological sources, including the 'creation-centred spirituality' advocated by the controversial Dominican priest Matthew Fox. Somewhat later still, NOS would move out of St Thomas's altogether and become an 'extra-parochial place' within the Church of England, taking over the cavernous Pond's Forge Leisure Centre for services which by then included a so-called 'Planetary Mass'.

Whereas Pete Ward insists in a recent article that for all his attempts to challenge evangelical worship he remains 'enthusiastic' about his evangelical identity,[3] Chris Brain's embrace of postmodern methods accompanied a conscious theological shift away from evangelicalism. In his compelling book *The Rise and Fall of the Nine O'Clock Service*, Roland Howard charts how NOS grew out of a fellowship group at St Thomas's, which had developed into a charismatic evangelical community based close by in Nairn Street. Initially, they had been influenced by the work of the Anglican charismatic David Watson, and then by the 'signs and wonders' teaching of the Californian evangelist John Wimber. At first, it was Wimber's spectacular form of

charismatic ministry which had inspired Brain and others at
Nairn Street to establish NOS in the mid-eighties. By the
end of the decade, however, another potent worldview had
entered the picture.

As Howard reports it, 'A couple of years into the experiment, Brain and the leaders decided completely to overhaul
the service . . . Brain was keen to react against the predominant reason-based approach to faith which he thought
had come with the Reformation and the Enlightenment.
He thought this made Protestants, and particularly evangelicals and charismatics, too matey with God.' In place
of this, says Howard, Brain 'wanted to stress the "other-
ness" of God, the distance between humans and God,
the mystery of the creator rather than the quantifiable,
reason-based perceptions which were derived from a wholly
rational, post-Enlightenment world view'.[4] Bearing in mind
our discussion so far, it will come as no surprise to discover what caused Brain to make this change of direction.
Howard recalls that 'Brain was reading postmodern texts
soon after they were published and, indeed, postmodernism
was to have a significant effect on NOS'.[5] In more specific terms,

> Not only was NOS's use of image-based multi-media
> effects and dance samples truly postmodern, but their
> emphasis on style and design and their attempts to
> communicate intuitively using visual and dramatic
> rituals, rather than reason-based texts, also reflected
> a postmodern view. Later their exploration and syn-
> thesis of a variety of Christian theologies (and also
> subsequently other faiths) was another expression of
> postmodernism. Their interest in sexual roles and
> boundaries, in new science and the environmental
> crisis, in re-inventing pre-modern rituals with tech-
> nology, also owes much to a postmodern understand-
> ing. *Postmodernism was a significant subtext running
> through NOS's development* [my emphasis].[6]

The legacy of NOS

Naturally, reflecting on NOS prompts the question whether its collapse was due simply to the aberration of one man, or whether there was something about its embrace of postmodernism which was bound, intrinsically, to lead it astray. Especially given NOS's evangelical roots, this is a question which strikes at the very heart of our concerns here. I put it to a number of those who were involved with, or influenced by, NOS. Perhaps not surprisingly, I met with a range of responses.

Graham Cray had been closely linked to the development of NOS, and his reflections on this point were extensive. Not only did he move in NOS circles and help lead NOS services; he now lectures in postmodernism to students within the Cambridge Federation of Theological Colleges. He is an immensely gracious and thoughtful man, and the two hours we spent talking in his study simply flew by. He even handled my cruellest question with insight and poise. I had noticed that in a paper he wrote for the Church of England's Board of Mission in the early nineties, Cray had offered a dedication to 'Rev. Chris Brain and the Sheffield Nine O'Clock Trust for their work in creating an expression of Anglicanism suited for mission in the post-modern world'.[7] How did he feel about this now? 'The collapse of NOS *was* partly down to something inherent within its approach to church and worship,' he admitted, 'but it was also partly down to Chris Brain himself.' He went on to explain:

I knew Chris and the Nairn Street community for at least five years before NOS came into being. I was closely tied in with NOS for the first half of its time. I had gradually had *less* contact even before moving to Cambridge, and now actually know I was cut out, to put it plainly. I visited the Pond's Forge Leisure Centre on one occasion – I was a celebrant at a Planetary Mass at an early stage. What I never knew – and the wool was pulled over my eyes as much as anyone's – was Chris's abuse of people. And I've got to take responsibility myself as a Christian leader involved there: I did not see it coming. There's no doubt that if at the heart of something there's a self-centred, systematic abuse of power, something distorted must be at the heart of the thing itself. It's no good saying simply, 'It was one bloke having his fun.'

With hindsight, Cray traces a link between NOS's worsening relational problems and the postmodernist turn taken by Brain in the later years:

At some point, NOS got into a theological helter-skelter, and that was the point at which I found myself less and less asked to participate. At some point, it shot out of orthodoxy. No doubt this went hand in hand with the adopting of certain postmodern philosophical assumptions, though I didn't see this at the time. One of the ways Chris managed to maintain power and control was to keep things moving intellectually. So, someone who was committed more to power than truth started to use truth as a weapon to manipulate people, and to create an instability in which the only way to be stable was to hang on to him. Ultimately, Chris used truth, and everything else, as a vehicle to get power. And that is called sin.

Despite his more 'traditional' charismatic pedigree, Gerald Coates told me that he was nonetheless open to alternative styles of worship. What had bothered him about NOS was not its techniques, but its leader. Coates had been on the Executive Committee of the annual Evangelists' Conference when Brain had been asked to speak. He recalled Brain as 'rude, offensive, abusive and superior. He never smiled, which is usually a bad sign. I remember saying at the time, "Anyone who has been blessed by God like he has should be humble and grateful." But he was hostile. So it was no surprise to us when NOS fell apart.' Coates reiterated, however, that the problem exposed by NOS 'is not an Anglican problem. It's not a problem to do with music. It's a problem to do with relationships.'

Similarly, Graham Cray remains convinced that NOS contributed a great deal to the Church, and that its methods should not be damned by its moral and theological failure. 'It released an enormous burst of creativity in which many people were involved,' he told me. 'A lot of it was good, and I would happily commend much of it to people today. It triggered a large number of worship projects, many of which are absolutely superb.' Cray's optimism is admirable considering his own disappointments with NOS, but he is not the only one trying to pick up the pieces of what happened in Sheffield.

'NOS was the greatest tragedy in the Church this century.' This was the startling reaction of Brian Draper, the London Bible College student who so powerfully unpacked postmodernity for the Bournemouth Assembly of Evangelicals. Hyperbole aside, Draper feels continuing anguish at what happened in Sheffield – and with good reason. He helps lead another self-consciously postmodern alternative worship service, 'Live on Planet Earth', in Cranbrook, Kent. Even now, he finds himself having to assure people that his own project will not turn into 'NOS 2'. 'Ultimately,' Draper told me, 'Chris Brain used postmodern theology to justify what he was doing personally. And that *was* a tragedy because it gave people an immediate excuse to reject alternative worship as such. We have NOS quoted at us month by month. We're still trying to recover as an alternative worship movement from NOS.' Nonetheless, he added, 'We're desperately, desperately trying to do what we can to make church relevant. And we're desperately trying to do it within the mainstream.'

This last comment underlines an accountability which, as Howard's book shows, was all too vague at NOS. Despite

the events of August 1995, Graham Cray is right to observe
that a growing number of alternative worship events have
developed since. The difference is that many of the practitioners have formed more coherent and more responsible
networks. There is now a national Alternative Worship
Conference, a journal (*re:generate*) and an 'alt.worship'
forum on the Internet.[8] 'Live on Planet Earth' is linked into
the local Council of Churches, and in September 1996 was
even visited by the Archbishop of Canterbury – no doubt
at the prompting of Pete Ward.[9] Indeed, it is Draper's zeal
to see alternative worship more generally accepted which
keeps him aboard the evangelical ship: 'I'd still want to
call myself an evangelical,' he insists, 'because I long to
see what we are doing at 'Live on Planet Earth' adopted by
mainline evangelicals – I long for them to understand us.'

Draper's dream may not be so far off. Recent Spring
Harvest weeks have featured a distinct 'youth service' strand
which has borrowed liberally from the alternative worship
movement. Jenny Baker, who works with her husband
Jonny in Youth For Christ, has helped to lead it. From
her point of view, 'The collapse of NOS was a big threat
to many people. They worried about it signalling the end of
alternative worship. But what's happened is that people have
said, "We mustn't throw the baby out with the bathwater;
there's so much good in the whole movement."'

While the Bakers' approach may be tempered to a degree
by the Spring Harvest ethos, it still manages to challenge and
provoke. 'After one service,' Jenny told me, 'we got a letter
saying that the kind of dance music we were using had an
unhealthy hypnotic beat. It reminded me of the "backward
masking" debate about rock music which evangelicals had
a few years ago.' Likewise, 'We were also criticised because
the slides we were using didn't have any capital letters in
them – not even for God and Jesus. But we were simply
using a typographic style rather than making any theological
point. Sometimes the whole thing can provoke a quite hostile
reaction.'

In the wake of NOS, alternative worship is often stereo-typed by 'Christian rave' and 'rave in the nave' headlines. Despite this, the high-octane image suggested by such tags is often misleading. Certainly, there is a move in some quarters towards 'DJ-led', rhythm-dominated events: the youth services of the Revelation Church on the South Coast often begin in this way, and the music at 'Live on Planet Earth' does at times reflect the faster 'techno' and 'house' styles common in clubs during the last few years. Nonetheless, the dominant genre at the latter is 'ambient' – or what Brian Draper describes as 'meditative and contemplative'. This, he says, represents a conscious attempt to move away from more established patterns of youth praise: 'When the Archbishop of Canterbury came to visit us, he was surprised to have come from *another* youth meeting in our area, which was a happy-clappy, fast-chorus affair, straight into our low-lit, downbeat atmosphere.' Draper seemed pleased to have challenged archiepiscopal assumptions: 'The penny dropped with Dr Carey that young people aren't just after the happy-clappy stuff, but want more in the way of contemplation.'

A similar approach is to the fore at 'Grace' – a monthly service held regularly in St Mary's, Ealing. Its originator, Mike Starkey, told me that, like Draper, he had drawn a great deal of inspiration from NOS, but had sensed the need to do something different: 'The first time I ever got very, very excited about a worship experience was at a NOS service – years before all the weird stuff started going on. They were much more orthodox then, with a charismatic bent, but they were integrating that with the rave culture.' Impressed though he was, Starkey realised that he could not produce a carbon copy: 'In my curacy at Ealing, I started "Grace" as a less dance-oriented event. We still used incense, gothic bits and pieces and eclectic readings from various sources, but things were quieter.'

Understandably, such postmodern plundering of the past has led some to investigate more thoroughly the traditions from which they have drawn. Just as Steinar Kvale has seen in postmodernity a paradoxical yearning for pre-modern paradigms,[10] so several evangelicals with connections to the alternative worship scene have begun more fully to embrace historic church liturgy and symbolism.

Evangelicals on the 'High' Road

It is indicative of a growing trend that Mike Starkey has now moved to an Anglo-Catholic parish in Finsbury Park, North London. Indeed, in a November 1996 article for the *New Christian Herald*,[11] he saw his own embrace of 'higher' liturgical forms as part of a movement which has developed not only from Anglican evangelical experiments with alternative worship, but in other parts of evangelical-ism, too. Starkey pointed out that the new and intensely liturgical Charismatic Episcopal Church in the United States had grown from Pentecostal rather than Anglican roots, and already boasted 180 congregations. Likewise, Peter Gillquist of Campus Crusade for Christ had led 2,000 evangelicals into the Antiochian Orthodox Church of North America. Chichester-based New Church leader Roger Ellis had begun to re-emphasise neglected aspects of Celtic worship for a new generation of teenagers, while other evangelicals had turned to the calm, repetitive chants of the Taizé Community in order to 'chill out' from their Christian raving.

Within the Church of England, the growth of such 'high church' evangelicalism had come about, wrote Starkey, for both pragmatic and theological reasons. First, there was the simple fact that 'half the C. of E.'s ordinands are now evangelicals, and there are simply not enough evangelical churches to go around'. Also, however, it appeared that many of those who ended up in Anglo-Catholic congre-gations had seen the potential for a re-marriage of Word and Sacrament, exposition and image, rational preaching and sensory ritual. When we talked at the City Temple,

Starkey linked all this quite explicitly to the postmodern shift from verbal-linear communication to visual-episodic communication – from the abstract and the cerebral to the sensate and the theatrical:

> The church where I now serve much more has a tradition of things not being word-based. If my predecessor gave them two minutes for the sermon they thought it was overdone. They now get ten or fifteen minutes from me, which they think is an eternity, but because it's full of stories and anecdotes it's all right – it sweetens the pill a bit. But I do have a lot of embodied liturgy and I deliberately use a lot of the so-called 'manual acts' from the Catholic tradition. At the prayer of consecration over the elements, I raise up my arms in a big dramatic gesture. When I say, 'He died for us on the cross,' I stretch out my arms. We also swing incense – though I'm always careful to explain what the symbolism is there.

Such borrowing is not indiscriminate, however. Starkey disavows features of the Catholic rite which he finds doctrinally unacceptable – the 'Hail Mary', and those parts of the eucharist which imply transubstantiation, for example. All the same, he reflects that he has found a real openness to this new approach, 'especially from people with an evangelical background, who are bored with the very wordy services of their tradition'.

This observation was echoed by Nick Mercer, whose background as a Baptist minister and Vice-Principal of the London Bible College offers a fascinating variation on the theme. For him, enacting the liturgy every day as a parish priest has recovered the defining story of life. 'This is a good re-emphasis,' he said. 'It has to do with the power of rhetoric, symbol and dramaturgy. It's about a return to *shape* within worship. We're realising that there's more to words than the Enlightenment scientific analysis of words.'

We have already seen that Dave Tomlinson's embrace of the Anglican way has led him towards similar conclusions. Nonetheless, it should not be inferred from this that all evangelicals who take church ritual more seriously can be dismissed as 'post-evangelicals'. Starkey and Mercer certainly expressed reservations about Tomlinson's broader arguments, while alternative worship leaders like the Bakers and Roger Ellis remain clearly within the evangelical camp. Having said this, other more subtle critiques of postmodern evangelical approaches to worship have been offered, and these deserve further consideration.

From Kendrick to Club Culture: the Scope and Validity of 'Postmodern' Worship

Sight versus sound

Not surprisingly, 'alternative' and 'high church' forms of evangelical worship have their fair share of detractors. Most of the concerns expressed focus on a perceived downgrading of the Word of God – an assumed dilution of that biblicism which has so long been a badge of evangelical identity. One of the sharpest critiques along these lines has been offered by Os Guinness.[12] Observing that we now live with the consequences of a 'graphics revolution' in which 'the image has triumphed over the word', Guinness attempts to show how this has adversely affected traditional evangelical emphases on worship as a celebration and exposition of Scripture.

Specifically, Guinness associates a stress on visual elements in worship with sin and idolatry. An emphasis on seeing, he says, puts our intentionality at the centre of things: we can choose whether or not to look at something, and therefore become the focus of power and control. By contrast, sound is something which addresses us 'whether we like it or not': it tends to make us the object of another's intention. Furthermore, images strike us in an immediate, spatial way, whereas words demand a sequential, directional concentration. Sights are effortless whereas sounds are more demanding; sights have to do with surfaces, whereas words have to do with meanings, and sight is common to all animals, whereas 'language and the ability to communicate in a specialised way is one of the distinctive features of human beings'.[13] Just as God is unapproachable by sight, argues Guinness (Exod. 33:20), so also the 'lust of the eyes' (1 John 2:16) led Adam and Eve to reject him, and the rebellion of Israel in the desert was manifested in idols who were dazzling but dumb (Exod. 32). Further still, Jesus called those who believe without seeing 'blessed' (John 20:29), and we are enjoined by Paul (2 Cor. 5:7) to walk by faith and not by sight.[14]

On these bases, Guinness questions what he believes is an eastward search for 'something we can see and contemplate', a creeping 'hunger for icons', and the present charismatic 'fascination' with signs and wonders. By contrast, he proposes that true evangelicals must be 'iconoclasts' – repudiating such excessive visuality with a recovery of intelligent preaching marked by 'correct doctrine married to cultural diagnosis'.[15] Likewise, David Jackman could well have been reading Guinness when he told me:

> I think we're a little too quick to accept the analysis that because we're a visually oriented culture, we should downgrade preaching. Jesus didn't say, 'Let him who has eyes to see . . .', but 'Let him who has ears to hear . . .' The distinctive feature of the God of the Bible is that he is not visually imaged, except as smoke and fire: 'No one can see God and live' (Exod. 33:20). But he *is* a God who speaks. Therefore, our responsibility to the God who has spoken is to listen, learn and understand.

There are a number of things which might be said in response to all this. First, Jesus himself clearly encouraged people to

look, as well as listen, for the truth. He told the disciples to
report to John the Baptist what they had *seen* – 'The blind
receive sight, the lame walk, those who have leprosy are
cured' – as well as what they had heard – the preaching
of good news to the poor (Matt. 11:5). He urged them to
learn lessons from nature (Matt. 6:26; Luke. 13:7; 21:25),
and to examine his resurrection body to convince them he
was alive (Luke 24:39). Admittedly, Guinness contends
that there is something unique about Jesus as the visible
representation of God, which is lost when he returns to
the Father, and which will not be perceived again until
he returns in glory.[16] It would be hard to deny this as it
stands, but Guinness pushes his point too far when he infers
from it that the years of Jesus's ministry on earth are thus
'the only time . . . when sight can be believed'. If this is
the case, why did the Spirit of Christ continue to produce
'signs and wonders', even after the ascension (Acts 2:43;
5:12; 6:8; 8:13; 14:3; 15:12)?

Guinness asserts that once Christ has gone up to heaven,
disciples make contact with God 'through believing and
receiving the apostolic message', as if this were simply
a matter of reading the Bible and listening to sermons.
And yet surely it is also about *demonstrating* that message
visually and tangibly – even if you are a conservative
evangelical who reckons that *supernatural* manifestations
died out with the apostles! I am sure Guinness would accept
this, but his failure to say so typifies a common conservative
fault – namely a lack of recognition that worship is about
much more than verbal exposition, important though verbal
exposition may be. If it is something which should engage
the whole 'body' in a 'living sacrifice' (Rom. 12:1), then it
is a fair assumption that more than our ears and minds must
be engaged!

To be fair, Guinness does accept that 'word and vision
are inseparable and complementary in human experience',
but his insistence that 'images are legitimate only when they
deal with what can be seen and shown' could be taken to

imply a very literal-minded aesthetic – one which has little place for the elusive dreamscapes of Ezekiel, Daniel and Revelation, or the rather fragmentary glimpses offered by Scripture of the angelic and demonic realms. No doubt, these more inscrutable things will be made plain when we see God face to face, but until then we look 'through a glass, darkly' (1 Cor. 13:12). In such circumstances, there must surely be a place for sanctified artistic abstraction, just as there is a place for praise which goes 'beyond words' (2 Cor. 9:15).

As for the distinctions Guinness and Jackman draw between sight and sound, while it is true that much visual information is less demanding of our minds than speech or writing, it would be hard to argue that, say, the crucifixion as painted by Matthias Grünewald or Malcolm H. Johnson does not carry considerable intellectual power. Granted, the images are dependent on an original verbal source (the gospels), but the plain fact of the matter is that they do a better job than many sermons on the theology of the atonement! This is not to denigrate preaching *per se*, but it does suggest the need to develop a theology of the Holy Spirit which charts its work of inspiration beyond the text of Scripture and the exposition of the preacher.

Ironically, the conviction that sounds are more demanding than sights neglects to recognise a point often made against charismatic, alternative and High Church services alike – namely that they are too much driven by the sound of music, and by the potentially empty sounds of sung or spoken repetition. This is certainly something that worries David Jackman. He told me: 'One of the problems of evangelicalism today is that "worship" has become almost synonymous with music.' No doubt he was thinking of how song tapes massively outsell sermon tapes in Christian book-shops, and of the way certain services appear to spend far more time on praise than preaching. No doubt, too, both he and Guinness would be disturbed by Brian Draper's account of the evolution of 'Live on Planet Earth': 'The service has metamorphosed over four years from being quite a churchy thing with a preacher and some jazzed-up choruses, to *no preaching and a backdrop of continuous music.* Now we gut the whole church. We put up banners. We've got loads of TVs, a giant video screen and slides' (my emphasis).

The contrast here is not so much between the visual and the aural as between the rationalistic and the impressionistic. There is still something to be heard, but ambient music (like the contemporary dance music used in other alternative worship services) is by its very nature resistant to explanation. Like many of the images projected on to Draper's video screens, it simply *is* – and you make of it what you will.

Music-centredness is something which Phil Wall links specifically to emergent postmodern evangelicalism. As we talked at his Salvation Army base, he made a bold prediction: 'The preachers and theologians of the future will be worship leaders. People will engage with theology through music and the arts.' He then drew a provocative comparison with the birth of British evangelicalism: 'That's how it was done in Wesley's and Whitefield's day, when John's brother Charles communicated new theological concepts through hymns.' Having said this, Wall was conscious of the fact that once music had become dominant, as with NOS, there would be a danger of services being motivated more by 'the worship of worship itself' than by the worship of God through his living Word. Without doubt, the scope for letting alternative services become performances – with audiences and spectators rather than congregations – is substantial.

Pick 'n' mix worship

Another reservation expressed by some of those I spoke to about alternative worship concerned its 'pick 'n' mix' approach to tradition and culture. We have already seen how certain evangelicals have moved beyond this to a more coherent embrace of classic liturgies. Nonetheless, the Methodist evangelist Rob Frost still saw good cause for concern: 'If we lose touch with the origins of what we borrow we'll become like a ship cut loose from its moorings,' he told me. 'If things are done without any context, we could end up worshipping anybody or anything.' For David Jackman, this context must most crucially be determined by Scripture: 'What we have to do is assess everything biblically and ask, 'Why are we doing this? What's the point of this? Are we doing it simply because we want to attract and accommodate people, to make it easy for them?' The danger in such an approach is that the message itself can also be accommodated.'

These worries are understandable, but it must be admitted that, even in the mainstream, there are worship leaders who confirm Clive Calver's characterisation of evangelicals as pragmatic magpies.

So, is Graham Kendrick postmodern?

Someone who gets singled out for a lot of criticism on the alternative worship scene is the popular charismatic songwriter Graham Kendrick – creator of 'The Servant King', 'Shine, Jesus, Shine' and a host of other evangelical smash hits. Indeed, to read a number of the messages on the 'alt.worship' Internet list, you would think that the whole post-NOS movement had developed as an alternative to Kendrick himself! Pete Ward summed up the tone when he told me: 'You might say it's a postmodern observation, but plastic chairs and Graham Kendrick don't cut it any more with young people. They desire something which is, quite frankly, *more religious* – more connected with historic spirituality.'

Aware of Kendrick's association with Ichthus, the influential South London House Church network led by Roger and Faith Forster, Ward continued by highlighting a paradox: 'The house churches went for a radical break from the historic Church, and what they've ended up with does not connect with the new generation's desire for something more authentic.' He then put forward a neat analysis: 'There's a sense in which the charismatic movement demythologises church, and thereby accommodates to *modernity*, whereas young people are now much more intrigued by the ancient wisdom and mystery to be found in historic liturgies.'[17]

This is a perceptive point, but I am not sure it tells the whole story. Kendrick may well attempt to demythologise church music by channelling it through accessible 'secular' styles like folk, rock and pop. But these are not the *only* styles in which he writes – indeed, there is an eclecticism about his work which might *itself* be described as postmodern. In 'The Feast is Ready to Begin', he appropriates calypso. 'And His Love Goes On' has a soft jazz accompaniment. 'O Lord, the Clouds are Gathering' and 'We Believe' are more theatrical. 'Jesus Put This Song into Our Hearts' has a consciously Jewish feel. Alternative worshippers may not actually *like* these songs, but they can hardly deny their variety. They may critique the evangelical sub-culture with which such songs are associated, but they must at least acknowledge Kendrick's attempt to vary his sources and mix his treatments. They may think his borrowings artificial – but then artificiality is hardly absent from an alternative worship scene which relies widely on synthesised sampling, drum machines and anachronistic symbolism. They may think him safe and populist, but postmodernists routinely exalt populism in the arts and media – from Abba to soap operas, from Madonna and Michael Jackson to *Blade Runner* and *Baywatch*.

I met Graham Kendrick in Bournemouth, during rehearsals for the National Assembly of Evangelicals. Over coffee, he happily confirmed his 'magpie' credentials: 'Down the years the pragmatic approach has tended to succeed best. It says, "Look – God made everything good, so let's redeem things; let's snatch them back." It happened when the Salvation Army began to use tavern tunes, and it happens in my music today.' He continued, 'The flag I wave is one which says that we should use everything that's helpful, mix it up together, and not get stuck in one style or another.'

The global and pluralised aspects of postmodernity are also prominent in Kendrick's thinking and composing. 'Travelling quite extensively, as I do, I get exposed to different cultures and learn to appreciate the variety of expressions of the Christian faith. If you only ever encounter things monoculturally, then you might not even begin to think about other styles.' Still, he added, 'there are people who imagine that the way they worship is the definitive method. Until you hear Aborigines singing a worship song, and can't even find a key, you might not realise that they, too, have a legitimate way of worshipping God. They just have a different language.'

This prompted me to share an experience I had had in a church service near Austin, Texas. The music group were kitted out as a Country and Western band, and played accordingly. Kendrick's songs were in their repertoire, but they came out sounding like a cross between Hank Williams and Johnny Cash! It had taken a while to get used to this, but in the end the effect was wonderfully refreshing. Kendrick smiled; he had heard stories like this from all over the world.

Despite his multicultural awareness, the accusation most often levelled at Kendrick by the alternative worshippers I spoke to, and by those who post e-mails on the Internet, is that however far he may stray for his musical inspiration, he always somehow heads back towards the middle of the road. Brian Draper typified this feeling when he told me that Kendrick offers 'Radio 2-style compromise music which is meant to keep everybody happy'.

Perhaps surprisingly, Kendrick himself is not too put out by such sentiments. Indeed, he freely admitted to me that he was 'trying to provide music which is accessible to the broadest number of people – trying to hit somewhere in the middle'. Unlike his critics, however, he does not see this as a bad thing: 'I want to be inclusive rather than exclusive.

Music can be a keep-out sign or a welcome mat. I'm aiming for the welcome mat.'

Specifically, Kendrick is concerned to produce music which can be enjoyed by a broad age range. In this sense, he sees his task as distinct from that faced by alternative worshippers. 'Over a certain age, people are largely monocultural. And unless they have been exposed to the vast variety of musical styles which has come into some of the Church in the last twenty years, they will find it difficult to adapt.' As a consequence, 'we have to take this into consideration in church worship: we must meet the challenge of being inclusive.'

Is alternative too exclusive?

Even as a practitioner, Mike Starkey has warned that alternative worship is in danger of becoming so concerned about its 'cool' or 'hip' image that it could exclude less trend-conscious sections of the younger generation – let alone those of more mature years. Writing in the *Church Times* he reflected that 'By the 1990s [an] aloof attitude of cool has become the normative attitude of the emerging culture. The yardstick of experience is not so much "Is it true?" or even "Does it feel good?", but "Is it cool?"' He went on to offer a real (unnamed) example of what he meant: 'Nobody welcomed the worshippers; the service consisted of fragmented images projected on to a screen, over some rock music backing. It was a show, a celebration of post-modern fragmentation, without any hint of where God might be . . .'[18]

Brian Draper appreciates such concern, but is keen to stress that his is more than a narrow 'youth' ministry. As he sees it: 'The middle-of-the-road approach fails to satisfy a lot of middle-aged and older people, too. More of them have started to come to "Live on Planet Earth" – for theological rather than musical reasons'. Draper linked this quite directly with post-evangelicalism: 'I think there's a greater crisis in the church than people are willing to admit at the moment. Dave Tomlinson's book didn't just speak to young people; it has spoken to a whole cross-section of ages, and I find that very, very interesting.' He had seen this reflected starkly in his own personal life: 'My girlfriend's parents are the most charismatic, evangelical, church-oriented people you could hope to find, and yet now they're saying that the church is becoming increasingly irrelevant. That speaks volumes to me.'

If Draper is right and such disillusionment is as wide-spread as he implies, a crucial question arises. Even if alternative worship is taken into the mainstream, even if its ideas are accepted by an older generation – how could it be practised on a regular, Sunday by Sunday basis? At present, we have seen that most of such worship takes place within 'special' services, which are so complex to prepare that they can only be held once a month.

This problem is of particular concern to Martin Wroe. Wroe is a journalist and author who writes on religious affairs for the *Observer*. As well as this, however, he serves on the Executive Committee of Greenbelt and is a churchwarden at St Luke's, Holloway – Greenbelt's year-round base. 'My interest,' he told me, 'is in whether it's possible to create a service for a local community – say a parish – which is informed by the attitude of the so-called alternative worship movement, but which is not "alternative", because it is the main service. After all, in the end, people do need to be together.'

Wroe sees a possible resolution of this difficulty in the move towards simpler, ambient services. 'As people get older, they're more likely to be into ambient music, which is much mellower. Besides which, there are major technical problems in the set-up of rave-style worship.'

Even this may, of course, be some way off. What is more, as I hinted in Chapter 3, many mainstream evangelicals have already been through an experience which now looks to have had a powerful – if inexplicit – postmodern impact on them. It is worth returning to this in the light of what we have been discussing.

Toronto in Postmodern Perspective

I have already suggested that with its emphasis on 'acted signs' and sensory experiences, and its preference for anecdotal rather than forensic preaching, the Toronto Blessing could be classed as a postmodern phenomenon. As I write, its initial impact seems be waning, but to an extent this makes considered reflection on it somewhat easier.

No doubt, Toronto might be seen as an intense form of Pietism, or of Pentecostal-charismatic activity.[19] On the other hand, whereas the manifestations which marked earlier movements were routinely 'expounded' from a biblical base (so that, for instance, the experience of 'slaying in the Spirit' was linked to Paul's falling down on the road to Damascus in Acts 9), the willingness of some Torontoites to let the manifestations 'speak for themselves' may signal an unconscious move from a modern to a postmodern sensibility.[20] This point has been developed incisively by Philip Richter in a little-known article, and his comments are worth quoting at length:

It is not without significance that evangelicals have, in the Blessing, enthusiastically embraced a non-verbal form of religious experience and expression . . . Although evangelicals sincerely believe that they have 'absolute truth' on their side, post-modern society cannot admit this possibility. One response, already predicted by the sociologist Ernest Gellner, is that religious expression may dissolve in this way into 'speaking in tongues or (logically) silence'. Paradoxically, charismatic evangelical churches may be reflecting two quite different responses to post-modernity: fundamentalism and either meta-language or non-language.[21]

Richter goes on to suggest that Toronto's supra-rationalism may derive not only from the difficulties which evangelicals have communicating with the outside world, but also from the problems which arise when they try to relate their faith to everyday life:

> It is not simply that *other* people find the gospel unintelligible, evangelicals themselves may be finding traditional religious language implausible when they themselves are 'full participants in cultural modernity' – because, for instance, of their everyday work milieux. The world of 'information superhighways' seems a million miles from the world of faith. If intellectual middle-class evangelicals are finding that the gospel does not seem to be 'speaking the same language' any more, one solution is to adopt the inarticulate meta-language of glossolalia, another is to embrace the non-verbal Toronto Blessing.[22]

As leader of the charismatic Ichthus fellowship, Roger Forster sees some mileage in such analyses, but adds certain qualifications. Aptly enough, I talked with him just after he had spoken to a meeting of Ichthus leaders about postmodernism. In his address, he had emphasised that the relationship between postmodern theory and Christian faith is more complex than many suppose. This applied especially to Toronto. 'In the early days,' he told me, 'John Wimber did say "Don't try to interpret the signs." But *I* always have done, because interpretation speaks to the person engaged and says more than just "Run on the spot to be bizarre." It says, "Look – there's something you should be doing in your life."' Forster elaborated: 'Running on the spot could relate to running with perseverance the race set before you

[Heb. 12:1]. And running backwards – which we've seen in Ichthus – could mean that someone needs to go back and start again in an area of their life.' He was clear that such interpretation went beyond the kind of straight 'rationale' which postmodernists would question. Rather, 'It's saying simply that when God speaks, he speaks, and it helps to find out what he's saying.'

It is a central tenet of Ichthus that God communicates in an integrated way through 'words, works and wonders'.[23] This accounts for Forster's apparently paradoxical conviction that God can 'speak' through visual and physical media. Having said this, it is clear that in using Scripture as the 'standard' by which such media must be judged, he remains very much attached to the primacy of words. On this point, he lines up with several others whom I questioned on Toronto.

For John Drane, the Blessing presents a dilemma. To some extent, he sees it as part of the positive postmodern yearning for 'holistic' spirituality. Then again, he senses that, in its push to balance words with feelings, it may have tipped the scales too far against good things which come from the 'verbal' approach to worship. When we spoke, he illustrated this by comparing Toronto with a more obvious postmodern trend – namely, the recovery of the Celtic tradition: 'While Celtic spirituality is mainly non-rational, it has room for rationality insofar as it stresses the *integration* of the mind with the body, soul and spirit. Toronto, on the other hand, is less apparently rational, and may in this sense have more in common with the New Age movement.' A very similar view was taken by Brian Draper, who added when we talked on this subject that, like much New Age religion, Toronto too often 'turns people in on themselves rather than getting them to look outward, at broader social concerns'.

Perhaps not surprisingly, David Jackman's conservatism leads him to an even more critical view: 'My problem with Toronto has been the absence of any biblical justification for it. And when one sees something which is so much a reflection of the culture, one at least has grounds for asking, "Is this really what it's been claimed to be, or is it a Christianised version of what's going on in the world?"'

Jackman's comment recalls one of the key issues of the evangelical–post-evangelical debate – that is, how far Christians can legitimately assimilate 'what's going on in the world', and how far they must stand apart from it. How much of the gospel is to be inculturated, and how much is to be preserved from culture? Is Toronto an example of God using the postmodern emphasis on visuality and sensuality to highlight the less rationalistic aspects of his revelation, or is it simply a devilish attempt to corrupt the Church?

It may sound woolly to say it, but the truth probably lies somewhere between these two extremes. From one angle, it could be argued that a theology which sees God appropriating culture to serve his own ends actually offers a stronger view of his sovereignty over the world than one which seeks to separate, and even protect, him from that world. This point came over forcefully when Graham Cray outlined his own more positive stance on Toronto: 'Toronto doesn't necessarily bypass the mind,' he told me, 'it bypasses those remnants of modernity's education system which persist in white, middle-class Christianity – the rationalistic intellectualism, the dissociation of mind and body, and so on. With Toronto, God has said, "There are things I have to do which cannot be done through that system."'

Clearly, advocates of divine inculturation can also call on the evidence of the incarnate Jesus – 'God with us'; the 'Word made flesh'; the Saviour of the world as a first-century Palestinian Jew. In Phil Wall's terms, 'God was incarnate within culture. Theology cannot be done in a cultural vacuum. That much is plain. What Toronto has raised is the question of how far God allows his manifestation of himself to be *shaped* by the prevailing culture.' To put it another way: Toronto may be God's way of overriding modernity, but could it not at the same time be a sign of his willingness to work through postmodernity?

Mike Starkey thinks so. He told me: 'Toronto probably was God accommodating himself to postmodern culture. It was positive in the sense that it was a thoroughly experiential thing which worked for people who live in an increasingly experiential society where logical, systematic argument is losing some of its force.' This is a more positive version of Richter's line that Toronto represents a weary *retreat* from logic by evangelicals who can no longer resist the doubts of scientists and philosophers. It was echoed by Rob Frost, who told me: 'What God has said to the Church through Toronto is "Shut up and listen!" A lot of what we are about as Christians is words, words, words; activity, activity, activity. I have problems with the Toronto Blessing, but I do think that in this respect it is a postmodern thing.'

Idolatry can be verbal, too!

Frost's point serves to underline another important aspect of this whole 'worship and culture' debate. Central as the Word of God is to Christian faith, it must be stressed that this Word can never be limited by words alone – not even by the words of Scripture. The Word is certainly never less than Scripture; but it is much more besides. As the Word made flesh, Jesus told the Pharisees, 'You diligently study the Scriptures because you think that by them you possess eternal life. These are the Scriptures that testify about me, yet you refuse to come to me to have life' (John 5:39–40).

Indeed, any view of words which abstracts them from their context is liable to mislead. Not only this: divorcing words from their field of reference, their users and receivers and their place within human discourse and dialogue has more to do with occultism than true Christian faith. Those who are so keen to link visual images to idolatry would do well to remember that there is such a thing as an idolatry of language. Pagan faith in 'spells' and 'incantations' derives from an assumption that words *themselves* possess innate power, whereas Christian orthodoxy understands that this power derives from an external source – from God himself, from human beings made in his image, or from Satan.

Just as the divine Word was embodied in Jesus, so godly words are meant to be embodied – within relationships and communities of faith. The text of the Bible is not there simply to be admired as print on a page: it is meant to be read, shared and lived out by the Church! In and of themselves, words are not morally superior to images and feelings: indeed, they are better seen as the tools with which God chooses to point us back to the visual and tangible life of Christ, and forward to the colour, beauty and sensuality of the New Jerusalem. If postmodernity prompts us to realise these things, then maybe it is being used by God in a positive way. If Toronto has reminded us of them, then maybe he has been at work within it. But these points apply far beyond Toronto. They relate to the whole structure of the church service – to preaching and liturgy in general.

From Exposition to Enactment: Preaching in the Context of Liturgy

The Reformation legacy

Modernity liked to expound things – to break them down and reason them out. This has been reflected in the development of evangelical preaching through the modern era. The problem is, postmodern culture is far less wedded to 'expository' forms of communication. This could well precipitate a crisis for evangelicals, in which our understanding of 'the sermon' is challenged and changed to a significant degree.

The roots of modern evangelical preaching can be traced to the Protestant Reformers. It was they who, after centuries of neglect, re-established preaching at the heart of worship.[24]

Whereas large numbers of priests in the medieval Church had either recited homilies from a book or ignored the sermon altogether, Luther restored the sermon to a central place within the liturgy, counterbalancing Roman emphasis on the eucharist with detailed preaching in the language of the people. In Zurich, Ulrich Zwingli went a good deal further, convening a special 'Service of the Word' distinct from the celebration of Holy Communion. Also, whereas Luther had mainly stuck to the themes of the lectionary, Zwingli updated the practice of the great fourth-century preacher John Chrysostom, working systematically through a book of the Bible phrase by phrase. Fired by a Renaissance drive to go *ad fontes* – back to original sources – Zwingli interrogated the text for its original meaning and intention, deriving key doctrinal and apologetic points from it, and applying it to the lives of the congregation. Calvin proceeded in the same vein, covering virtually the whole of Scripture in this way.[25]

Crucial though these developments were, it was the Puritans of the seventeenth century who went even further in making the preached word determinative of worship as a whole. Whereas the sixteenth-century Reformers had redeveloped expository preaching alongside established patterns of church ritual, later Puritans forced the expository model out beyond the pulpit and into every other part of worship. Whereas Calvin, for instance, had at various times used ancient liturgical discourses and corporate responses like the *Kyries, Gloria, Nunc Dimittis,* Ten Commandments, Apostles' Creed and Lord's Prayer, Puritans in general – and Separatists in particular – did away with the use of set forms and unison prayers in favour of continuous didactic monologues.[26] Prayers of adoration, confession and thanksgiving turned into detailed theological disquisitions by the minister – sometimes lasting an hour or more![27] What had once been meant as shared responses were flattened into dense doctrinal prose.[28] Puritans frequently cited 1 Corinthians 14:16 as a proof that only one person at a time should speak in worship, and took this as a prohibition against corporate participation. The single word 'Amen' was often the only exception to this rule.[29]

All this went hand in hand with the Puritans' rejection of the Prayer Book, and their preference for unscripted, extemporary worship. Although there are indications that in the early days this issued in a genuinely spontaneous sharing around the Word of God,[30] Puritan services soon became not only 'preacher-led' but 'preacher-dominated'. As a result, an expository mentality affected almost everything that was done. Hence, even when he took the unusual step of publishing 'suggested' prayers, Richard Baxter had them printed with marginal Scripture references, just to assure everyone of his exegetical soundness![31] As Erik Routley describes it, this Puritan drive to explain and expound the whole of worship led to an excess of 'literalism' in which 'nothing [was] left to the imagination', and in which the long-held belief that concise, canonical liturgies can aid meditation was rejected outright. In many cases, the result was what Nicholas Wolterstorff calls a 'suppression' of the 'worship dimension' by the 'proclamation dimension'.[32] This imbalance remains all too common among evangelicals and nonconformists today – and it is distinctly out of sync with postmodern culture.[33]

As we have seen, the expository model is being overthrown by alternative worshippers keen to return to a 'premodern' emphasis on ritual, mystery and communality in worship. For many evangelicals, this might just be acceptable so long as the sermon remained in didactic form. But the indications are that, in postmodernity, it will become increasingly difficult to 'ring fence' preaching in this way.

Bolstered by Enlightenment rationalism, the expository approach was consolidated in eighteenth-century America by Calvinists like Jonathan Edwards and Gilbert Tennent, in nineteenth-century Scotland by Thomas Chalmers and Thomas Guthrie, and in twentieth-century Britain by Alexander Whyte, Martyn Lloyd Jones and others.[34] Without doubt, it represents a major strand of evangelical worship, and is still common in more Reformed churches today. Its leading practitioners include Dick Lucas of St Helen's, Bishopsgate, R. T. Kendall of Westminster Chapel and Roy Clements of Eden Baptist Church, Cambridge. Its persistence is also evident at conservative evangelical preaching conferences like Word Alive, and in the ministry of the Proclamation Trust.

Other evangelical models of preaching

To read some advocates of the expository tradition, you would think that theirs is the only authentic biblical and evangelical model of preaching and worship.[35] At the very least, this is highly questionable. At least since Wesley and Whitefield, there has been another, more emotional and more experiential emphasis in evangelicalism – one which, across the Atlantic, was personified by Charles G. Finney and Dwight L. Moody. Since the early 1900s, this tide of experientialism has been swelled by the upsurge of Pentecostal and charismatic spiritualities, with their emphasis on what Walter Hollenweger calls a 'correspondence between body and mind'[36] – that is, on the corporate expression of charismata as balance to the didactic, expository approach. More recently, a number of Anglican evangelicals have shown how their basic convictions have been enriched by a re-emphasis on ancient liturgy, and have in turn made a valuable contribution to liturgical reform.[37]

More fundamental than this, though, is the fact that the Bible itself seems to endorse models for worship and preaching which are neither exclusively, nor even mainly, expository. Several Psalms are drawn from Temple rites in which the people participated actively and responsively in praise and confession (e.g. Pss. 15, 24, 84, 121, 122). Certain of Paul's letters appear to borrow from hymns or creeds which express the faith in a doxological rather than expository fashion (Phil. 2:5–11; Col. 1:15–20). When the New Testament describes worship, it is very often multivocal and discursive: when Paul speaks at length in Troas in Acts 20:7–12, the Greek suggests that he was actually engaging in a dialogue;[38] when he instructs the Corinthians on order in worship, he assumes several different contributors (1 Cor. 14:26–33). Furthermore, the style of heavenly worship described in the book of Revelation – of which our worship should at least be a foretaste – is exclamatory, adorational and corporate rather than didactic (Rev. 4:8, 11; 5:9–14; 7:11–17; 11:16; 15:3–4; 19:1–8).

Now it is certainly true that Jesus expounded Hebrew Scripture in the synagogue (Luke 4:16–30; John 6:59), as indeed did Paul (Acts 13:14–43). Nonetheless, most of the preaching done by Jesus happened in less structured settings, and deployed rather different methods. Indeed, as David Norrington has pointed out, much of it took place in the open air, with Jesus using a wide range of communicative techniques including 'enigmatic sayings, Jewish history, visual aids, familiar ideas, projects, figures of speech, irony, poetry, logic, problem-solving, humour, looks, gestures and movement, silence, repetition, questions, discussion, rest and relaxation, together with frequent avoidance of dogmatic answers and precise definitions, withholding of material until it was requested, emphasis on how to think rather than what to think, and sparing use of correction'.[39]

Preaching and narrative

Although there is much room for debate about the distinction between teaching and preaching,[40] it is hard to get away from the fact that when Jesus declared the Good News of God, he relied a great deal more on *stories* than on abstract propositions. We have already noted that postmodernism has been marked by a new emphasis on narrative. The seminal postmodern theorist Jürgen Habermas has stressed the need to see rationality as communicative, discursive and social rather than merely instrumental – something which emerges more from conversations than from atomistic formulae.[41] I have already mentioned that one of the most eloquent interpreters of the postmodern world is the novelist Douglas Coupland. There is as much to be learned about this world in Coupland's sharp, sad tales as in any number of academic articles.[42]

Until recently, postmodern emphases on narrative and discourse were for the most part applied to theology by those operating outside the evangelical constituency – most strikingly by postliberals and liberation theologians.[43] Now, though, evangelical scholars have begun to suggest that when addressing postmodern people, preachers will need to recover Jesus's own bias towards storytelling.[44]

When we look at the ministry of Jesus in the Gospels, we see that he preached and taught substantially through the media of parable and conversation. All in all, the sixty-odd parables and parabolic sayings of Jesus represent about one-third of his recorded utterances. The majority of his other teaching was dialogical: it arose in debate with various experts in the Jewish law, in discussion with his disciples, and in the discourses he had with those he met on his travels. Sure enough, he made more formal didactic speeches from time to time, but these were relatively infrequent by comparison.[45]

A parable is a form of narrative speech. A still common evangelical view is that it is a story or saying intended to illustrate a certain doctrinal point. The assumption is that it is an adjunct to a theological proposition worked out in advance – a proposition which can be recovered by good exegesis and sound expository preaching.[46]

The problem is that Jesus rarely presents parables in this way. Indeed, he offers detailed explanations of only two – the parable of the sower (Matt. 13:18–23) and the parable of the tares (Matt. 13:36–43) – and in each case the interpretation is compound and allegorical rather than singular and transparent. Elsewhere, a clear context is given which provides a clue to the meaning (Luke 10:25; Luke 7:41; Luke 19:11). Mostly, though, Jesus anticipates Steinar Kvale's point that stories are best left to speak for themselves.[47]

In many of his dialogues, Jesus undoubtedly gives straightforward moral or doctrinal instruction (Matt. 4:1–11; Matt. 5:21 to 7:29; Matt. 10:8–14). At other times, however, he seems content to let his respondents make their own distinct points, and to assimilate them into his message (Matt. 8:5–13; 15:21–8).

Clearly, not everything Jesus did could or should be replicated: only he could die to save sinners; only he could legitimately claim to be the Son of God. But when it comes to models for preaching and worship, it can hardly be blasphemous to suggest that those forms of discourse favoured by Jesus might be a useful guide. Furthermore, in a postmodern world which has become wary of straight rationalistic assertion, it may be that his preferred, story-based approach will offer a constructive model of worship and preaching for the twenty-first century.

The future of preaching

Several of the leading evangelicals with whom I spoke agreed that the 'modern' age of expository preaching might well be drawing to a close. Graham Kendrick's father was a Baptist minister whose pulpit style ensured that the songwriter 'absorbed good expository preaching by osmosis'. Nonetheless, Kendrick reflected that he had 'probably caught the end of the expository era'. Similarly, from his strategic vantage point at the London Bible College, Derek Tidball observed that for all LBC's attempts to get students to preach on the text, 'We now have a much harder job to do in applying that text. The assumption that our congregations will either be interested or able enough to handle Scripture in a propositional, didactic way cannot be made. We need to go beyond the classic expository model.'

Gerald Coates echoed these sentiments, but went on to raise a provocative point about the elitism of straight expository thinking. As he put it, the expository line, with its stress on close exegesis and cerebral deduction, 'may be *a* valid approach, but it is not the *only* approach. We don't all have the same academic qualifications, and to suggest that every church must do classic expository preaching is immediately to exclude nineteen-twentieths of the world's population!' Coates went on: 'This in turn begs a pragmatic question about where revival is happening in the world today. It's happening in China, Argentina, parts of the USSR, India and Africa. Very few of the Christians in these places adhere to the expository model: many of them haven't even heard of Luther, Zwingli and Calvin!' Despite this, Coates insisted that 'All of them have a strong emphasis on Scripture. They just have a different way of *communicating* Scripture. I'm not saying the expository approach is always wrong. But it's interesting that where there is revival today it is generally absent, while in Europe and North America, where it is maintained, the Church is mostly in decline.'

Other interviewees focused on the example of Jesus, and saw considerable divergence between his methods and those of the expository school. For Nick Mercer, 'You've got to ask why Jesus didn't major on expository preaching. He could have done a wonderful job on Isaiah 53, for instance, but he didn't touch it! The claim that expository preaching is the only true preaching is misplaced.' Graham Dale and John Drane were more concerned to highlight the age range of Jesus's audience. As Dale expressed it, 'Jesus attracted little children. Children tend not to flock to hear "sound" expository preachers.' In Drane's view, 'If God had chosen to, he could have come to earth as a fully-grown articulate man. But the fact that God chose to become a child legitimates non-cognitive, non-verbal ways of communicating and celebrating the gospel. This is a whole area which has been neglected by evangelicals.'

Another criticism made of the expository approach in my conversations was that it tended to exalt a single 'expert' interpreter while keeping the congregation too passive. For Gerald Coates, the charismatic movement's recovery of lay giftings and shared ministries had challenged this dominant 'pastor-teacher' model. More specifically, Clive Calver warned that in certain cases it can breed a 'hagiography of preaching'. This, he said, looks to the pulpiteers of three or four hundred years ago and 'bestows on them a stature and dignity they wouldn't themselves have recognised'. Even today, Graham Dale noted the potential of expository models to produce a 'cult of the preacher' in which 'leaders are judged primarily on whether they are good or bad at preaching', and in which 'people will travel miles to hear someone who is deemed to be good'.

As a counterbalance to all this, Clive Calver did go on to remark that an expositor like Roy Clements 'can go through a verse-by-verse exposition and break all the rules of postmodern communication, and yet have people riveted'. Then again, Calver voiced an intriguing doubt about whether it was only within postmodern culture that such figures seemed exceptional. 'We talk about the irrelevance of expository preaching today,' he said, 'but I suspect the irrelevance has been there for a long time. Even in modernity, people would not flock to hear the exegetical, verse-by-verse sermons of evangelical preachers unless they were brilliant.' On this point, at least, David Jackman would tend to agree:

> One of our problems is that most of the sermons which remain in print from the past are those preached by the men of genius. In any age, there will be preachers who seem almost uniquely gifted. You could argue that Martyn Lloyd Jones was one of these. Yet there are hundreds of jobbing pastors who will never attain

to this, but still have to do something worthwhile every Sunday.

Jackman is adamant, however, that the best model for such church leaders remains the expository one. Neither is he convinced by claims that it is too intellectual and word-based for the mass of contemporary people.

> When I led a church in Southampton, we had a very wide-ranging congregation, from medical consultants to shipworkers, and I learnt the lesson there that good expository preaching is not primarily an intellectual business. Where there is a spiritual hunger, people will make enormous strides, even if they have very little formal education. And I don't mean that they become more 'middle-class', but that they progress in understanding Scripture because they've got an appetite to know God.

This, of course, begs the question 'How do postmodern people *acquire* such an appetite?' What should those who proclaim the gospel do to *foster* it in the first place? There is a trace of 'take it or leave it' in Jackman's comment. It could seem rather patrician. It presents a single true model of proclamation, which 'the world' is invited to learn and accept. If such acceptance is not forthcoming, then that is because the world is sinful and hard of heart. This somewhat self-justifying cycle fits in well with the classic Reformed view of the Church, which tends to rationalise others' rejection of its preaching by inferring that they were predestined to reject it anyway! This may be something of a caricature, but Gerald Coates's point about global revival cannot be brushed aside. With all the changes being wrought by postmodernity, and the relative failure of 'modern' Western exposition to spark wide-scale renewal, it is surely time to get beyond the talismanic status of expository preaching

– to see past its status as a 'badge' of evangelical orthodoxy and ask just how much it really has left to offer.

My own view is that as long as we drop the hype about the expository model and cease treating it like a sacred cow, it could continue to make an important contribution to the Church's diet. Nonetheless, where preaching is concerned, we need to recognise that this diet will contain ingredients which have not usually been associated with exposition, or which have been relatively marginal to it. This brings us back to narrative.

It is wrong, of course, to see story and exposition as mutually exclusive. Expository preachers have always told stories, while today's proponents of 'narrative' preaching usually still root their storytelling in a particular text. Tom Houston, for instance, was keen to defend Dick Lucas on this point: 'Dick is supposed to be very propositional, but if you actually listen to him preaching on a character like Elijah, you will find an excellent matching of "story then" with "story now". It is all highly contextualised.' Conversely, I well recall an Evangelical Alliance discussion on preaching at which a wise participant declared that he had never once heard a story which did not contain some kind of proposition! It is just that, in the expository model, stories have tended to serve and illustrate a propositional point, whereas, to quote Gerald Coates, 'Very often nowadays, the stories *are* the point!' R. T. Kendall put it another way: 'Stories and illustrations could be compared to commercial breaks in a TV programme – except that in many cases the adverts have become more interesting than the programmes!'

Once again, the parables loom large here. Without doubt, Jesus came to the parables with a wider agenda – the agenda of the Kingdom of God. He had studied the Scriptures from an early age and had earned the title 'Rabbi'. We have already seen that, where appropriate, he was quite capable of formal expository preaching. And yet, with the common people, he wore all this learning lightly. The parables may be deceptively simple, but they are simple nonetheless. They scratched where people were itching. They made contact. My suspicion is that to be effective in the postmodern world, evangelical preachers will need much less to show people the expository wheels going round. The exegetical apparatus will still be necessary, but it will function less as the framework of the sermon and more as its scaffolding. It will have to be removed from view before the sermon is preached. Mike Starkey confirmed something similar when he spoke from his own parish experience:

> Story is definitely becoming more important. Even when I was at theological college, which was not very long ago, we were taught that the ideal sermon was one in which you went through the passage point by point and expounded the text. And the argument was that this would stop you imposing your own agenda on the text. Even then I had big problems with that, but after being here in Finsbury Park I have come to disagree with it completely. To me, the work of exposition needs to go on in the minister's study before he gets into the pulpit. He must then find an appropriate way of making the expository point. And the way I now usually do that is to begin with an anecdote or humorous quip, make a link with the passage, and begin to draw out practical implications, moving back and forth between story, text and application. To me, this is a more creative approach, and it certainly suits this parish better than a wordy, expository style. I think, in fact, that the expository model has passed its sell-by date.

Nick Mercer is equally frank about his own preaching. He told me: 'Even those of us who were taught the classical expository model know the experience of preparing a sermon and realising – or even admitting to the congregation – that something you want to say isn't exactly exegetical. Nonetheless, you say it because you have been prompted by prayer to do so.' He went on to make an admission which might well be made by other designated expositors:

> Although for a long while I claimed to be an expository preacher, a lot of the time I wasn't doing straight expository preaching. I was linking themes from the text to current pastoral needs. But I'm not sure that is so bad. I look at congregations which have had thirty-odd years of solid expository sermons lasting forty minutes or more, and then I look at congregations who have been used to a typically non-exegetical Anglican homily, and there's hardly any difference in them as Christian people.

Many would balk at Mercer's claim, but it does at least seem that in postmodernity preachers will need to pay more attention to personal testimonies, anecdotes and stories. Whether in worship generally or preaching particularly, what Rick Gosnell calls the 'inductive' model[48] is likely to come more and more to prominence. Evangelicals who wish to reach the next generation will have to start with specifics and practicalities before moving towards grand principles and systematic doctrines. Further still, those principles and doctrines will need to be narrated rather than simply declaimed. Even R. T. Kendall agreed with this to some extent: 'One has got to be aware that if the average attention span for TV is, say, seven to eight minutes, it will be even shorter for sermons. Stories and illustrations can help to overcome this problem.'

To those of us reared on the classic expository model, all this may appear strange. It may seem like putting the cart before the horse. And, no doubt, the inductive model has great potential drawbacks. It could easily drift off into self-indulgence, sentimentalism and gimmickry. Stories may be told less to make or even constitute a point, and more to get a laugh. The personal experience of the preacher and people may override what God has actually revealed, or the sin he wants them to confront. Likewise, the assumption of decreased attentiveness may ignore the power of God's Word to engage and deepen our concentration. As Clive Calver expressed it to me, 'There's a danger that consciously postmodern preaching will end up peddling "snapshot" theology. Indeed, evangelical preaching already derives too much from postmodernity's emphasis on method over message.' Tom Houston was similarly circumspect: 'As long as we have rationalists around in our congregations, insisting on the categories established by science over the last one hundred and fifty years, the expository approach will remain valid.'

These are important qualifications, but they cannot be used to justify a 'King Canute' approach. As I have shown, it is not just that the tide of postmodernity is threatening the classic expository form of church service; Scripture itself suggests that this tide could be surfed effectively, despite the danger of drowning. No doubt some congregations are still solidly modernistic; no doubt some will continue to be so for quite a while. But where churches comprise a mix of young and old, well-educated and less well-educated, literate and less literate, text-oriented and image-oriented, analytical and intuitive, a good dose of postmodern eclecticism may not go amiss. Furthermore, there is warrant for this not only in the diversity of Jesus's own worship and preaching, but also in the example of St Paul. It is to this example that we now turn.

9

BIBLE REFLECTION: 2 TIMOTHY 2:1–13

You then, my son, be strong in the grace that is in Christ Jesus. And the things you have heard me say in the presence of many witnesses entrust to reliable men who will also be qualified to teach others. Endure hardship with us like a good soldier of Christ Jesus. No-one serving as a soldier gets involved in civilian affairs – he wants to please his commanding officer. Similarly, if anyone competes as an athlete, he does not receive the victor's crown unless he competes according to the rules. The hardworking farmer should be the first to receive a share of the crops. Reflect on what I am saying, for the Lord will give you insight into all this.

Remember Jesus Christ, raised from the dead, descended from David. This is my gospel, for which I am suffering even to the point of being chained like a criminal. But God's word is not chained. Therefore I endure everything for the sake of the elect, that they too may obtain the salvation that is in Christ Jesus, with eternal glory.

Here is a trustworthy saying:

> *If we died with him,*
> *   we will also live with him;*
> *If we endure,*
> *   we will also reign with him.*

> *If we disown him,*
>   *he will also disown us;*
> *if we are faithless,*
>   *he will remain faithful,*
>   *for he cannot disown himself.*

Of course, 2 Timothy is neither a liturgy nor a sermon. It is a pastoral letter, written from prison by the apostle Paul to his young protégé around AD 66–7. Nonetheless, it is often quoted by those who seek to defend expository-style church services. Summing up its contents, David Jackman has written:

Search as we may, we find nothing here about a sacramental, priestly ministry, or one of signs and wonders. It is all about ministry of the Word as the church moves from the certainty of apostolic inspiration to an uncertain future, when a generation of eyewitnesses has passed on to heaven and the church on earth still awaits the King's parousia [i.e. the Second Coming of Jesus]. Without an effective ministry of the Word in the congregation, there cannot be a strong and effective ministering church in the world.[1]

Few, if any, evangelicals would argue with the last sentence here. Neither can there be much doubt that 2 Timothy is urgently concerned with sound teaching. Timothy's church at Ephesus was under severe pressure. Like many other churches, it was threatened with persecution by the emperor Nero. As well as this, it was being assailed with heresies. We know from 1 Timothy that the Ephesian Christians had been infiltrated by people devoted to 'myths and endless genealogies', who promoted 'controversies rather than God's work' (1:4). The heresies in question probably combined Gnosticism, decadent Judaism and bogus piety (4:1–5).

In the face of all this, Paul encourages Timothy above all else to hold fast to that which will stand for ever – the divine Word of God. Specifically, he is to do this by 'fanning into flame' his long-nurtured gift of teaching (2 Tim. 1:6; 2:15; 3:14–15). He is 'to keep the pattern of sound doctrine' (1:13), 'correctly handle the word of truth' (2:15) and 'preach the Word' (4:2). Not only this: in the passage from chapter 2 quoted above, he is charged by Paul to pass on his skills to those 'who will be qualified to teach others' (v. 2). This task is far from purely cerebral: it is deeply spiritual and, as such, extremely taxing. Paul compares it with the hard labour of soldiery (vv. 3–4), athletic competition (v. 5) and farming (v. 6). Clearly, this exacting work of proclamation and instruction will be rooted in Scripture, since it is Scripture which is uniquely 'useful for teaching, rebuking, correcting and training in righteousness' (3:16).

As a former Pharisee, it is quite possible that Paul gives all this advice to Timothy with regular, synagogue-style exposition in mind. It must be said, though, that there is little evidence for such an assumption in the letter. Even if this is the context, it ought to be noted in any case that 'preaching' in the Jewish assembly was some way removed from the rhetorical monologue which has come to stand for exposition in many evangelical churches. Recent research into Jewish preaching in the New Testament period has shown it diverging from the modern expository style in a number of respects. It may well have involved a good deal of dialogue, discussion, and even debate (cf. Matt. 13:54–7; Luke. 4:28ff.; Acts 18:6; 19:8). The expositor was not necessarily an ordained professional, and on occasion preaching was omitted from the service altogether.[2]

None of this detracts from Paul's high regard for biblical exposition *as such* – but it does raise questions about the actual *form* and *context* of that exposition. Most specifically, it raises questions about the relationship between exposition and worship as a whole. In the passage quoted, Paul speaks only of those qualified generally to *teach* (v. 2): there is no direct link to a regular act of worship. Even when he later talks more specifically about proclamation (using the Greek verb *kerussein* in 4:2), it is not at all certain that he has in mind a rhetorical sermon to be delivered by Timothy alone on a weekly basis. There is no doubt that Paul was prepared to discourse on the Scriptures 'every Sabbath' in the synagogue (Acts 18:4; 19:8) but, again, it seems clear that this process was an argumentative one, with others interrupting and answering back (Acts 18:6, cf. 17:2). Neither is there any doubt that, like Jesus, when the occasion demanded it he would deliver a sustained oration (e.g. Acts 13:13–41; 17:22–31) – but this was usually in a non-ecclesial, evangelistic setting. Besides, such orations were not always expository: they were just as likely to have comprised narrated personal testimony (Acts 21:39 to 22:21). As David Norrington has said of 2 Timothy 4:2:

> The reference may be to a sermon, or even a series of sermons, but it need not be . . . The sermon, if such it was, was an aid in the battle [with the Ephesian heretics] but there is nothing here to suggest that it was already a regular feature of church life or that it should ever become such . . . The precise meaning of 'in season and out of season' is not clear, and in any case there is no reason to restrict its application to preaching the word [i.e. it could refer more generally to the pastoral discourse of 'correction, rebuke and encouragement' mentioned in the latter half of the verse].[3]

The second epistle to Timothy staunchly supports good biblical explication, but this does not mean that it endorses the kind of didactic pulpit speech which is still assumed by many to be the nub of evangelical church life. I am sure that there will always be a place for straight verbal proclamation by a single expert, but whether this place should be in every act of corporate worship in every church every Sunday is questionable not only from a postmodern perspective, but from a biblical perspective, too. Paul's dominant concern in this letter is with good teaching in general, rather than with 'the sermon' in particular. Postmodernity cannot be allowed to dilute evangelical commitment to 'correct handling of the word of truth', but to make this commitment dependent on classic expository preaching is to assume rather too much. Indeed, there is good evidence to suggest that such preaching owes its style more to the influence of Greek and Roman rhetorical methods on later generations of Christians than to the methods exemplified by Scripture itself.[4]

Despite having favoured the expository approach all his life, Tom Houston's background as a classicist compelled him to admit this distinction: 'My preferred model does come out of a European, Graeco-Roman tradition. It still has relevance to many people, but the thing which ultimately determines the style of preaching is the audience in each case, and if narrative is the way to communicate to an audience which no longer thinks rationalistically, then preaching will need to change.'

Like Houston, I do not entertain such change lightly. I myself am temperamentally drawn to expository preaching. The problem is simply that while the classic expository model may have suited the book-driven, linear mindset of the modern West, it is hard to see how it will suit the screen-driven, multi-media mentality of postmodern culture. It may continue to work for those who still spend more time reading books than watching TV or working a computer, but the percentage of such people is falling. Given that the Bible offers a much wider range of options for teaching and proclaiming God's Word, it would be foolish to cling to the classic expository approach simply because we are afraid of otherwise seeming 'unsound'. Far better, surely, to explore the possibility of biblical-style parables and dialogues, the interrelating of words with images, and a more general integration of preaching with the rest of worship.

These points connect to another interesting feature of our

passage from 2 Timothy 2 – namely, its use of liturgy. Amid
all his advice on good teaching, Paul inserts a poetic block
which most scholars believe to be either a hymn or the creed
from an early baptismal rite (vv. 11–13). As I have shown,
it has been a common assumption of 'modern' evangelicals
that worship is a 'commentary' on Scripture and doctrine.
Where they have entertained liturgy at all, it has often
been as a 'preliminary' or 'appendix' to the sermon. This
has been especially true of my own Reformed tradition.[5]
What often gets forgotten in such a view is the liturgical
content of Scripture itself! I have already mentioned the
Psalms, the book of Revelation and Paul's own use of
hymns and responses elsewhere. In this text, he reminds
the Ephesians that the truths they need to defend are already
being recited by them corporately in church. What is more,
the Hebrew parallelism of this stanza would almost certainly
have helped them remember such truths more effectively.
In addition to all Paul says to Timothy about teaching, he
wants the church at Ephesus to be much more than a Bible
school: it should be a community in which worshippers offer
intercessions and thanksgivings, lifting up 'holy hands in
prayer' (1 Tim. 2:1–8), chanting Psalms and singing hymns
and spiritual songs (Eph. 5:18–20). It is to be a community
with a dynamic liturgy, as well as a deep commitment to
proclamation.

Even if we accept that the decline of signs and wonders
after the apostolic age pushed the sermon to a more central
place in the Church's life,[6] the Pentecostal-charismatic
'rediscovery' of such phenomena has at least challenged
the view that preaching should control everything else in
the service. Neither can the evangelical exaltation of 'Word'
over 'sacrament' be defended on the grounds that baptism
or communion 'died out' after the first century. One must
presume that Paul wanted the Ephesians to celebrate the
Lord's Supper whenever they 'came together', just as he
had instructed the Corinthians to do so (1 Cor. 11:17–33).
Neither is there any indication that this practice should ever

be revoked. Even the arch expositor John Calvin believed
that communion should be celebrated weekly.[7]

No doubt when it is treated as a *substitute* for sound teaching, liturgical celebration runs the risk of degenerating into
the sort of 'vain repetition' scorned by Jesus himself (Matt.
6:7). But when the two are creatively intertwined – when
preaching becomes as interactive as the best Christian liturgy
and liturgy becomes as instructive as the best expository
sermon – we might yet recover the sort of worship which
Christ described as worship 'in spirit and in truth' (John
4:24). For all its other dangers, if postmodernity prompts
us to this, then postmodernity will have done us a favour.

10

WITNESS AND DISCIPLESHIP

Three Examples of Faith-Sharing

The youth group leader

I owe a great deal to Gill. She was a leader in my church youth group. All my youth group leaders were dedicated: they had to be with teenagers like me around! But there was something different about Gill. She shared her faith with such ease. I remember her testimony to this day. It was so matter-of-fact – so down-to-earth. She was having a bath, she said. She had been thinking about Jesus for some time, but she had not done anything about it. The bath was a good place to think some more. By the time she got out to dry herself off, she had made a commitment. Ever since then, she told us, she had wanted to let others know about the gospel.

I was impressed. I sought to find out more. Gill used to invite people to Bible studies and speaker meetings. I went to a few, and they persuaded me that mere attendance at church would not make me a Christian. But they did not finally convert me. Then, one night, Gill took a group of us to a Christian concert. It was a bit of a culture-shock. Not long before, I had been at Led Zeppelin's last ever gig in Britain. That had been awesome – an earsplitting, gargantuan swansong. This was more like the Carpenters, but not as slick. There was no preaching or exegesis – just a brief talk by the lead singer after the encore. He invited people to pray a simple prayer of commitment. Amazingly, I was stirred to join in. My heart raced and my mind went into overdrive. I checked intellectual reservations, asked myself crucial questions: 'How can you be sure Jesus rose from the dead? What will this do to your musical taste?' But God was at work in me. He had somehow become real. His love was irresistible. I said the prayer and raised my hand to confirm what I had done. There was no doubt about it: I had become a Christian.

The misguided enthusiast

Five years later, I found myself sitting in a study bedroom at university with Dave. Dave was a geographer. He lived next door to me. For six months, we had chatted about football, television, hall food – the usual stuff. But this week things were different. This week was Christian Union mission week. This week, I had become David Hilborn – Evangelist!

The conversation started ordinarily enough. We were both beginning to worry about our coursework. Then there were the exams. Oh, and what about that New Order single? But I was getting impatient. We had been going for half an hour, and I had not mentioned Jesus once. Then I saw my chance. Dave let on that he was having problems with meteorology. I told him not to fret – the important thing to remember was that God was in control of the weather, just as he was in control of everything else: as the Bible had said, 'He sends his rain on the just and the unjust' (Matt. 5:45). Dave looked at me as if I had gone mad. But I persisted. Every time he tried to move the subject away from God, I forced it back again. However tenuous the link, I would shoehorn yet another chunk of evangelical apologetics into the conversation. Things got decidedly uncomfortable, but I only saw that as a sign that I was doing my duty. After a

while, Dave said he had to go out. I left, satisfied that I had
seized another opportunity to bear witness to my faith.

I cringe when I think about it now. I had befriended Dave
over half a year. He knew full well that I was a Christian.
But suddenly, he had seen me in a different light. It was as
if my whole personality had changed. Things were never
quite the same after that. We did not talk as openly again.
I lost touch with Dave after we graduated.

The happy minister

Ten years further on. Easter Day at the City Temple. I had
just preached on the resurrection, and was chatting with
people over coffee after the service. A group of Korean
students approached me. They were staying in England and
had come to London for the weekend. All were Christians
– bar one. His name, they said, was Yang. He had been
seeking God, but had yet to take a decisive step of faith.
Nonetheless, having heard the sermon, he had told them
that he might now be ready. Could I help?

It was the sort of moment for which I pray often, but
which rarely proves as straightforward as it did with Yang.
He, his friends and one of my church members came with
me into the chapel. I made sure Yang understood who Jesus
was, and what he had done for the world. I shared some key
Scriptures, and Yang responded positively to them. Then I
told him that I was going to pray a prayer of commitment
with him, and he said that would be fine. To make sure he
understood every phrase clearly, I got one of his friends –
a good English speaker – to translate as we went along.
He then repeated each phrase in Korean. I was nothing if
not thorough. We went through creation, sin, incarnation,
atonement, resurrection, judgment, discipleship and a few
more things besides. At each stage, Yang affirmed his belief.
Then finally, he repeated, 'I accept Jesus Christ as my Lord
and Saviour.' People were in tears; Yang himself was serene.

We parted, and I put him in touch with a Korean pastor near to where he was staying.

Some reflections

I guess that, for many, the last of these three stories would still represent the ideal model of evangelism. The Scriptures had been expounded; the gospel had been proclaimed; a sinner had been convicted and had been led through clear doctrinal explication to a 'crisis' conversion at a particular time, on a particular day, at a designated Christian meeting. But look again at what happened, and look also at the previous two stories . . .

Yang came to church with his Christian friends. He had travelled from Korea with them to study English. They were staying in the same place together. They had been demonstrating the good news of Jesus to him for quite some time before he came to us. Our church service, and my leading him to commitment, were but links in a long chain. He had been brought to the point of conversion by patient people who had taken time to build up a trusting relationship with him. In fact, they had helped him far enough along the way that, in the end, it was *he* who asked *them* to approach *me* for prayer. In no way had he been coerced: he had seen faith at work in his companions, and had been given sufficient information to make a free choice for himself.

The same sort of thing happened with me. Gill shared her story with my youth group, and taught us regularly from the Scriptures. But I do not remember her sitting us down one by one and taking us through a catechism, or issuing an altar call. Instead, she got alongside us and helped us to realise that the Christian life was the most natural thing in the world. She made us see that it was the life all of us were meant to live. She did not try to preach to us, but sometimes she took us to hear other Christians who would challenge us in different ways. All this took a fair time: I was in her group for two years before I prayed that prayer of commitment. When I began to share the gospel with others myself, I should have learnt from my own story. It took me a while to do so, however, and Dave was just one victim of my naiveté.

Suddenly, with the onset of a student mission week, I had roused myself to what I supposed was 'proper evangelism'. Every contribution to every conversation would have to carry some kind of doctrinal punch, and if I did not go for a knockout there and then, I would feel that I had let the side down. This aggressiveness was not so much the fault of the Christian Union, which had tried hard to stress the value of non-confrontational, non-propositional evangelism. But I *had* picked up on a prevailing stereotype – a stereotype which may partly have been imposed on evangelicals by others, but which evangelicals themselves have often helped to perpetuate.

Event and Process in Evangelism

James Emery White has stressed that as Western culture moves from modernity to postmodernity, Christians will need to view evangelism less simply in terms of an *event,* and more in terms of a *process.*[1] This, he says, goes hand in hand with the increasing scepticism of postmodern people towards 'packages' of truth which fail to connect with their own personal growth. As we have seen, postmodern culture tends to persuade us that something is true by appealing to our desire for self-exploration and self-realisation. It is at once pragmatic and narcissistic. John Drane has analysed this trend helpfully:

> The development of psychotherapies of various kinds
> – foremost among them the rise of transpersonal psy-
> chology – is providing [the postmodern] person with

access to the same kind of transformational experiences as mystical traditions offer, but without the initially unwelcome baggage of religious dogma. Hence the popularity of transformational video and audiotapes, bodywork, and other related therapies.[2]

As modernity recedes, so also must attempts to change people's worldview merely by gaining their assent to a set of logical 'proofs'. No doubt the self-absorption of today's style magazines, exercise programmes and New Age therapies can be hard to reconcile with a gospel of sacrifice and servanthood. Even so, it must be admitted that standard evangelistic methods have frequently overlooked people's God-given capacity for maturing towards wholeness rather than 'buying into' a ready-made religious 'product'. As Kevin Ford has observed, the outreach programmes of modernity often paralleled the 'cold selling' of secular commerce: rallies, door-knocking and street campaigns would present folk with a one-off opportunity to take up the 'special offer' being made, the aim being to 'close the deal' there and then.[3] By contrast, Emery White writes that in a postmodern setting, 'Effective churches will create a context for [an] adoption process to take place in the lives of nonbelievers. The "event" of coming into a personal relationship with Christ as Lord and Saviour is but the culmination of a spiritual pilgrimage as a "seeker".'[4]

These metaphors of adoption and pilgrimage are, of course, thoroughly biblical. But they have tended not to feature in evangelical outreach. We have preferred the crisis-driven language of being 'born again' and 'turned around' at some decisive moment.[5]

From re-birth to adoption?

Paul speaks of our being adopted as God's children in Romans 8:15–23 and Ephesians 1:5. As Chris Hudson has

suggested, this may for many be a more helpful model of
starting the Christian life than the model of 'second birth'.[6]
For one thing, Jesus only uses the concept of being born
again when among fellow-Jews who assumed they already
belonged to God (John 3:1–21; 8:31–47). In this context,
it is a warning to the religious that faith is not genetically
inherited. For the general mass of people, however, the idea
of adoption could be more appropriate. In Hudson's terms, it
is more realistic about the past: just as adopted children bring
the baggage of their former life into a new home and just as
it may take some while to deal with that baggage, so new
Christians do not immediately shed every vestige of their
former life. A long process of sanctification usually awaits
them. What is more, adoption is not tied to early infancy.
As Hudson puts it, adoptive relationships can develop over
a period of time:

> I knew my children for eighteen months before they
> were officially adopted. Already, our lives were becom-
> ing connected through the interviews, the visits with
> social workers and then when they came to live with
> us. The adoption order came later, a legal seal set
> on something which was already taking place – and
> which is still developing. In the same way, the Holy
> Spirit begins working his miracles in us long before
> we realise it, and certainly long before we claim to be
> Christian.[7]

This process is certainly recognised in classic evangelical
doctrine: it is called regeneration. No doubt, it could be
related to rebirth in the sense that a foetus must develop
in the womb before being delivered. Likewise, I recently
pointed out to one of my congregation who was insisting on
the 'born again' model as the norm that some labours take
minutes, whereas others can last for days! Relatively speaking, the length and nature of the birth process can vary a great
deal. Even so, it would seem that postmodern evangelism is

likely to rely on more obviously developmental images – of which 'journey' and 'pilgrimage' are already becoming very popular. Furthermore, this is not simply a shift in theological fashion: it is being dictated to a large extent by plain, hard, modernist facts.

In 1992, John Finney published the results of a survey on over five hundred English Christians who had made a recent profession of faith.[8] Even among those who designated themselves 'evangelical', 63 per cent reported that they had experienced a 'gradual' conversion, and only 37 per cent a 'sudden' commitment. Among Christians in general the ratio was even higher: 8 to 2 in favour of 'gradualism'. Finney explained that 'the gradual experience was said to take anything from one day to forty-two years, though many people saw it as an ongoing process which had not yet finished'.[9] Understandably, he went on to use the language of journey to summarise this perception.[10]

From crisis to journey

As those who believe in a Saviour who described himself as 'the Way' (John 14:6), and who depicted the life of faith as a 'road' (Matt. 7:13–14), Christians should have few qualms about the language of journey. Nonetheless, the fact that such language has been rarer in evangelicalism than in other church traditions could present problems for us in the postmodern context. Unless we are prepared to diversify from an 'event' mentality into a 'process' mentality, we could end up prioritising a style of evangelism which does more to fulfil our own desire to 'get things done' than to help those who do not yet know Christ. One facet of evangelical pragmatism is its urge to see tangible results. This is both good and bad. It means that we set clear goals and objectives. On the other hand it can also make us impatient, and this could be counterproductive in a postmodern world where people simply want more time to make up their minds.

Now I quite understand the evangelical desire for urgency and directness in outreach. I understand, too, that 'journey' and 'pilgrimage' can become vague terms which cease to have much to do with making people Christians. As a member of a liberal-majority denomination like the United Reformed Church, I often hear such metaphors bandied about, but they sound rather hollow given that the URC has failed to employ even one full-time evangelist, and that evangelism is at best a secondary element in our lay and ordination training. Often, I have heard evangelicals defend the 'crisis' and 'event' models on the grounds that if people are not explicitly challenged on a first encounter, they may never again hear the gospel, and may thus end up in hell (cf. Rom. 10:14). Certainly, if, like many in the URC, you are a universalist who believes that everyone will be saved in the end, it is a lot easier to go for the 'gradualist' approach! However, since virtually all evangelicals reject universalism as unbiblical, we shall need to balance our pressing sense of responsibility for the lost with a calm assurance that the work of conversion is ultimately done by God, and proceeds at his pace in his way.

In *The Post-Evangelical,* Dave Tomlinson does not get very far in addressing this balance. He mentions that people at Holy Joe's have appreciated John Saxbee's *Liberal Evangelism* – but Saxbee hardly acknowledges the more urgent aspect of faith-sharing.[11] Indeed, when he expresses his own preference for 'journey' and 'pilgrimage', Tomlinson does so at the expense of the more radical transformation conveyed by the New Testament when it speaks of people moving from darkness to light, death to life, old creation to new creation, condemnation to liberation, Satan to God, idolatry to true worship and disobedience to belief (Acts 14:15; 26:18; Rom. 6:1–14; Col. 2:10–12; 1 Thess. 1:9; 1 Pet. 2:25).

No doubt any or all of these processes can take place over a period of time. Even so, they still evoke a contrast, rather than a continuity, between one way of being and another.

No doubt most people are on some kind of 'spiritual
journey', but when that journey leads them to mass suicide
or schizophrenia, it must surely be distinguished from the
authentic Christian journey. David Jackman may not have
put it very subtly, but he had a point when he told me that,
for all our need to understand postmodern paradigms, 'In
the end people have got to repent and believe – in the end
it comes down to that.' There is a clear 'over-againstness'
in the gospel – a radical *counter*-culturalism which may
get forgotten as we try to reconcile everyone's pilgrimage
with our proclamation. Jesus may be 'the Way', but where
people's paths diverge from his, he can also become a
'stumbling-block' (1 Cor. 1:23). As Jackman warned, 'Even
believers try to avoid what God is saying in his Word,
because it's so uncomfortable. If you truly preach the gospel,
you're always likely to get a negative reaction, and when
that happens you need to pray for conviction of sin.' Such
distinctions are hard to detect in what Tomlinson writes:

> The usual approach to presenting the gospel assumes
> that 'We've got it – you need it!' But such dogmatic
> claims are unlikely to cut any ice in today's world. It
> is much more helpful to use the language of journey. It
> is quite wrong to think of the world as 'Christians over
> here on the right and non-Christians over there on the
> left', with evangelism understood as the task of shifting
> people from left to right. It is much more helpful to see
> that people are already on a spiritual journey, in which
> we can expect that God has been evidently present and
> at work, even if he is unrecognised by that name. And
> evangelism should . . . be understood as an opportunity
> to 'fund' people's spiritual journey, drawing on the
> highly relevant resources of 'little pieces' of truth
> contained in the Christian narrative.[12]

Perhaps Graham McFarlane questioned this approach most
astutely when he asked the congregation at Holy Joe's

whether they saw any difference between a journey and a wander. His point was that journeys usually have clear destinations, whereas wanders tend to be aimless. When I spoke with Dave Tomlinson, I pursued the same line and asked him where, if anywhere, he was hoping to lead folk. 'We do see people come to a place of faith in Christ,' he told me. 'They would say that they have become Christians here. But they have not done so by jumping through the standard hoops.' He continued: 'We try not to behave like privileged insiders who say, "We've got the truth – you need it!", but on the other hand we want to avoid becoming trivialised outsiders, wondering all the time what we're going to say. Our role lies somewhere between these two extremes.' Tomlinson spoke warmly of Walter Bruggemann, from whom he had drawn his more modest version of Christian witness in which evangelism 'funds' the postmodern imagination rather than invading it.[13] Beyond this, however, he could only say, 'I think there *is* a place for evangelism in the post-evangelical outlook, but it's an area which requires a lot more thought. I hope it will be a target of future discussion.'

But what of 'continuing' evangelicals? How is their practice matching up to the theologians' emphases on 'process' and 'journey'? At the coal face with Youth For Christ, Jenny Baker confirmed that such ideas have begun to filter through. 'Missions in the past have very much entailed a team coming into an area and holding a series of meetings, with someone preaching, doing an appeal and leaving those on the ground to pick up the pieces.' Although this may have worked for some years, Baker went on to tell me that YFC had revised its strategy in favour of '4-D Evangelism'. She explained: 'Previously, evangelism was run on a basic "2-D" model of "Declare and Decide". An evangelist would declare the truth, and people would decide whether or not to accept it. But we've been saying that it needs to include two more "D"s – Demonstration and Discipleship.' She added: 'It's just as important to show the love of God to people – not least in social action – and to emphasise that "making a decision" is just the beginning of a whole, lifelong process.'

Phil Wall's experience with the Salvation Army has led him to similar conclusions. 'When I stand up and do evangelism now, I say, "We're not here to tell you what you should think, or to tell you that you're wrong."' Instead, he begins by asking questions:

I tell them my presupposition is that every human being on planet Earth is on a spiritual journey, whether they be Christian, Buddhist, atheist or Hindu. From there, I ask just two key things – "Where are you on your spiritual journey?" and "What does the next step need to be?" I then take it that people want to move on in their journey, and I present Christianity as a step forward.

Wall was keen to distinguish this approach from the more 'doctrinaire' style of previous generations: 'I stress that Truth is a person called Jesus. Once you step outside that and define it more as dogma or systematic theology, you are in trouble.' Looking at things from his urban parish, Mike Starkey echoed all this: he told me, 'Going out into my community with propositional messages or hit-and-run truths which are not embodied in any way is a complete waste of time.'

Where these reflections may differ from Tomlinson's is in their assumption that wherever people are on their spiritual journey, it is still imperative that they end up at Jesus Christ. They still hold this – quite literally – to be a matter of life and death. The methods may have become more inductive and subtle, but the same message is still there in the background, fundamentally unchanged by the shift from modernity to postmodernity. By contrast, I cannot help wondering whether Tomlinson has somewhat relativised his Christology. Tough as it may be for them to do so, post-evangelicals will need to grapple more thoroughly with the consequences of unbelief. What if someone's pilgrimage never gets them to Jesus, despite clear signposts having been placed along the way? It may be distastefully 'modern' even to ask such a question, but people will go on asking it for some time to come, and anyone who takes the Bible seriously simply cannot avoid it.

Having said all this, it is clear that approaches had to change, and that changes are being made. R. T. Kendall highlighted this quite inadvertently when we spoke together. He was actually defending the more traditional methods of the 'Pilot Lights' street evangelism programme, which he co-ordinates from Westminster Chapel. As it happens, we were talking about the doctrine of hell:

> One of our 'Pilot Lights' is a taxi driver. I gave him a tract one day. He came back to me and said, 'I must have had thousands of these given to me in the last thirty years, but for some reason I've pulled up in a rank with nothing to do, and I've read this. It shook me rigid!' He said, 'Can you take me to the man who wrote it?' I told him that I'd written it. He asked me to talk with him. He said, 'If what you say is true, I'm going to hell. Am I going to hell?' I said, 'Let's talk, and find out.' I led him to the Lord. His name's Charlie Stride. He was a modern man. He was in his fifties. He'd seen it all. And he'd been converted to this gospel – absolute truth. That goes against anything being put forward by postmodernism.

The significant details here are Charlie Stride's age, and R. T. Kendall's (admittedly colloquial) description of him as a 'modern' man. As someone born in the 1940s, he would indeed have still been responsive to the thought-forms of modernity, and it is not so surprising that he received Christ in the way he did. It would be interesting, though, to analyse how many of today's twenty-somethings are converted in this manner. No doubt their eternal destiny remains an issue, but my suspicion is that fewer of them would resonate with the way it was explained to Charlie than would those of Charlie's own generation.

To be fair, there is at least one aspect of this story which would carry over quite easily into postmodern evangelism. The conversion came out of dialogue and interaction rather than passive reception of a message. Charlie and R. T. Kendall set out on a relationship in which questions were asked and answers offered. The tract may have been deductive and propositional, but the actual faith-sharing was inductive and interpersonal. This takes us on to other key facets of evangelism in a postmodern world.

Witnessing through Dialogue and Story

If proposition-based evangelism is losing its impact, dialogue and narrative offer the most obvious alternative modes of discourse through which to express the gospel. I have already made this point at length with regard to worship and preaching, and similar principles apply here. Both forms of communication are thoroughly biblical, and offer the prospect of a more personal, communitarian kind of faith-sharing. Dialogue dynamically engages those who are being witnessed to, while stories can tell us a great deal about the history and society from which they have emerged – they can 'embody' the good news.

From his vast experience as an evangelist in the Methodist Church, Rob Frost reflected thoughtfully on the changing emphases in communication since he started out in the early seventies. He told me: 'Postmodernity entails a recognition of other people's right to believe what they believe. In some ways, this makes evangelism more difficult. It is no longer enough for me simply to evangelise you by proclamation; we must enter into a meaningful relationship and a meaningful conversation.'

For Phil Wall, this shift towards dialogue relates crucially to an increased emphasis on *choice* in contemporary Western culture. With the options for belief and commitment increasing all the time, he insisted when we met that it has become nothing less than a 'pastoral necessity' to present Christian belief within the busy 'marketplace' of ideas. Certainly, postmodern consumerism seems to have extended far into the realm of philosophy and faith: one only has to look at the bewildering range of life-paths offered in bookshop 'religious' sections to realise this.

There are, of course, deep inherent dangers in accommodating the gospel to this choice-fixated world. As Gene Veith has written:

> For Luther, Calvin, St Augustine, and many other biblical theologians, the human will is in bondage to sin, so that our choices drive us away from God. In salvation we do not choose God; He chooses us. We are not saved by our wills, but by God's grace which transforms our sinful wills by the power of the Holy Spirit. Then and only then can we be said to have freedom of the will and are enabled to 'choose Christ'. Even theologians such as Arminius, Wesley, and Aquinas, who believed that the human will is free and must cooperate in the process of salvation, did not view salvation as a sheerly autonomous choice . . . Evangelicalism, having perhaps neglected its theology, thus seems attractive to postmodernists for its warm emotionalism and its exaltation of choice. Other practices evangelicals have followed for years (such as Bible studies and prayer groups) suddenly have a new resonance for postmodernists (with their fondness for support groups and cultivation of group identity). While such traditions of evangelicalism might be good ways of attracting postmodernists in order to evangelize them, sometimes the conversation has gone in the other direction.[14]

Pete Ward of Oxford Youth Works elaborated on the same theme: 'A market is good for us inasmuch as it assumes that we have a right to sell what we are offering. But it is more problematic inasmuch as people feel no obligation to buy.' Where once Christians in Britain could rely as a matter of course on the best pitch and brand recognition, the public's knowledge of what is on the Christian stall is reducing all the time. Hence, their choice is becoming less informed, and their confidence and ability even to enter into dialogue is receding. Emery White reports how John Stott once told a small group that if written today, his bestseller *Basic Christianity* would have to be approached in a totally different way. The reason he gave was that the level of general Christian knowledge assumed by him when he published the book simply no longer exists.[15]

This suggests that, for all it has to offer, the dialogical model brings certain postmodern difficulties to the surface. Dave Tomlinson may have told me that 'the model of evangelism through dialogue is a good thing to play around with', but the more I 'play around' with it, the more double-edged it seems. For one thing, to be fruitful, dialogue must find 'common ground'. In postmodernity, however, Christian assumptions about that common ground can get seriously challenged. Jenny Baker articulated this problem well: 'I think there's more friendly acceptance of Christians in our culture than there was, say, twenty years ago. But I'm not sure that Christians are equipped to deal with that change!' She explained:

> We often can't cope with people who say, 'You're a Christian; that's nice for you; don't bother me about it.' A lot of our evangelism has started with questions like 'Are you sad?' 'Are you lonely?' 'Are you depressed?' And we have given the answer, 'Then come to Jesus!' But there's a lot of people who reply, 'No, I'm not especially sad, lonely or depressed – I'm quite happy with what I am and what I believe.' And we struggle

with them because we've been so used to assuming that there are holes, and then looking to fill them. But if someone doesn't think they have any major holes in their life, what do you say?

One answer to Baker's question is to tell stories – stories which in turn relate to 'the greatest story ever told'. Given the growing ignorance of Christian 'facts' in postmodernity, story provides a way of reintroducing the gospel in more 'user-friendly', inductive form. The American evangelist Leighton Ford has made much of this. He has stressed that stories are not only biblically authentic but also culturally appropriate, integrative and relational.[16] His son Kevin expands on these points fluently:

> Story reaches not just the intellect, which is contained in the thin, outermost layer of the human brain – the cerebral cortex. Story reaches to the most deeply buried parts of the human personality, to the emotions, and even to that mysterious, elusive part of us that we know only as the human soul. A powerful story tingles our spine, surprises us with laughter, melts us to tears, moves us to righteous anger, tugs at our heart-strings, rivets our *psyche* [soul], involves our *pneuma* [spirit], refashions our worldview, colours and filters our perspective, renegotiates our belief structure, calls into question our assumptions and ultimately leaves us a changed human being.[17]

This, of course, is a very optimistic viewpoint, and it is worth saying that Jesus himself recognised that his own stories would prove impenetrable to some (Luke 8:10). Nonetheless, there is no denying the primacy of narrative from Genesis to Revelation,[18] or the power of personal storytelling and testimony to bring others to commitment. These days, it is not only my sermons which have become more narrative: the years when I would try to argue Dave and others into the Kingdom with a stock of abstract formulae have largely gone. Even when evangelising Jehovah's Witnesses, who themselves still approach things in a highly modernistic way, I have made far more impact telling my story than scoring doctrinal points as I used to. No doubt my testimony often *leads on* to discussions about doctrine, but where once I treated it as an aside, it is now of primary importance. So, rather than debating the judgment of God, I tell of my relationship with him and then ask the JWs whether, after all I have shared, they really believe that he will reject me.

In the same research on new Christians which I mentioned above, John Finney found that the commonest factor leading his respondents to faith was the witness of a Christian friend.[19] 'Witness' in this context clearly means verbal restating, but it must also entail Youth For Christ's third 'D' – Demonstration.

Witnessing through Demonstration and Presence

Evangelism through words, deeds and signs

I have been stressing throughout this book that, for good or ill, evangelical Christianity connects with the postmodern ethos above all in its pragmatism. As we enter a more demonstrative age in which people are concerned less with whether something is logically verifiable and more with whether it works, the evangelical drive to 'do the gospel' could turn out to be a real asset. In his charter for postmodern evangelism, James Emery White has stressed that 'Christianity should be portrayed as practical . . . The attention of many nonbelievers will not be initially arrested through truth, but through practical assistance.'[20] Kevin Ford bears this out when he writes of his Baby Buster peers, 'Previous generations assumed that the barrier to conversion was intellectual and the way to remove that barrier was to answer all cognitive doubts. But Xers live in an age of intellectual ambiguity, when cognitive answers carry considerably less weight. The question my generation asks is not "Can Christians prove what they believe?" but "Can Christians live what they believe?"'[21]

You would be hard pushed to find a more dedicated proponent of practical evangelism than Roger Forster. Since he helped establish the Ichthus Fellowship in 1974, he has insisted on the fullest integration of proclaimed and demonstrated truth. Hence, alongside more obviously evangelistic initiatives like street work, overseas mission and the Worldwide March for Jesus, Ichthus supports an award-winning employment project (Pecan), a community launderette and a Christian school. As Forster put it to me, 'The New Testament teaches that everything in the end is measured against the primacy of love. If this is not evident in our witness, our witness "profits nothing" [1 Cor. 13:3]. Our cerebral claims to statements of faith really have no meaning whatsoever without that priority.' He went on: 'Of course, reaching out to people in compassion will include telling them of the love of God seen in Christ, and how they can get their lives ordered to the Kingdom of God. But there are plenty of other ways to show compassion. These ways are summed up by what we call "presence evangelism".'

Embodied in Ichthus's threefold credo of 'words, works and wonders', this 'presence evangelism' has a quite distinct theological lineage. Forster pointed to the seminal Lausanne Congress on World Evangelization in 1974, when many leading evangelicals pledged to re-establish their commitment to social action. Even so, Ichthus has taken this commitment in a particular direction:

At Lausanne, John Stott put over the idea of husband and wife being the totality of mission – the husband as the preacher of the gospel and the wife as the doer of good works. But with all due respect to John, to whom we owe a great deal, we've resisted that in Ichthus.

We've always maintained that those two things are not just walking hand in hand. They are one.

Forster underlined this from Scripture:

Paul says in Romans 15 that he fully preached the gospel from Jerusalem to Illyricum 'with words, deeds and signs mighty in power' – all done in the Holy Spirit. And again, in Acts 10, Jesus is described as having preached peace, having done good and having delivered people from the enemy. Those areas are all fundamental to the gospel. The good news is the whole lot.

Evangelism through the Church itself

If 'presence evangelism' entails a greater emphasis on deed and demonstration, it must also take more seriously the role of the Church itself as an expression of God's purpose. As Stanley Grenz has put it, 'The existence of the Church declares that Christ has come and has instituted the new community; that the Spirit is here and is constituting us as God's people; and consequently God will act decisively to bring his purpose to completion.'[22]

All this becomes especially important for a postmodern generation which is in many quarters yearning for a new sense of community. Just as Steinar Kvale has detected in postmodernity a desire for something more tight-knit than the alienating individualism of the modern city,[23] sociologists and philosophers like Robert Bellah, Alisdair MacIntyre and David Shelbourne have outlined a new 'communitarian' ethic based on mutual responsibility, participation and a renewed stress on shared narratives.[24] Grenz rightly sees this as a trend from which evangelicals can learn, and to which they can contribute: 'Communitarians point out the unavoidable role of the community or social network in the life of the human person,' he writes. 'We must take seriously the discoveries of contemporary communitarians. They are echoing the great biblical theme that the goal of God's programme is the establishment of community in the highest sense.'[25]

Ideally, the Church would model community in a positive way for postmodern people: it is, after all, the body of Christ – diverse in personalities and giftings but held together by his love (1 Cor. 12:1ff.). It is at once plural and global, local and international. The problem is that the reality often seems so far removed from this ideal. The Church is widely perceived as disunited, and this can be a genuine obstacle in evangelism. A recent study of non-churchgoers in Charlotte, North Carolina, which has no fewer than 600 churches, found that the second most common reason given for not attending services was perceived denominational division.[26]

When pressed, evangelicals will usually admit the link between church unity and mission. They may even cite John 13 and 17 on the same point. But they are often reluctant to make much of the issue, for fear that their pragmatic edge might be blunted by the institutional nature of 'official' ecumenism. Although many evangelicals are involved in ecumenical work, the ecumenical movement as a whole has often been viewed by evangelicals as a liberal diversion from the Church's primary task of winning souls for Christ.[27] Structural convergence is seen as an end in itself, rather than a means to the end of converting the world. Such perceptions at least influenced the Evangelical Alliance's decision not to join the Council of Churches for Britain and Ireland in 1990.[28]

To some extent, this hesitancy is justified. I have already mentioned the evangelistic weakness of my own denomination, the United Reformed Church. Yet of all mainline British churches, the URC is the most clearly committed to ecumenism. This is a fairly common corollary: whereas the main ecumenical players are mostly losing members, those Christian groupings which are growing fastest here tend not to be so heavily involved in ecumenical activity.[29] Even on the international stage, where the picture of growth and decline is more complex, the World Council of Churches seems hardly to have made evangelism its top priority in recent years. Although John Drane's admirable work owes something to the WCC's efforts in this area – and not least to the vision of its Evangelism Secretary Raymond Fung[30] – Lesslie Newbigin has become very disillusioned. He poured a great deal of energy into the WCC in his earlier years, and still retains some involvement on the evangelism side. Nonetheless, he feels that the WCC's view of 'mission' has become far too dominated by social and political activity, at the expense of personal conversion and discipleship. He told me:

> The present leadership of the WCC has lost all interest in world evangelism. Fifteen-odd years ago the Council endorsed a splendid statement on mission and evangelism, but they have just ignored it ever since. The whole emphasis has been on programmes like *'Justice, Peace and the Integrity of Creation'*, but I have to say this seems to have added up to very little.

Paradoxically, evangelical reluctance to fall in with institutional ecumenism could in itself have postmodern overtones. 'New Communitarianism' may well be a reaction to modernist individualism, but it is also a reaction to modernism's other face – that of unwieldy, centralised bureaucratic conformity. Tom Houston took up this theme controversially when we spoke together at his home in Oxford:

> The historic Western churches have what I would call 'nation state' structures. They have modelled themselves on a particular kind of nation state. For example, the Catholics modelled themselves on the Roman Empire; the Reformed modelled themselves on

the oligarchies of Switzerland, Holland and Scotland. These movements have tried to develop the church as a hierarchy, with written rules administered by committees which do things 'by the book'. And in the main, these are the churches which are declining today. By contrast, when you look at where growth is happening, in the West and in the Third World, it's happening largely through denominations which encourage autonomy, and parachurch organisations which have a high inbuilt flexibility. The 'old line' denominations are thus destined to become the dinosaurs of ecclesiastical history.

Many, of course, would argue with this. Proponents of the ecumenical movement in Britain might claim that they now put local partnerships before the dream of a national 'superchurch'. Even so, the looser, more *ad hoc* links fostered among the New Churches, and by the Evangelical Alliance, may actually have more in common with postmodern communitarianism than the ethos of the Council of Churches for Britain and Ireland. If postmodern evangelism is to take place in the 'free market' of religious belief and experience, the evangelical willingness to maintain a variety of Christian 'brands' could very well prove more effective – even if, in the end, it remains theologically problematic.[31]

Witnessing through the Media

One of the defining phenomena of postmodernity is *deregulation*. With its accent on difference and autonomy, the postmodern world is privatised not only at the level of religious belief, but also at the level of commerce and communication. The advance of computer, satellite, cable and digital technology in the past fifteen years or so has led to a phenomenal multiplication of media outlets and companies. In Britain, Margaret Thatcher's commitment to media diversification in the 1980s broke the hegemony of the print unions and gave hundreds of new licences to independent broadcasters.

Pragmatic as ever, evangelicals have been quick to seize on all this. In Chapter 3 we saw how they have led the way in the marketing of religious software, but their magpie instincts have been evident in many other media, too. As computerisation has made books, newspapers and magazines cheaper to produce, and as the number of titles has grown accordingly, so the evangelical print media have turned out more and more paperbacks, weeklies, glossies and journals. Thirty per cent of the UK's Christian publishing houses have been formed since 1985 – and most of them have been evangelical. Much the same goes for Christian newspapers and periodicals, more than a quarter of which have been launched in the same period. In the last decade there has been a 110 per cent increase in Christian design, layout, advertising and marketing services; 59 per cent more audio-visual, film and video companies have emerged; and 47 per cent more radio and TV producers have come on to the scene. Not all are evangelical, but evangelicals have been at the forefront of the growth.[32]

The increased choice and competition which follow from all this are themselves features of postmodernity – and more often than not they have quite suited evangelicals. Whereas evangelicals have frequently criticised the state-sponsored BBC for a perceived liberal bias on Christian issues,[33] the opening up of the airwaves has offered them the chance to do things more on their own terms. When in 1995 a new tranche of licences for London-wide radio was made available, Premier – a station conceived, funded and run by a majority of evangelicals – was one of the winners. Although it soon suffered serious teething problems and had to lay off several staff, it has since achieved a degree of stability, finding its niche in an ever-expanding market. The radio output of United Christian Broadcasters (formed in 1986) is more modest, but functions on a similar basis.

There are, of course, gains and losses for evangelicals in this new, highly pluralised situation. On the one hand, it presents more opportunities and more outlets for the communication of the gospel. On the other, it tends towards 'narrowcasting' rather than 'broadcasting'.[34] The postmodern world may offer evangelicals the chance to make more distinctive programmes, but even as it does so it threatens to dissipate their potential audience.[35] As a result, the evangelistic opportunities offered by the new media explosion could be illusory. As specialisation becomes the order of the day, we could well end up making programmes only for one another! There may yet be a certain pastoral benefit in this, but we ought to hesitate before we equate it with the conversion of the world.

Nowhere do these issues arise more starkly than in the realm of television.

The role of television

One cannot discuss postmodernity without coming round sooner or later to the telly. It might well be argued that TV is *the* postmodern medium. Although its invention was a product of modernity, its development has gone hand in hand with the emergence of postmodern culture. Some would say it has even *constructed* that culture. At the very least, its place in the lives of most people is highly pervasive. Not only is TV ownership in Britain up to 97 per cent of all households: TV viewing is by far and away the most popular leisure activity, consuming an average nineteen hours per week of our free time – 400 per cent more than anything else.[36] Some surveys put the figure even higher.[37]

It was Marshall McLuhan back in the sixties who declared 'the medium is the message' and predicted a 'global village' in which television and other forms of electronic communication would erode distinctions of nationality and

race and form their own dimension.[38] Although the detail
of McLuhan's analysis is often dismissed these days, the
worldwide impact of the Cable News Network (CNN),
with its live battlefield footage and instant analysis, is
but one confirmation that his basic vision was right. The
Internet is another, and there are already signs that the lines
between this and television will become increasingly blurred
by digital and cable technology.

What McLuhan less clearly predicted was the way TV
reflects, and even creates, fragmentation. We have come
back a number of times in this study to the great postmodern
paradox: as some things are globalised, others get more
dispersed. This paradox lies at the heart of Jean Baudrillard's
writing on TV. For Baudrillard, as TV becomes more central
to our existence, so it breaks down the very structure
of reality itself. We enter a world of 'hyperreality' and
'pure simulacra' in which life dissolves into a series of
images – images which cease to refer to anything 'beyond'
themselves, and begin to lose coherence even *among* themselves.[39] Notoriously, Baudrillard went so far as to suggest
on this basis that the Gulf War had never taken place –
that it had existed only as a hyperreal projection on our
screens.[40] However sick and ridiculous this may seem, it is
at least true that millions more 'experienced' that conflict
in the way Baudrillard described than fought in Iraq. Most
of us were served, at best, sharply edited 'highlights' of the
action. At times, the resemblance to a video game was hard
to avoid.

When images appear on screen now, they do so increasingly in a non-linear, fleeting, disconnected way. From
pop videos to *The Big Breakfast*, from documentaries to
drama, shots, scenes and items are shortened to accommodate briefer attention spans. Camera angles are multiplied.
Viewers are assumed to be more 'TV conscious' than a
generation ago, and more gaps can be left for them to fill. As
Stanley Grenz has put it, 'by offering its collage of images,
television unintentionally juxtaposes the irreconcilable. But

in addition, it obliterates spatial and temporal distinctions. It merges the past and the present, the distant and the local, bringing all together into one perpetual here-and-now – the "present" of the television viewer.'[41]

By pandering to us in this way, TV tends to encourage passivity. I am not suggesting that it always or inevitably does so. At its best, it can engage and stimulate more effectively than any medium. But when your remote control allows you to flip uninterestedly from death camps to panel games, from hard news to soft porn, your capacity for involvement or concern is likely to be numbed somewhat.

I should make it clear that I am not 'anti-TV'. As a Baby Buster, I grew up with it, and I get frustrated with evangelicals who portray it as the root of all evil. As we shall see, it has much to offer as an aid to Christian discipleship. Nonetheless, there is room for doubt over how much use it really is as a tool of witness to *non*-Christians. If the aim of evangelism is to stir active commitment, how well is it likely to penetrate the world of the casual viewer, the channel-hopper and the couch potato?

These questions were uppermost when I spoke to Alan Rogers.

Ark2 and Christian broadcasting

Alan Rogers was the Managing Director of Ark2, which had set out to be the first national British Christian cable TV channel but which has since gone into liquidation. Previously a producer with the BBC, he helped launch Ark2's publicity campaign in 1995, with a view to going on air by April 1996. When we met, that transmission date had been delayed almost a year due to lack of funding.[42] Doubts about witnessing through TV are, it seems, more than just theoretical! Still, he was convinced that there was a market for his product, and he had the research to prove it.

Although involved in the evangelical scene for many

years, Rogers was seeking to reach a largely 'unchurched' audience. He told me:

> Our aim is quite consciously to broadcast rather than narrowcast. We're trying to communicate with people who've never come within the ambit of Christianity. Seventy-one per cent of the population believe that God exists, but only 10 per cent go to church. Take away those committed to other faiths and you're left with about 56 per cent who believe but are not active. That's a majority audience – one which has lots of questions but very few answers.

He added: 'This is our target audience at Ark2. In fact, I think it must be the target audience for any medium that claims to be doing outreach. I don't think there's any justification for a Christian station which simply services Christians.'

These comments begged a comparison with American 'televangelism'. Rogers was happy to make it: 'American Christian TV relies on specific bands of financial support and is quite narrow in terms of audience. Although televangelists like Benny Hinn and Morris Cerullo claim that they're broadcasting to the unconverted, the reality is that they're mostly reaching keen Christians. In fact, the statistics show that they're reaching mainly older, female Christians!' He continued: 'Of course, they can point to some wonderful conversion stories, but these occur within the confines of what is already a very small audience. The hard truth is that the really "hot gospel" shows are watched by non-Christians mainly for a laugh.'

How, then, would Ark2 be different? Rogers's instinct was to steer away from direct evangelism and proselytising. Instead, he talked of 'putting Christianity on people's agenda' and 'leaving them to make up their own mind rather than shoving the gospel down their throats'. He told me: 'Even in this kind of television there's an honest journalistic job to be done. If truth is a good Christian value, it must include presenting different sides of an issue; the Holy Spirit is quite capable of convicting people in such a context.'

This less explicit approach may reflect Rogers's 'public service' past, but at least some potential backers have seen it as a dilution of the gospel. With a wry smile, Rogers told me of a meeting with a wealthy evangelical businessman in the North-East.

> He said that he loved the American televangelists, and I had to admit that wasn't where we were at. And then he said, 'My sort of Christian TV may only have ten viewers, but two of them might get saved. Your sort may have a hundred viewers, but none of them are likely to get saved!' But I replied, 'Maybe – but ten of mine might be persuaded to go to church, and they can get saved there!'

It remained to be seen whether the 'softly, softly' ethos of Ark2 would catch on, or whether the more in-your-face style of the televangelists would reach beyond a limited number of evangelicals. Yet the points raised by Alan Rogers bore more generally on the place of indirect and implicit witness in postmodern evangelism. This issue related not only to the media, but also to the arts.

Witnessing through the Arts

Painting: the case of Cornelius Browne

Some time ago, my church hosted an exhibition by Cornelius Browne. Cornelius is an evangelical Christian painter. Having worked on the graphics side of advertising, he is adept in a number of different styles. As a mark of thanks to us for letting him display his art, he gave us two of his paintings. The larger of the two is a luminous interpretation of Psalm 139:7–10. The text appears beneath the canvas:

> Where can I go from your Spirit?
> Where can I flee from your presence?
> If I go up to the heavens, you are there;
> if I make my bed in the depths, you are there.
> If I rise on the wings of the dawn,
> if I settle on the far side of the sea,
> Even there your hand will . . . hold me fast.

The picture shows two figures hiding their faces. One is crouched awkwardly; the other is using an arm as a shield, eyes closed against an overwhelming presence or light. They recall the human forms of Matisse, but are rather more angular. The barest features are shown, yet every emotion expressed by the Psalmist is evoked – awe, bewilderment, beauty, estrangement, aspiration, faith. Both are set against a cosmic backdrop of shifting colours and moods, dotted with stars and planets. The whole is superbly composed and balanced. It is not a strictly representational painting, but neither is it purely abstract. Like the Psalm itself, it is psychologically rather than geographically located. Also like the Psalm, it is profoundly honest and yet gloriously transcendent. It hangs alone on a wall in my office.

Without wishing to sound ungenerous, the other painting is much less successful. The composition is more heavy-handed, but this is not the main problem. Cornelius has portrayed a glass of water being stirred up by a bolt of lightning from a black sky. The text below the image is not from Scripture as such, but offers a theological explanation of the work, which is entitled *Living Water*:

> The lightning depicts the awesomeness of the power
> of the living God. The glass represents the believer.

The water is stirred by the potency of the lightning
but miraculously, the glass is not broken. This is a
metaphoric reference to what happens when the power
of God comes upon the believer.

The difficulty here is that everything is just too literalistic.
As the Romantic poet John Keats would have said, the
artist has too palpable a design on us. Browne has taken
a potent biblical symbol, which Jesus used to stimulate our
imagination (John 4:10; 7:38), and has gone and done all our
imagining for us! To have to be told what every element in
the piece means is, effectively, to kill the piece as a work of
art. This is painting as an adjunct to rational theology, rather
than painting *as* theology. The ideas behind the canvas are
more important than the canvas itself. We simply do not need
to be told that the reference is 'metaphoric', but we are told
anyway, in spite of the fact that lightning forking directly
into a glass cannot be anything *but* metaphoric. The work is
undoubtedly sincere, but it is too self-conscious, too man-
nered. In a nutshell, it represents modernistic evangelicalism, whereas the first picture is much more in keeping with
what I would call a postmodern evangelical artistic witness.

It is not insignificant that the first painting is accompanied
by straight Scripture, whereas the second uses the more
distanced language of exegesis and doctrine. Psalm 139
deploys intimate dialogue and questioning to get to the
heart of humanity's relationship with God. It moves from the
personal to the cosmological, the particular to the general.
On the other hand, Cornelius's text for the second painting is
driven by propositions about the way God deals with people
generally, and fails to root these propositions in anything
specific.

Historically, evangelicals have had problems with art
which goes much beyond a literal depiction of positive biblical motifs and concepts. We have tended to be uncomfortable with the obliqueness, analogy and mystery which lies at
the heart of much great art. And yet, ironically, Psalms like

139 show us that complex poetic emotions can be thoroughly scriptural. At different times, the Psalmist asks questions of God, voices angst, cries out in pain, articulates confusion, celebrates beauty, revels in joy and sings with wonder. Art can suggest all this and more – for, as I have already stressed, there is that of God which lies beyond words (2 Cor. 9:15).

If artists like Cornelius Brown are to paint as a means of witness and outreach in the postmodern world, they will have to explore these more challenging themes with an integrity which comes from their own search for the will of God, rather than solely from the prescriptions of doctrinal theologians. At times, they may appear ambivalent and even dubious; at times they may exceed the limits of his revealed order. But in an age of doubt and uncertainty, we must at least entertain the possibility that they could express their Lord's empathy for postmodern people, and draw them into Christian communities where a more definite message can be heard.

Rock Music: the 'U2 question'

Issues similar to those seen in painting arise in the field of rock music. At the end of *The Post-Evangelical*, Dave Tomlinson picks up a debate which has long been close to my heart. He writes, 'When Bono of U2 said "I still haven't found what I'm looking for," many evangelicals despaired, thinking that he had lost his way spiritually.' But, as Tomlinson rightly adds, 'he was quite clear: "You broke the bonds, you loosed the chains, you carried the cross and my shame. You know I believe it, but I still haven't found what I'm looking for."' This, says Tomlinson, is not a statement of confusion or spiritual ambivalence: 'quite the reverse, it is a positive recognition of the frailty of human experience and human comprehension. We know only in part, we experience only in part, and in a postmodern world it is crucial that we are honest about this limitation.'[43]

The four members of the Irish quartet U2 comprise one of the most successful rock acts ever. Remarkably and unusually, three of the four have at various times identified themselves as Christians. In their late teens, Bono, the Edge and Larry Mullen became involved in a charismatic fellowship on the outskirts of Dublin, and the influence of that community shows through on their first two albums – *Boy* and *October*. I vividly remember a student friend telling me about this 'weird, sort of spiritual' band with a fresh guitar sound, liking what I heard and going to buy these LPs together. The music had an innocent, optimistic quality which moved me deeply, but then I started to pick up on the lyrics, which were not printed on the album sleeves. Bono sang soaringly of faith, hope and love: many tracks were addressed directly to the Father or the Son. The call to discipleship was strikingly affirmed in 'I will follow'; in an extraordinary way, 'Gloria' became a post-punk hymn of praise, shifting into Latin as it sought to express the inexpressible:

> Oh Lord, if I had anything, anything at all
> I'd give it to you.

And so it went on. 'Rejoice' celebrated God's capacity to change the world outside and the the world inside – the world of the heart. 'October' drew on Psalm 46 to affirm his steadfastness; 'With a Shout' yearned for both the splendour of Zion and the drama of Calvary – the place 'where blood was spilt, and we were filled with love'. But my favourite song of all was 'Tomorrow', in which Bono matured from seeking the soul of his dead mother to anticipating the return of his Lord:

> Open up, open up to the Lamb of God,
> To the love of He who made the blind to see;
> He's coming back, He's coming back:
> I BELIEVE! Jesus is coming!

In later years, it emerged that around *October,* the three Christian members of U2 had thought seriously of quitting the music business altogether. They were finding it difficult to reconcile their evangelical faith with the values of the rock world, and were worried that they might be compromised by it. After a great deal of soul-searching, they decided to persevere, and the result was *War* – a far more political record, but one which still clearly affirmed Christian values. Even 'Sunday, Bloody Sunday', which bemoaned the violence in Northern Ireland, ended by looking to Christ as the only way through:

> The real battle just begun
> To claim the victory Jesus won.

The achingly beautiful 'Drowning Man' quoted Isaiah 40 on God's giving strength to the young, while '40' set the Psalm of that number to a haunting melody. The latter closed U2's concerts at this time, and more than once I remember walking out of theatres and stadia singing it with thousands of others: worship is the only word fit to describe the experience.

I suppose it was around 1984 that evangelicals began to worry about U2. Their next album, *The Unforgettable Fire*, seemed more vague about its spirituality. 'Pride (In the Name of Love)' did exalt Jesus, but more as a champion of goodwill to be placed alongside figures like Martin Luther King and Gandhi. Then came *The Joshua Tree,* and that song: 'I Still Haven't Found What I'm Looking For'.

No doubt, the zealous fervour of the early albums had gone. But in its place came something which in its own way was equally biblical. The combination of faith ('You know I believe it') and restless searching ('I still haven't found . . .') reminded me of the honest humility of the demoniac's father in Mark 9:24, who says to Jesus, 'I do believe; help me overcome my unbelief.' The commitment behind the song comes through even more profoundly in the version of it which appears on U2's live album, *Rattle and Hum.* There, the group are backed by an exuberant black gospel choir, who leave the audience in no doubt that the chorus is about aspiring to God's purpose rather than abandoning it.

Graham Cray felt similarly when he first heard the song, and continues to do so now. A long-time student of the rock scene, he told me:

> It always takes me to Philippians 3:12 – 'Not that I have already obtained all this, or have already been made perfect, but I press on to take hold of that for which Christ Jesus took hold of me.' The few connections I have with the U2 camp have confirmed what I have always felt – that this song was never a statement of disbelief. It was a profoundly Christian statement of the truth that just when you think you've worked God out, he draws you on to something else.

Cray elaborated: 'At the very heart of Christian experience there is a sense of things being "already, but not yet". That tension between what is and what is still to come is the very motor of our faith, because it prevents complacency and spiritual pride.'

Since *The Joshua Tree,* it is significant that U2 have engaged increasingly with postmodern themes. Stage shows have featured a backdrop of random images and slogans; there is a great deal more parody, pastiche and camp, and the spiritual restlessness has intensified. The theological content of their 1997 album *Pop* is actually much greater than that of the previous four or five albums – even if it hardly reflects standard evangelical doctrine. In 'MOFO' Bono seeks to 'fill that God-shaped hole', and in doing so finds others 'lookin' for baby Jesus under the trash'. It is an arresting image of incarnation – of light in the midst of darkness. Elsewhere, he asks, 'If God will send His angels, would everything be alright?' There is a palpable struggle between personal faith and public religion, summed up ironically in the same song:

> Jesus never let me down
> you know Jesus used to show me the score
> then they put Jesus in showbusiness
> now it's hard to get in the door

Maybe this is the self-justification of compromised pop stars: maybe it is U2's immersion in 'showbusiness' which has made it hard for *them* to get through to *Christ*. Even so, the *desire* to get through is tenaciously maintained – not least on the closing track, 'Wake Up, Dead Man'. Bono declares himself to be alone in a fallen world, but pleads with Jesus to offer a grand narrative solution:

> tell me, tell me the story
> the one about eternity
> and the way it's all gonna be

No doubt some evangelicals would despair that U2 feel the need to be told again a gospel message which once seemed so clear in their music. Could they possibly have forgotten? I doubt it. Rather, I suspect they feel the context has changed so much that the 'story' needs to be related in a new way to the new situation. There are parallels here with the many different Old Testament settings in which the people of Israel go back and re-present the Exodus narrative, and in doing so discover new things about their past, as well as their present. The great value of stories is that they can be re-lived and re-experienced rather than just re-stated; while their basic meaning may not change, they can be applied and adapted in fresh ways to fresh circumstances. This possibility is at least entertained in the closing question of the song:

> if there's an order
> in all of this disorder
> is it like a tape recorder?
> can we rewind it just once more?

Granted, such quizzical ambivalence is unlikely to win many new converts. No doubt, there are committed Christian artists who aim more obviously to lead their audiences to faith. But not least in a postmodern world, the main job of such artists is unlikely to be at the hard edge of conversion. If anything, they will contribute more to 'pre-evangelism'. They will raise people's awareness, suggest possibilities, build bridges to a generation which is at once more open to, and yet more ignorant of, God – a generation which is less textual, and more used to receiving its stimulation in symbolic, metaphoric and analogical form. This is certainly Cornelius Browne's intention. Whether it is the intention of U2 is harder to say, and I suspect their work will relate more to those who are *already* committed, but who are coming to terms with the complexities of faith in the postmodern situation.

Sometimes, it is unclear just where U2's embrace of complexity is leading, and this can be unsettling. Even so, Graham Cray, for one, errs on the side of generosity:

> The band's fame and wealth, coupled with the negative reaction of the evangelicals among whom they found faith, has detached them from regular engagement with the Church. This means that at times they make strange statements and present an odd lifestyle. I don't want to bless everything U2 do, but my sense is that their central instinct has not travelled as far as a lot of people think.

Certainly, around the release of *Pop,* Bono told an interviewer, 'It's hard to be a believer when you see the way things are in the world, but I *am* a believer.'[44]

General reflections

In the sacred sphere as much as the secular, art which

merely proclaims and ideologises is rarely good art. Since evangelicals are so much defined by proclamation and 'sound' belief, they are often wary about the place of art, and view it at best as a supplement to the Church's mission. As John Drane put it to me:

> The arts are being used in congregations, but mostly just as illustrative material – to back up what is still a propositional message. Most evangelicals in Britain are still unhappy with any creative presentation carrying its *own* Christian message. You might have a 'drama slot' in a service, but mostly it will be there to back up the key point of the sermon.

Or, as Jenny Baker reflected, 'We seem to accept any old art, good or bad, as long as it has a fish stuck on it!'

There are, of course, exceptions to all this – one of which is the Greenbelt Arts Festival. As a Festival Committee member, Martin Wroe was keen to stress when we met that 'Greenbelt has always valued "art for art's sake", rather than treating art as a way to propagandise. For instance, we've shied away from putting musicians on stage who want to preach. We've also shied away from formal evangelism.' Not surprisingly, this non-explicit approach has attracted criticism. I can well recall a keyboard player at the Festival sporting a t-shirt with the legend 'Born Again' printed across the chest. When I asked him why he had gone for this attire he said it was to answer someone who had told him there were no true Christians at Greenbelt!

This view may have been extreme, but Greenbelt's ethos has caused growing unease within the mainline evangelical constituency. Having started out as a radical, but still clearly evangelical, event, many feel that it has now drifted into post-evangelicalism, or even tacit liberalism. Certainly, Dave Tomlinson claims it as a major inspiration for his own recent work.[45] Martin Wroe is keen to avoid labels, but insisted that 'Greenbelt is unashamedly Christian. Every year we get hundreds of letters, many of which say, "I became a Christian at the festival." We are evangelistic inasmuch as we are about the good news of Christ.'

As postmodern culture relies less on verbal–propositional forms of communication, it seems likely that artistic models will come to occupy a more central place in Christian witness. In keeping with the move from 'event' to 'process', the power of these models to convict may be less immediate. Even so, for many postmoderns their impact may well prove to be more profound and more durable than that of the tract, the soapbox sermon or the altar call. Indeed John Finney's suggestion that we see conversion more as an unfolding experience than an immediate act implies that the general distinction between 'evangelism' and 'discipleship' may have to be reviewed.

Evangelism and Discipleship

When Jesus called people, the call to conversion was closely bound up with the call to discipleship. People were prompted not only to repent, but also to follow him, and in turn to 'make disciples' of others (Matt. 4:19; Luke 14: 25–35; Matt. 28:19–20). The New Testament word for repentance denotes a change of mind, and the word for disciple means quite literally a pupil or student – someone who is being taught. Given the obvious point that our minds are changed as we learn more, it is not difficult to see the connection between turning to Christ and being 'trained' or 'schooled' by him.

Where Jesus was concerned, verbal profession was not enough; it had to be accompanied by an ongoing absorption of, and obedience to, God's will (Matt. 7:21; Luke 6:46–9). Even when there was a clear 'crisis moment' of recognition or commitment, Jesus would often map out the long, tough journey of faith which lay ahead (Matt. 8:18–22; Luke 5:8–11). As John Drane has shown, although Peter could date his decision to go with Christ (Mark 1:16–18), his 'conversion' can also be charted as an emerging story, reaching back to his past as a godfearing Jew and into his future experience of theological understanding (Mark 8:27–30), denial (John 18:15–27), re-commitment (John 21:15–17), witness-bearing (Acts 2:14ff.), 'worldview revolution' (Acts 10:1–48) and the instruction of others (1 and 2 Pet.).[46]

Now, as I have said, my liberal past makes me only too aware of how the vocabulary of 'pilgrimage' and 'growing into faith' can be used as a cover for nominalism and lukewarmness. To put it bluntly, some people need a good, sharp kick up the backside to get them started on the journey! If my youth group leader had not persisted with me in the belief that I needed to make some kind of clear commitment, I might barely have left the starting-blocks. Even so, increasing numbers of evangelicals are aiming for a much closer integration between 'saving souls' and 'making disciples'. One manifestation of this is the growing use of small groups as a means of inculcating the faith.

The house group as a postmodern development

From modest, largely evangelical beginnings in the early seventies, the phenomenon of the 'house group' or 'home group' has mushroomed, extending across a wide range of traditions and churchmanship.[47] Whether this development can be directly related to postmodernity is a moot point, but it does at least mirror certain postmodern trends. Not only has it provided an important bridge between conversion and discipleship: at its best, it has 'democratised' the Word of God, ensuring that Christian teaching has become much less the sole preserve of professional clergy. It has fostered a 'dialogical' model of learning as compared with a 'didactic' one. And it has set study and prayer in a more general context of community and fellowship, rather than confining them to formal church services or private devotions. Rob Frost confirmed all this when he told me that house groups have helped to 'de-institutionalise Christianity', contributing greatly to a 'relational' model of church. For all his commitment to classic expository preaching, David Jackman observed that 'while the preacher may offer a degree of application, the house group can take it much further'. Derek Tidball went so far as to suggest that 'the move in house groups from a single authoritative teacher towards self-discovery and exploration is very postmodern'.

Despite all this, nearly everyone I spoke to was quick to qualify the positive aspects of house group learning. Nick Mercer told me of an Anglican cleric he knew whose attempts in this area amounted to an evening in the vicarage lounge at which chairs were arranged in serried ranks and the priest told everyone what the Bible meant! Graham Dale saw the potential for postmodern-style learning in house groups, but warned that they can easily offer little more than 'a guy preaching from the sofa rather than the pulpit'. Rob Frost told me: 'The downside of house groups is that they can very quickly get set in concrete, and can turn into cliques. They need to be mixed up every so often if they are not to lose touch.' Derek Tidball saw a further problem arising out of such stasis: 'In truth, house groups can sometimes make for a sophisticated sharing of ignorance rather than knowledge. They can be places where a lot of rubbish is taught and a lot of heresy generated. They may allow people to reflect on their own experience, but if that experience has no clear biblical framework, there can be real problems.'

Alpha: modernist apologetic meets postmodern presentation

More recently, another initiative has emerged from within evangelicalism which has sought very consciously to balance informed biblical input with the relaxed air of the home group. Importantly too, it has modelled a 'process' approach to evangelism, and has also done much to elide conversion with discipleship.

The *Alpha* course started in 1977 as a modest four-week introduction to the Christian faith at Holy Trinity, Brompton – a charismatic Anglican church in West London. By 1981, it had been lengthened to ten weeks, and had incorporated a weekend of teaching on the Holy Spirit. In 1991, the course was running four times a year, and involved some six hundred people. As other churches saw *Alpha* working, they imported it. In 1996, around five thousand courses were being run all over the world, attended by approximately a quarter of a million people.[48]

Although initially conceived as a programme for new Christians, under the guidance of curate Nicky Gumbel *Alpha* was oriented increasingly towards the unchurched, with further, integrated courses being made available for those who had come to faith and needed to consolidate their commitment. The merging of evangelism and discipleship comes over clearly in the *Alpha* publicity, which states that it is designed 'for non-churchgoers and new Christians' and can also be used 'as a refresher course for mature Christians'.

Alpha builds on the relational context of house groups, and many smaller *Alpha* courses are held in people's homes. Even when it takes place within a church building, however, great efforts are made to reduce formality. A typical evening begins with supper at 7.00 p.m., followed by notices at 7.45, a main talk at 8.00, coffee at 8.45 and small-group discussion from 9.00 until 9.45. Those taking part are encouraged to 'ask anything', and space is allowed for laughter and more casual conversation. The communal aspect of the course is underpinned by the weekend away, which offers time to deepen friendships and develop openness.

No doubt all these elements could be traced back to previous evangelistic and discipling initiatives. *Alpha*'s success has come from its skilful blending of them into a non-threatening, rolling programme – and from impressive marketing which allows less well-resourced churches to use it 'off the peg'. Indeed, it might well be argued that the most postmodern thing about *Alpha* is its presentation and packaging, rather than its theological content. Books, videos, cassette tapes, newsletters, conferences, a web site and endorsements from key church leaders all add up to a corporate strategy which is very much in tune with the branded, 'synergised' world of postmodern commerce. This is not meant as a criticism: Holy Trinity, Brompton, have simply recognised that in order to reach contemporary people who take high media standards for granted, the gospel must be 'sold' in a professional way.

One of the most intriguing things about *Alpha* is that for all its efforts to make Christianity 'user-friendly' in a postmodern world, its core forty-five-minute talk remains closely wedded to a modernist apologetic. L. G. Witlock Jnr has defined apologetics as 'discourse in defense of the divine origin and authority of the Christian faith'.[49] A biblical text often cited in relation to apologetics is 1 Peter 3:15: 'Always be prepared to give an answer to everyone who asks you to give a reason for the hope that you have.' At least since the eighteenth century, evangelicals have approached this task not just in a 'reasonable' way, but in a typically rationalistic way. As we saw in Chapter 5, not all evangelicals signed up lock, stock and barrel to the Enlightenment. Nonetheless, many leading evangelical apologists since then have worked from its foundations and premises.[50] Even my own generation of evangelicals caught the tail-end of this movement. We were brought up on Josh McDowell's forensic textbook *Evidence that Demands a Verdict*, and Francis Schaeffer's *Escape from Reason*, with its exposition of the 'unchangeable facts' of Christian faith. We memorised the 'logical proofs' for the resurrection and waited eagerly to stun atheists with C. S. Lewis's dictum that Jesus must either have been mad, bad, or God. But as Kevin Ford has pointed out, those coming after us have demanded 'a different apologetic –

an embodied apologetic – a flesh-and-blood, living and breathing argument for God'.[51]

Embodied and relational though it may be in other respects, *Alpha* still relies heavily on the McDowell–Schaeffer model for its core teaching. In the official video of the course, Nicky Gumbel certainly punctuates the doctrinal content with plenty of stories and jokes, but that content is still presented in the classic, deductive way. Hypotheses are established, possible responses posited and evidence adduced before the proper evangelical conclusion is drawn. It is all there: from the manuscript attestation of the New Testament to that C. S. Lewis aphorism, from eleven reasons to believe in the resurrection to four theories of the atonement.[52]

And yet, *Alpha* has been a phenomenal achievement. What does this tell us? Gumbel himself is well aware of the challenges of postmodernity, and offers some helpful insights into his philosophy in *Telling Others*, his account of the development of the course:

> I have found on *Alpha* that those from an essentially Enlightenment background feel at home with the parts of the course which appeal to the mind, but often have difficulty in experiencing the Holy Spirit. Others coming from the New Age movement find that rational and historical explanations leave them cold, but at the weekend away they are on more familiar territory in experiencing the Spirit . . . The gospel involves both the rational and the experiential and it impacts both those from an Enlightenment background who need to experience God and those who have sought experiences but who need to understand the truth about God.[53]

This explanation suggests that *Alpha* has very deliberately tried to hold the modern and the postmodern in tension. Indeed, Gumbel refers to the prevailing cultural situation as 'transitional'.[54] The key question for a future in which postmodernity is destined increasingly to *replace* modernity is how much longer the more postmodern, experiential elements can remain confined simply to the weekend away and the practical teaching on the Holy Spirit. Will there not be a need to revise the more modernist apologetics of other sessions along similar lines? And, if so, how might this revision be done without compromising the basic purpose of *Alpha*, which is to engender conviction and commitment, rather than a mere sense of well-being? Nick Mercer pinpointed this dilemma when he told me, 'One of the strengths of *Alpha* which both postmoderns and post-evangelicals find difficult is that it does look clearly for *closure*. In the end it still says, "You've heard all this; so do you want to be a Christian or not?" Postmoderns and post-evangelicals hardly dare ask that, because it suggests something other than journey.'

This is a problem which goes much wider than *Alpha*, of course, and it merits deeper reflection.

Teaching in transition

Rob Frost is one who feels very much caught up in the transition from modern to postmodern discipleship. He told me about two university Christian Union meetings which he had led a few weeks previously. 'Each CU sent me a list of instructions. The first asked for a twenty-five-minute address, but said that this was negotiable. The second asked for a forty- to forty-five-minute address, and would not negotiate.' Frost duly bargained with the first group: 'I hauled people out of the audience, and we re-enacted the story of the woman caught in adultery. It was very funny, but very poignant. I had them talking together. I got them to ask questions, and the Bible exposition flowed out of the discussion. There were more questions at the end, and I mingled with the students afterwards.' The second university was a quite different matter. Frost recalled, 'I was told to preach, verse by verse, in an expository fashion. I was even given five points to bring out. People came with Bibles and notebooks to *receive*, and there was no encouragement to dialogue over coffee afterwards. I had done my bit, and I went away.'

It may seem that Frost much preferred the first experience to the second. But he put things differently: 'I did in fact enjoy the second CU. It's good for the ego to do that kind of preaching in front of 400 eager students who have their Bibles open and notebooks at the ready. But I don't actually believe that in terms of contemporary communication it worked as well as what I did at the other meeting.'

From her perspective at Youth For Christ, Jenny Baker very much echoed Frost's assessment. She told me:

The predominant model is still one person up at the front, and it *is* hard to get away from that. But I do think people are recognising that the young in particular are more inductive. They pick up bits and pieces of information from here and there, so it might be necessary to communicate the gospel in smaller chunks, interspersed with other material, rather than having a long exposition.

Another young evangelist, Phil Wall, was passionate about the need for a more embodied apologetic, and for him this had clear socio-political implications. Despite the fact that my wife is a minister, I have not looked here at a subject which many would regard as crucial to any debate about Christianity and postmodernity – namely, the place of women in the Church. This is mainly because it is so vast a topic that it merits a book in its own right. Nonetheless, I will say that Wall's comments resonated deeply with what I have thought for some time about both hard-core expository preaching and modernist apologetics, each of which often correlate these days with a denial of female leadership: 'A lot of this has to do with male power. When we talk about communication in a postmodern society, the power debate meets the crisis in masculinity. What we are seeing now is a generation of men trying to sustain a role which is unsustainable because it is ungodly – a role of dominance rather than partnership.'

However you react to this, it suggests that the way we do church – whether in prayer book traditionalism, rave worship, 'event' or 'process' evangelism, one-man rhetorical preaching or relational apologetics – has implications for how we relate to the world *outside* the Church. It underlines the need for evangelicals to discern those points at which they must be *counter* to postmodern trends, and those at which they might fruitfully *learn* from such trends. This in turn implies a broader ethical agenda. How can Christians truly 'embody' the gospel in a postmodern world? How might our message be demonstrated in such a way that 'all people will know' that we are Christ's disciples (John 13:35)? I shall address these questions first by looking at the example of Philip and Nathanael, and then by tackling the vexed question of private and public morality.

11

BIBLE REFLECTION: JOHN 1: 35–51

The next day John was there again with two of his disciples. When he saw Jesus passing by he said, 'Look, the Lamb of God!' When the two disciples heard him say this, they followed Jesus. Turning round, Jesus saw them following and asked, 'What do you want?' They said, 'Rabbi' (which means Teacher), 'where are you staying?' 'Come,' he replied, 'and you will see.' So they went and saw where he was staying, and spent that day with him. It was about the tenth hour.

Andrew, Simon Peter's brother, was one of the two who heard what John had said and who had followed Jesus. The first thing Andrew did was to find his brother Simon and tell him, 'We have found the Messiah' (that is, the Christ). And he brought him to Jesus. Jesus looked at him and said, 'You are Simon son of John. You will be called Cephas' (which, when translated, is Peter).

The next day Jesus decided to leave for Galilee. Finding Philip, he said to him, 'Follow me.' Philip, like Andrew and Peter, was from the town of Bethsaida. Philip found Nathanael and told him, 'We have found the one Moses wrote about in the Law, and about whom the prophets also wrote – Jesus of Nazareth, the son of Joseph.' 'Nazareth! Can anything good come from there?' Nathanael asked. 'Come and see,' said Philip.

> *When Jesus saw Nathanael approaching, he said
> of him, 'Here is a true Israelite, in whom there is
> nothing false.' 'How do you know me?' Nathanael
> asked. Jesus answered, 'I saw you while you were
> still under the fig-tree before Philip called you.' Then
> Nathanael declared, 'Rabbi, you are the Son of God;
> you are the King of Israel.' Jesus said, 'You believe
> because I told you I saw you under the fig-tree. You
> shall see greater things than that.' He then added, 'I
> tell you the truth, you shall see heaven open, and the
> angels of God ascending and descending on the Son
> of Man.'*

In this text, six people come into contact with Jesus. In every
case, the contact is verbal. John the Baptist tells others who
Jesus is as he walks by (v. 36). Two of John's disciples
hear this (v. 37) and one of them, Andrew, tells his brother
Simon (v. 41). Then Jesus speaks to Philip and says, 'Follow
me' (v. 43). Then, in turn, Philip grabs Nathanael and tells
him, 'We have found the one Moses wrote about in the
Law, and about whom the prophets also wrote – Jesus of
Nazareth, the Son of Joseph' (v. 45). And the circle is
completed when Jesus and Nathanael have a conversation
(vv. 47–51) which ends with Nathanael's great confession:
'Rabbi, you are the Son of God; you are the King of Israel'
(v. 49).

So words are important here. We should never under-
estimate their power. But we still need to look more
closely at this passage. We need to examine more deeply
what is going on. And when we do, we realise that
here, as elsewhere, words are not enough. Certainly, one
person told another about Jesus – just as Jesus had told
them about God. But for every verb of speaking in this
chapter, there is a verb of seeing, and embodying, and
demonstrating.

John the Baptist sees Jesus before he tells others about
him (v. 36). And even as he tells them he says, 'Look! Look!

There's the Lamb of God!' John's disciples ask Jesus where he is staying, but he does not simply give them directions. He says: 'Come, and you will *see*' (v. 39). Having spent time with Jesus, Andrew tells his brother Simon about Christ, but he also *brings* him to Christ – he takes him to see Jesus. Philip tells Nathanael about Jesus, and explains that he has fulfilled what the prophets told Israel about a Saviour for Israel. But when Nathanael questions Jesus's credentials, Philip's first response is: 'Come and see.'

William Temple was Archbishop of Canterbury during the dark days of the Second World War. One of Temple's best-known books was his *Readings in St John's Gospel*. When he deals with this chapter, Temple writes of one leading another to Christ, 'Perhaps this is as great a service to the Church as any men ever did.'[1] Temple recognised what many who are trying to define an authentic postmodern Christian witness are stressing – namely that the best evangelism and gospel explication is relational.

Nathanael was no pagan. He was already on a journey of faith. He was a studious, prayerful Jew. He knew his Bible very well. He had read the Law and the prophets (v. 45). He had spent time under a fig-tree (v. 48), which was a symbol of meditation and scholarship. Jesus himself describes him in verse 47 as 'a true Israelite, in whom there is nothing false'. He even compares him with the great patriarch Jacob, by promising that like Jacob at Harran, Nathanael would see angels ascending and descending between earth and heaven (cf. Gen. 28:12–13).

But for all his religion and all his spirituality, Nathanael is slow to cotton on. For all the time spent under that fig-tree, he has not quite understood. Like many postmoderns today, he was instinctively religious. He knew *about* the Messiah, but knowing *about* him was not enough. He had read all the right books, but words alone would not suffice. *He had to go and see.* The gospel had to be embodied for him. He had to be *shown* Jesus. What is more, Philip had to introduce him *personally*, in the context of a relationship.

One of the great themes of the fourth Gospel is that in Jesus we see God. He is not just God's Word – he is God's Word made flesh. The invisible made visible. The divine become human. Earlier in this opening chapter, John says that in Jesus, God 'made his dwelling among us. We have *seen* his glory; the glory of the One and Only, who came from the Father, full of grace and truth' (John 1:14).

Unlike Nathanael, we today do not have the privilege of seeing Jesus 'in the flesh'. In the words of the Nicene Creed, we declare that, 'On the third day he rose again; He ascended into heaven, and is seated at the right hand of the Father.' As I have shown, more conservative evangelicals have often taken this as a pretext for emphasising verbal over visual or demonstrated witness. But Jesus has not left the world without any visible reminder of his life! St Paul tells us in 1 Corinthians chapter 12 that the *Church* is now the visual representative of Jesus on earth. He even goes so far as to call it his body! In a very real way, all Christians are visible representatives of Jesus. We must all embody his truth in our lives, as well as in our words.

Later in this Gospel of John, Jesus prayed for his disciples as he prepared to die on the cross. He said: 'May they be one; as you, Father, are in me, and I in you; so also may they be in us, that the world may believe that you sent me' (John 17:21). That prerogative still applies. Our witness and our teaching can be expressed in words. But that will never be enough. The evangelistic impact for which Jesus prayed also depends on the Church's visible and practical demonstration of what the gospel is. This may not necessarily imply 'nation state' ecumenism, but it cannot merely mean 'spiritual' unity. It must in a very real sense mean physical, enacted unity. In the visual and pragmatic culture of postmodernity, this point simply has to be acknowledged if the Church is to be credible in its mission and teaching.

Having said all this, there is clearly a danger of confusing the means with the end. A while ago, I had the pleasure of preaching at St Paul's Cathedral. In such a magnificent setting, it is not hard to *see* the glory of God. Nonetheless, for all its visual grandeur and beauty, I made the point that St Paul's is but a pointer to something else. That something is a relationship with Jesus. Whatever form it might take, postmodern evangelicalism cannot neglect this end. It cannot allow itself to get so caught up in the mechanics of 'process' evangelism that it forgets where the process must lead. To do so would be to take the 'evangel' out of 'evangelical'. It would also be to risk denying people the marvellous realisation of Nathanael when he declared of Jesus, 'You are the Son of God.'

12

ETHICS AND SOCIAL ACTION

Is Body-Piercing Biblical?: Personal Morality in Evangelicalism and Postmodernity

Shortly after I joined it, contributors to the alt.worship mailing list on the Internet began to debate the ethics of body-piercing. Most thought it was just fine, but many of those from evangelical backgrounds commented on the disapproval it had aroused in their churches. I am open to correction, but I cannot think of a biblical text which directly rules out this practice. After all, even very conservative evangelical women have their earlobes punctured, and in many tribal cultures it would hardly conflict with Pauline notions of modest attire (cf. 1 Tim. 2:9; 1 Pet. 3:3–6). Perhaps it is more a question of context and degree: the postmodern fashion for nose-rings and eyebrow pins can be quite disconcerting if you are not used to it. There is also a certain 'guilt by association': face-studs and the like often serve as an emblem of urban club culture, with all the drug abuse and promiscuity that implies. At the very least they signify rebellion and a departure from social norms – things with which evangelicals have often struggled.

For many evangelicals, body-piercing would represent one among several 'private' moral issues which occupy a blurred zone between outright unacceptability and cautious approval. As we have seen, moral ambiguity is a watchword of postmodern culture, and though even post-evangelicals seem unlikely to embrace the thoroughgoing relativism of, say, Michel Foucault or Richard Rorty, it does appear that the list of evangelical 'dos' and 'don'ts' has changed somewhat over the years. Dave Tomlinson makes this point when he recalls that during the twentieth century, mainline evangelicalism has shifted from condemnation to assimilation on a number of issues including theatre, cinema, drinking, Sabbath work, Sabbath sport and Sunday papers.[1]

No doubt Tomlinson has a point when he suggests that taboos which once appeared absolute and biblical turn out in retrospect to have owed more to cultural convention. Then again, not all the examples he cites fall so readily into this category. Swearing, for instance, has been around longer than Christianity itself,[2] and though warnings against it can be found in Scripture (Eph. 4:29), it has always been controlled *outside* the Church as well as within it.[3] Even in secular postmodernity, restrictions on its use in the media stem more from a desire to respect the feelings of others than from nostalgia for a 'purer' past. Perhaps it has been unrealistic of evangelicals to deny this verbal safety-valve as completely as they have. Perhaps many would be shocked by the fruity prose of Martin Luther, or even by St Paul's original Greek (cf. Gal. 5:12, Phil. 3:8). Nonetheless, curbing our expletives has at least as much to do with loving our neighbour and setting an example as with stuffy conservatism. I say this with feeling: it is not so long ago that my three-year-old son returned from his inner-city nursery mouthing the 'f'-word. Evangelical or not, most parents would become very moralistic in such circumstances!

A more obvious corroboration of evangelical ethics comes in the area of smoking. Tomlinson links smoking to the drinking and gluttony of which Jesus was accused, and implies that charges against it are just as misguided.[4] But this ignores the fact that whereas alcohol and food are not *in themselves* damaging to health, the secular medical community has long warned that nicotine is highly addictive and directly linked to cancer. Tomlinson also ignores the harm caused by passive smoking, which again raises the issue of respect for others. Indeed, pressure groups, local councils and companies have done far more than the Church to stigmatise smoking in the postmodern world.

Sexual Ethics in Postmodernity and Evangelicalism

Nowhere is the tension between 'relative' and 'fixed' views of private morality more keenly felt by evangelicals than in the realm of sex and sexuality. There has undoubtedly been some movement here. In the 1870s, the American Young Men's Christian Association (YMCA) lobbied Congress to prohibit the distribution of contraceptives and birth-control information. This was duly enshrined in the Comstock Act of 1873. Today, Protestant evangelicals take contraception for granted. Currently, around half the main British evangelical paperbacks on sex stop short of condemning masturbation outright. The official line was much more clearly opposed when I began to embrace evangelicalism twenty years ago.

Precedents like this have prompted some to push for a change of attitude on other sexual issues – issues about which society at large has become more tolerant. The most obvious examples are sex before marriage and homosexual practice. In *The Post-Evangelical*, Dave Tomlinson hints that authentic postmodern Christianity will accept such behaviour as long as it forms part of a committed, stable relationship.[5] This is not the place to rehearse the whole biblical debate on such matters: there is a truckload of detailed exegesis available elsewhere.[6] What I will say is that a good deal of work supporting the more 'open' view is driven not so much by pure textual analysis as by postmodern ethical reductionism.

Granted, marriage is defined in Scripture more by a sexual relationship than by a particular form of ceremony. Granted, the rising tide of divorce does call for a re-examination of marital stereotypes. Granted, marriage has often been used by men to suppress women. But to reduce it as Tomlinson does to lowest common denominator values like 'love, commitment, faithfulness and responsibility'[7] is misleading. As he uses them, these are vague concepts unqualified by the incontrovertible fact that Scripture defines marriage as an exclusively heterosexual institution, and links it to a covenant pledge which is not only sincere, but lifelong (Gen. 2:24; Matt. 19:6). In these promiscuous, individualistic, short-term times, it is quite deluded to suppose that if the Church redefined marriage purely as sleeping or living together, marriage would become more stable or healthy as a result.

Words like 'loving', 'committed', 'faithful' and 'responsible' are often also used by those who seek the ordination of practising gays and lesbians. Over the past few years, my own United Reformed Church has begun seriously to entertain the possibility of allowing homosexuals in 'a stable, long-term relationship' to become ministers.[8] The Methodist Church has followed a similar course, and the Church of England may well do so soon. In a book compiled by the URC Caucus of the Lesbian and Gay Christian Movement,[9] this policy is urged through appeals to an ethic which owes more to the Beatles circa 1967 than the witness of Scripture. One contributor writes, 'Jesus's actions tell me that no rule is sacrosanct except the rule of love.' For someone else, 'Gay sex is certainly not wrong, provided you have a commitment to and concern for your partner . . . The relationship must be right and caring, but not necessarily heterosexual, as long as there is love, clear, clean and equal.' The authors conclude by affirming 'long-term, committed partnerships as the ideal', but all this begs the question of exactly what is meant by 'long-term', 'committed', 'stable' and 'loving' in these contexts. Clear definitions are conspicuous by their absence! Are we talking about a form of 'serial monogamy' in which people restrict themselves to one partner at a time but may have a number of partners in their lifespan? If so, how many partnerships would be acceptable? Three? Seven? Twelve? How long is 'long-term'? Ten years? Five? Six months? What is a 'committed' relationship? One in which there is a 'commitment' to live together but allow other partners as and when? And what is 'love' if it is not supported by biblical prerequisites? Does it not simply become whatever lesbian or gay Christians make it?

John Lennon may have sung 'All you need is love', but Jesus was clear that although love may have 'summed up' God's law, it could not be used as an excuse to disobey his moral code (Matt. 5:17–20; 22:35–9). Indeed, the kind of love Jesus advocates is *inextricably* linked to specific ethical directions: 'If you love me,' he says, 'You will obey my commandments' (John 14:15–21). The apostle John adds, 'This is love for God: to obey his commands' (1 John 5:3). No doubt some Old Covenant regulations are abrogated by Jesus. No doubt his death on the cross cancels all kinds of ritual prescriptions (Heb. 9). But this does not mean that everything 'legal' is null and void. Jesus upheld God's creation ordinances (Mark 10:6–9) and reinforced the Ten Commandments (Matt. 19:17–19). More to the point, he amplified Jewish discipline on marriage, taking it to be an exclusively heterosexual institution and the sole acceptable arena for full sexual relations (Mark 10:9; Matt. 19:6).

All this cuts against the postmodern ethos. Not only is morality itself ambiguous in postmodern culture: the language used to express that morality is often elusive, slippery and incorrigible. As Gene Veith puts it, 'the fragmentation of language breeds schizophrenia. Where there are no external frames of reference, experience is reduced to "a series of pure and unrelated presents".'[10]

So instead of defining or campaigning for long-term political change, Douglas Coupland's Xers take refuge in the flux of friendships and sensations. They tell each other stories, but do not treat those stories as 'fables' enshrining universal laws of human behaviour. Insofar as they have an ethic at all, it is based on what Coupland dubs the 'Personal Tabu' – 'A small rule for living, bordering on a superstition, that allows one to cope with everyday life in the absence of cultural or religious dictums'.[11] Rules are privatised and customised. If there are codes at all, they are determined by companions and peer groups rather than by society as a whole. The only world Kevin Ford's 'New Generation' feels any allegiance to is the world of its friends.[12]

In the light of all this, it is not surprising that one of the defining motifs proposed by the gay and lesbian lobby in the churches is the motif of friendship.[13] At one level, of course, friendship is thoroughly biblical. Jesus called his disciples 'friends', and made friendship with God a feature of the New Covenant (John 15:14ff.). Even so, problems arise when friendship becomes a *substitute* for more specific ethical requirements, as it seems to for the Gay and Lesbian Caucus of the URC:

> Friendship is important to us all and is especially important to lesbians and gay men who for the most part see our relationships primarily as friendships. As friend, Jesus is the one whom we can trust and rely upon, who will not betray us, or judge us unjustly. As friend he will point out when we fail, celebrate when we succeed, laugh when we laugh and cry when we cry. This is a friend who does not cling on to us, and who loves us as we are, not as others would like us to be.[14]

This is the morality of 'Just as I am'. It may be fine for conversion, but it is hardly adequate for sanctification. There is not much obedience here, and little sense that Jesus is

Lord of life. The problem with a morality based wholly or
even mainly on friendship is that human friendships are not
self-validating: companions may care deeply about one other
yet still act immorally (see Bonnie and Clyde). What is more,
the above comment comes close to casting Jesus's friendship
with gays and lesbians in the image of gays' and lesbians'
friendships with *one another*, rather than vice versa. In true
postmodern fashion, experience precedes revelation.

These criticisms are important, but they must be qualified.
As much as it may threaten evangelical values, postmodern
sexual morality could at least remind evangelicals to view
sex *relationally* rather than *mechanically*. If it is true that
the dark side of contemporary culture depersonalises sex
(in pornography and some advertising, for instance), it must
also be admitted that modernistic evangelical approaches to
the subject have themselves often isolated it as a series of
'bodily functions' – functions which are then deemed either
'sound' or 'sinful'. But even if we disapprove of people's
sexual practice, it is vital that we do not *wholly* define them
by it, and either embrace or reject them on that basis. Even
if we regard someone as a sinner, we need to recognise that
God made them in his image, that Jesus died for them, and
that we need to love them as one sinner loving another.
Although love is dependent on law as much as grace, we
may need to learn humbly to put grace more up front. Phil
Wall illustrated this well with a moving example:

A Christian friend of mine was in a pub and got
chatting to the barman. He asked her what she did,
and she told him. She was at an evangelical theological
college. As soon as she mentioned this, he exploded
into a fit of anger. It turned out he was gay, and
had experienced terrible rejection at the hands of
evangelicals. He completely lost his temper. He was
shouting, berating the Church. My friend was stunned.
She couldn't speak. She just listened to all this pain
and hurt. When he calmed down, she was in tears. All

she could say was, 'I'm sorry.' For all that we believe homosexual practice is wrong, that may often have to be our first response.

From Private to Public Morality: the Problem of Rights

Gay rights and Christian duties

Homosexuality may be filed under 'personal' morality, but in the postmodern world it is being brought ever more into the public square. This owes a lot to its association with human rights.

In a letter dated 30 December 1994 Peter Tatchell, founder and chairman of the gay and lesbian pressure group Outrage!, challenged the Bishop of London, David Hope. Hope is a bachelor who has described his own sexuality as 'a grey area'. Tatchell wrote to him:

> It is our sincere hope that you will find the inner strength and conviction to realise the importance of voluntarily coming out as gay and of speaking out in defence of lesbian and gay human rights . . . Your openness and commitment to our human rights could help precipitate a dramatic change in Anglican attitudes and policies. No Anglican leader has ever crusaded for lesbian and gay human rights. If you take this step, you will be doing something uniquely honourable and worth while.[15]

In April 1997, Outrage! turned their fire on the evangelical Archbishop of Canterbury George Carey, disrupting a meeting at Lambeth Palace to press the 'right' of gay and lesbian Anglicans to ordination.

Peter Tatchell is not a Christian, but the defence of

homosexual ordination on human rights grounds is being made increasingly from *within* the Church. In 1985, the Fifteenth Annual Synod of the United Church of Christ (USA) affirmed 'the protection of rights without regard to . . . sexual orientation', and incorporated this into its employment practice for ministers.[16] In 1988, the United Church of Canada followed suit.[17] In each case 'sexual orientation' was taken to include sexual practice.

Despite odd hints in ancient philosophy,[18] human rights are a classic product of the Enlightenment. They were most formatively defined in the seventeenth century by John Locke (1632–1704) and in the eighteenth by Thomas Paine (1737–1809). Just as Locke believed that human nature was distinguished by the capacity for reason, so he proposed that all men and women possess certain rational 'natural rights'. These rights were seen as universal. Locke believed they were intrinsic to all people, and defined them most basically in relation to life, freedom and the ownership of property. Under Paine's influence, such rights formed the basis of the American Constitution, which holds it 'self-evident' that 'all men are created equal' and thereby have rights to 'life, liberty and the pursuit of happiness'.

In the twentieth century, 'natural human rights' have been extended and refined on a grand scale – most notably in the United Nations Universal Declaration of Human Rights (1948) and the European Convention on Human Rights (1950). Echoing Locke and Paine, the UN Declaration recognises that all human beings are 'endowed with reason', and that this reason demonstrates the 'inherent dignity . . . and equal and inalienable rights of all members of the human family'. The European Convention adopts the same philosophy.[19] These charters define a whole range of rights including rights to privacy, free association, marriage, thought, employment, racial equality, gender equality, education and – very significantly for evangelicals – freedom of religion.

Neither the UN nor the European documents specifically

enshrine the 'human rights' of gays and lesbians, but they are increasingly being inferred from other rights. When homosexuals have pressed for equal recognition in law, they have usually invoked rights to free expression, free association, privacy and protection from sex discrimination.[20] These are also the rights most often asserted by those urging the Church to ordain lesbians and gay men to ministry.[21]

But there is a massive problem in all of this. Although Enlightenment thinkers like Locke and Paine took human rights to be not only inherent but also coherent, postmodernity has highlighted the fact that rights often clash and contradict one another. To be fair, this can be detected in the more pessimistic, cynical philosophies of Thomas Hobbes (1588–1679) and Jeremy Bentham (1748–1832). Nonetheless, it has been accentuated in a postmodern world marked by growing numbers of special-interest lobbies, each asserting its particular rights in a marketplace of protest groups and single-issue campaigns. So Life and the Society for the Unborn Child stress the rights of the foetus in the womb, while numerous feminist lobbies insist on the right of the mother to choose. So ASH campaigns to ban smoking from public spaces, while FOREST fights for the freedom to use tobacco. So the Snowdrop Appeal urges Parliament to legislate against handguns, while gun clubs march to preserve them. Instead of a utopia of intrinsic human rights, we see the Nietzschean 'will to power' in full spate. As Graham Cray expressed it to me, 'The public square used to be the place of reason. It's now the place where people *use* reason to gain influence.'

Evangelicals enter this battle of rights not only in the sphere of abortion, but also when they set their own right to religious freedom against other rights. For example, although potential gay priests might argue their case by claiming a right to sexual equality in employment, in Article 18 of the Universal Declaration, and again in a Special Declaration on 'Discrimination Based on Religion' (1981), the UN upholds the right of religious bodies to observe their own teachings and practices without interference. The latter document makes it quite clear that these religious bodies have the right 'to train, appoint, elect or designate . . . appropriate leaders called for by the requirements and standards [laid down by such bodies]'.[22] In other words, they are under no obligation to appoint gays and lesbians to ministry: the right of some churches *not* to do so is as 'inalienable' as the right of others to go ahead with it!

The bitter stalemates which arise in such circumstances only confirm how inadequate human rights are as a basis for morality. On one level, of course, the modern Western concept of human rights ties in quite closely with biblical teaching. Rights to life and liberty seem to be implicit in the fact that God created men and women to live freely and be 'fruitful' on earth (Gen. 1:28; 2:16). In Deuteronomy 30:19, God charges Israel to 'choose life, so that you and your children may live'. Concern for the 'rights' of the poor, the alien and the victim run deep through the Law of Moses (Deut. 15:4ff.; Lev. 24:22; Exod. 22:21ff.). Likewise, Jesus began his ministry by promising 'good news to the poor, freedom to prisoners and release for the oppressed' (Luke 4:18).

Having said all this, the Bible itself rarely – if ever – uses the language of 'natural', 'inherent', 'inalienable' human rights. Even when it upholds what look like rights, it presents them not as products of our own autonomous reason but as things which we have a *duty* to respect because God has commanded us to do so. The moral truths of Scripture are not so much 'self-evident' as *disclosed* and *urged upon us* by God. Time and again, from the Ten Commandments to the Sermon on the Mount, the focus is on the *perpetrator* of an action rather than the *victim* of an action: upholding the rights of others obliges me to act responsibly towards my neighbour in submission to God's will. I must 'humble myself' in sacrificial love before I assert my grievances.

As I have hinted, this has implications for both sexually

active gay Christians and evangelicals who oppose their lifestyle. For gays, it will certainly mean taking the submissive, self-denying strand in biblical ethics seriously. It will mean accepting that the rights-driven morality of secular postmodern culture cannot suffice for the Church. And, yes, it will mean abstaining from intercourse just as thousands of single heterosexual Christians have done – even though they may never have pledged themselves to lifelong celibacy. But for evangelicals opposed to homosexual activity, it will mean recognising the more general rights of lesbians and gay men in society as a whole, and resisting the wanton hatreds of the past.

Let me stick my neck out and give an example of what I am driving at. British evangelicals may have grown in influence over the past few years, but we are still very much a minority group within wider postmodern society. This means that we simply cannot expect the law of the land to reflect every aspect of our own church discipline. We do not yet live in the New Jerusalem. Neither, more negatively, can we countenance putting a policeman on every bedroom door. It is unrealistic to suppose that Parliament could legislate against consenting adults going to bed together – even if we disapprove of their choice of partner. For better or worse, human beings have freewill, and the rights and laws of a democratic society can only go so far in preventing its citizens from exercising that freewill badly. In the end, we cannot legislate people into the Kingdom of God; we can only persuade them to seek that Kingdom, and pray that the Holy Spirit will convict them of their sins.

On these grounds, and as a nonconformist believer in the separation of Church and state, I see little point in the pretence of a two-year gap between the age of consent for gay and 'straight' people (eighteen and sixteen respectively). My evangelical convictions lead me to the firm belief that homosexual activity is wrong, and I have taken a lot of flak in my denomination for opposing the ordination of practising gays and lesbians. Nonetheless, believing something to be to be wrong and criminalising it are two different things. Evangelicals often forget this, and it is one reason why so many of us are so naive about the political process. I also believe that fornication, drunkenness, lying and usury are wrong, and yet I have to accept that the law does little to contain *them*. The principle of a minimum age for sexual relations is a vital and proper safeguard against the corruption of minors, but that corruption can come as readily through heterosexual paedophilia as through gay paedophilia. Both are *equally* abominable to God. I can see why certain evangelicals might hold the two-year differential to be better than nothing, and can at least understand why some view *any* 'liberalisation' of secular law as a thing to be resisted. But my point applies as much if the discrepancy were rectified upwards to eighteen as downwards to sixteen. Besides, the whole debate is muddied by the fact that lesbian sexual activity is clearly condemned by Paul (Rom. 1:26–7), but has not even been acknowledged in British law, let alone accorded an age of consent! If evangelicals want the statute book to be an instrument of revival, they must recognise the complexities which attach to such a desire.

The awkward issue of blasphemy

Another area in which the postmodern 'clash of rights' affects evangelicals is blasphemy. In 1979, the evangelical campaigner Mary Whitehouse secured a rare conviction for 'blasphemous libel' against the magazine *Gay News*, which had published a poem suggesting that Jesus was gay. She did so by appealing to a centuries-old common law which protects Christians alone. Later, the House of Lords dismissed an appeal against this judgment which had invoked the principle of free speech. It referred in doing so to Article 10.2 of the European Convention on Human Rights, which makes it clear that although 'freedom of expression' is fundamental, it is subject to 'such formalities, conditions, restrictions or penalties as are . . . necessary . . . for the *protection of the rights and freedoms of others* (my italics).[23]

Even as cases like this are won, however, the very idea of blasphemy law is being questioned.[24] Most recently, debate on it has been prompted by the 'Rushdie Affair'. After the Ayatollah Khomeni imposed a death sentence or 'fatwah' on the novelist Salman Rushdie for his allegedly blasphemous book *The Satanic Verses*, large sections of the British Muslim community and some politicians called for the extension of the law of blasphemy to faiths other than Christianity. By contrast, a majority report of the Law Commission around the same time argued that 'The imposition of criminal penalties upon such abuse or insults becomes, in our view, peculiarly difficult to defend in the context of a "plural", or multi-racial, multi-religious society . . . Here one person's incisive comment may be another's "blasphemy".' In effect, this amounted to a call to repeal the law.[25]

In 1989 John Patten, then Minister of State at the Home Office, stated that in view of the confusion surrounding blasphemy the government would be taking no steps to change the existing law. The following year, two Private Members' Bills were introduced – one to extend and one to abolish the law – but neither succeeded.[26] In postmodernity, it seems that for every assertion of religious freedom, there are moves to turn freedom *of* religion into freedom *from* religion.[27]

I may be wrong, but I do not remember evangelicals being prominent in the Rushdie debate. No doubt this was because it was (and indeed still is) an especially tricky area for us. On the one hand, we believe in the right of religious freedom. It is this that enables us to evangelise and publish. But when it comes to asserting that right on behalf of other faiths, we are more hesitant, because we believe those faiths to be misguided, or even demonic. Because we hold Jesus to be unique, it rather suits us to have a blasphemy law which applies to Christianity alone, and we are perhaps reluctant to give in to pluralism by supporting the extension of that law to Jews, Sikhs, Buddhists, Mormons and the like.

On the other side of the issue, we support the right of free speech, since this, too, allows us to maintain a public witness. But Rushdie is not a Christian, so we do not worry so much about him. Besides, he is a secular intellectual who has often expressed views with which we disagree, so we keep our heads down. Indeed, one prominent evangelical leader unforgettably told an audience of which I was a part: 'You don't need to read *The Satanic Verses* to understand where Rushdie's coming from; the title alone tells you to keep clear!'

I suspect I am one of the few evangelicals who have not kept clear. I have read the book, and the irony is that it almost anticipates the furore it has caused. One of its central motifs is the very idea of 'sacredness' in a postmodern world. Rushdie is engaged in a debate about the meaning and authority of religious texts in a pluralist setting. As far as I can see, he does not himself blaspheme Islam; he investigates the history and dynamics of blasphemy. Perhaps with all his intelligence he should have realised that the subtleties of this investigation would get lost, but this does not excuse us from ignoring his plight.

No doubt the Rushdie affair points up the problem of trying to order society on the basis of human rights alone. No doubt it exemplifies the clash of rights which is so much a feature of postmodernity. No doubt it shows how Muslims' right not to be offended conflicts with Rushdie's right to publish. No doubt, too, many evangelicals would say that if only society followed Christian rules, everything would be all right. But as things stand, that is wish-fulfilment. The plain truth is that society is *not* uniformly Christian, and we cannot bury our head in the sand until either it becomes so or Jesus returns in glory.

On the basis of biblical justice and respect for the alien, I believe that evangelicals should have supported an extension of the blasphemy law, but in order to protect artists like Rushdie should have sought its application only where a specific intent to cause outrage to religious feelings could be demonstrated. I realise that such intent can be hard to prove, but rather ambiguity in that area than no law at all – which is where things might end up if we do not break our conspiracy of silence on such matters. I also accept that, scripturally, blasphemy against a false god is not really blasphemy at all, and that there is a case for proceeding down the line of incitement to racial hatred instead. Even so, it is vital once again that we distinguish between secular laws designed to maintain peace in a multicultural society, and theological absolutes to which everyone's assent has yet to be gained (cf. Phil. 2:10–11).

If all this reiterates the tension between human rights and Christian values, it also suggests another legislative quandary for evangelicals – censorship.

Evangelicals, Censorship and *The Last Temptation of Christ*

The film

Jesus is on the cross. His whole body is contorted with pain. The camera zooms in on his face. He is swooning – visibly hallucinating. Victims of crucifixion do that: as breathing becomes more difficult, the supply of oxygen to the brain is reduced, and they begin to fantasise. The pulsating soundtrack halts abruptly. The focus shifts. We are now clearly inside Jesus's head: the territory is no longer geographical, but psychological. The world of history has given way to the world of supposition – supposition about what might actually be entailed by Hebrews 4:15: 'He has been tempted in every way, just as we are.'

A figure appears at the foot of the cross. She seems vaguely angelic. She says to the dying Christ, 'You've done enough; he doesn't want your blood.' She tells Jesus that the parables of love, peace and joy were sufficient, and that there is really no need for all this suffering. She adds that Jesus is under no obligation to regard himself as divine.

The scene changes. Jesus has come down from the cross and is getting married to Mary Magdalene. Another change, and Mary is soothing his wounds in their home. The intimacy heightens, and they have sex. Mary becomes pregnant, but dies tragically. At this point, the hallucination turns darker. The 'angel' says it was God who killed Mary, and leads Jesus to another Mary – the sister of Lazarus. The 'angel' remarks that 'there is only one woman in the world – one woman with many faces'. The second Mary marries Jesus. They have children, and he re-establishes himself as a carpenter.

One day, Jesus sees the apostle Paul preaching (remember: we are in dreamland). Jesus brands Paul a 'liar' for having misrepresented what 'actually' happened. Afterwards, Paul responds by declaring, 'I created the resurrection out of what people need.' He concludes by saying, 'I don't care whether you are Jesus or not!' and 'I'm glad I met you; now I can forget about you!'

Cut to Jesus as an old man. He is living in material comfort. In Jerusalem, however, the Temple is being destroyed. It is AD 70. Jesus's health deteriorates. He meets his former disciples on his death-bed. Judas has been fighting the Romans. There is still blood on his hands. He tells Jesus, 'Your place was on the cross, but you hid yourself in some man.' Then Judas turns to the 'angel' and questions her credentials. Jesus realises that she is, in fact, a devil. Judas remarks that 'without sacrifice, there is no salvation'. Jesus concurs.

A rush of sound and light. We are back at Calvary. The hallucination is over. Jesus regains concentration: 'It is accomplished,' he cries. The movie ends. We do not see the resurrection, but it has been alluded to several times throughout. The credits roll.

The protest

The sequence I have just described is from the leading American director Martin Scorsese's *The Last Temptation of Christ*. The film is based on a novel by the Greek writer Nikos Kazantzakis, and was made by Scorsese on a relatively low budget in 1988. When it was screened in British cinemas, many Christians objected, and evangelicals were prominent among them. The Evangelical Alliance rushed out an eight-page booklet on the orthodox version of Jesus's life, for distribution to audiences as they left the cinema. The Crown Prosecution Service was approached by a third party around the same time, but declined to initiate legal proceedings against the film.

Having been shown on satellite TV in early 1991, *The Last Temptation* was broadcast as part of a season of Scorsese films by Channel 4 on 6 June 1991 at 10.05 p.m. Prior to this first terrestrial transmission, the Independent Television Commission received a record 1,459 complaints about the film. Most of these originated from a campaign in the Roman Catholic newspaper the *Universe*, but evangelicals were again involved.[28] Following transmission, there were a further ninety-two complaints, only seventeen of which came from people who had actually seen the film.

The official response

Despite this tide of protest, the ITC deemed Scorsese's film acceptable for broadcast, as it had done for the original satellite showing. Nor afterwards did it conclude that there were grounds for intervention or censure. In its report on the matter, the Commission declared it 'did not believe that the intention of the film-maker . . . was to attack Christianity and to abuse and insult it'. It went on:

The film is controversial and undoubtedly some viewers

have taken strong exception to its showing on television. The ITC noted the conclusion of the British
Board of Film Classification, when it passed the film
for cinema release, that it was a faithful adaptation of
a novel, and not a film based on the Gospels. The film,
like the novel, does attempt to imagine the adult life
of Jesus and to deal seriously with the paradox that
Jesus was both fully human and fully God. It explores
the nature of Christ's humanity and ways in which he
might have been tempted sexually and might have been
tempted to reject his divine nature. These speculations
might be upsetting to some Christians, but there are
others who see the film as a thoughtful reflection on
Christ's life.

The report continued by stating that there had been letters and
articles written by Christians supporting the latter view. It
also remarked that 'The issues with which [the film] grapples
are those which are widely addressed in theological colleges
and seminaries.' In conclusion, the ITC said, 'Controversial
the film may be, but [we do not] believe that, in the words
of the Broadcasting Act 1990, it involves "any improper
exploitation of any susceptibilities of those watching".'

This is a fascinating case study of the dilemmas facing
evangelicals in postmodern culture. In Chapter 9, I highlighted the pitfalls for evangelicals of approaching imaginative, symbolic art in a literal way. When this approach
extends to the arena of public protest, the pitfalls become
even more precarious.

Superficially, Scorsese's film is shocking and disturbing.
It departs wildly from the biblical script. It dramatises things
which either did not happen or have no clear warrant in the
New Testament. And yet the opening titles are very clear:
'This film is not based on the gospels,' they say, 'but upon
[a] fictional exploration of the eternal spiritual conflict.' This
is more than a thin excuse to titillate and offend. It is a clear
signal that the film has been composed as a *theological*

narrative rather than as a *linear, temporal* narrative. Scorsese is concerned more with ideas about Jesus than with mere facts about Jesus. Like Kazantzakis, he is more interested in the *personality* of Christ than his *biography*. The result is more collage than reportage, more episodic than journalistic, more postmodern than modern.

As I have already suggested, and as the ITC report confirmed, the hallucination sequence which dominates the end of the film is a serious exploration of a biblical truth – the truth that Jesus experienced very human temptations. Since he was revealed at his most human on the cross, Scorsese depicts a delirious Christ imagining what for him would have been the most seductive temptations of all: renouncing his divinity, leaving sacrifice to others, settling for marriage, family, home and career, and living a long, secure life. No doubt it is uncomfortable to see Jesus in a sex scene, but the main point is not so much sexual as psychological: just as when Satan tempted him in the desert, Jesus could have chosen easy pleasures – but he did not. What Scorsese depicts in this dream sequence is everything Jesus *resisted*. No half-attentive viewer could miss the obvious signposts from fact into fantasy and out again. Scorsese's camera 'enters' the mind of Jesus, explores it, and then pans back with a jolt to the harsh physical world of crucifixion.

The ITC were also right to say that the issues explored by Scorsese are commonplace in academic theology. What they did not point out, however, was how conservative Scorsese's view of such issues turns out to be! Indeed, Scorsese implicitly condemns many liberal and radical views of Jesus by including them in a fantasy imposed on him by the devil. Anyone who misses this detail misses the whole point of the end of the film. Certainly, it is suggested that Jesus need not have been God incarnate; that the atonement need not have been sacrificial or propitiatory; that Jesus had sexual relations with women; that he did not die and thus was not raised, and that Paul 'mythologised' him. But these suggestions are identified as Satanic temptations *overcome* by Jesus, rather than as actual features of his life.

The implications

Despite the analysis I have just offered, many might still question why Scorsese felt the need to delve into areas which Scripture itself merely hints at. Of course we know Jesus was tempted 'in every way', but do we have to have graphic visual speculation on what his temptations were? Just as they were private to him at the time, should they not remain private now? This point lay behind the reaction of Roger Forster, whose Ichthus congregations had participated in the protest against the film when it first came out. He told me, 'Despite the fact that we live in a postmodern world, ordinary people don't know it yet: they still think things are either true or false. If something is put over as a reconstruction of what *could* have happened, rather than what *did* happen, they get confused. They think this is what Jesus actually did and said.'

If Forster is right, the analysis of the film which I have given here would go right over the heads of most viewers. But is this really the case, and even if it is, what are the implications for regulation and censorship? Forster himself would not go so far as to ban such films altogether. He confirmed when we spoke that Scorsese had a right to make his movie, but that access to it should be restricted in the same way that other potentially offensive material (e.g. pornography) is restricted to particular outlets. He recognised that the film's '18' certificate and distribution to selected theatres imposed a degree of restriction, and so had supported the EA's campaign of protesting *outside* cinemas *after* screenings. Gerald Coates took much the same line. Both were far more concerned, however, about the influence of terrestrial TV in such matters. Coates worked in advertising before moving into full-time church leadership, and had formed his views out of that experience: 'My whole job was to encourage people to buy a product in thirty to sixty seconds of airtime. I know how television images can persuade. Of course we have to be careful about curbing writers and artists, but there is a sensible debate to be had about what we do and don't find acceptable.' On similar grounds, Forster told me, 'The problem is that, for many, TV has come to be seen as offering authoritative statements about things, even while the truth or falsehood of those things gets blurred by the medium. Responsible TV would not show *The Last Temptation of Christ,* because it confuses and doesn't help people to know what are the authoritative statements concerning Jesus.'

At the ITC itself, these views are well understood, but seriously questioned. Keen to explore the Scorsese issue further, I spoke to Rachel Viney, Religious Broadcasting Officer at the Commission. She told me, 'My own background is an evangelical one, so I think I can see where these complaints are coming from. It's not my chosen path now, but I do have a lot of experience of what causes offence in that particular community.' For all this, she was sceptical about the Forster/Coates line on TV transmission: 'So much depends on what people mean by "availability" in the context of programming. *The Last Temptation* was shown at 10.30 on a weekday night and is a very long film; you'd really have to have been pretty motivated to watch it.' Viney went on to point out the context of the broadcast – that it had formed part of a season of Scorsese films, and was thus not shown in isolation.

According to Viney, the ITC is not convinced by the argument that since a more secular society is forgetting the Christian story, TV should steer away from unorthodox or 'misleading' versions of that story. 'The problem with this view,' she told me, 'is that the media are not simply there to represent church groups! The commercial companies in particular are there to satisfy an audience which reflects all religious convictions, and none.' She then made a point which goes to the core of the postmodern evangelical problem: 'There seems to be an attitude among some evangelicals which says, "We don't want to see this, and we don't want anyone else to see it either"! But the majority of the population would say, "Who are you to make that decision on our behalf?"'

Again, this brings us back to the distinction between moral condemnation and criminalisation. In a pluralistic, postmodern society, can Christians honestly expect all their ethical absolutes to translate into law?

Clive Calver thinks not, but he still insists that broadcasters fail to give evangelicals a level playing-field. He told me:

> I have no problem with the actual showing of films like *The Last Temptation of Christ.* I do not pretend that you can legislate exclusively for Christian values in a non-Christian world. But I do have a big problem with the arrogance and bigotry of Channel 4, which did not allow a response from the churches. I can cope with unorthodox views of Jesus being screened on TV, but I want the chance to debate the issues afterwards, and to put the orthodox view. Sadly, that happens far too little.

Having said all this, some of the evangelicals I met did not reckon *The Last Temptation* to be particularly immoral, anyway. Graham Dale thought it a challenging and important film. He told me: 'I found the whole evangelical reaction rather crass. I know of a doctor who phoned in to complain about it, not because he had seen it but because a vicar had told him to. We can appear really naive over things like this.' Nick Mercer reflected that 'Many of the evangelicals who protest at representations such as Scorsese's have a hard time with the full humanity of Jesus.' He illustrated this with a typically risqué anecdote: 'I once addressed a men's meeting at which I dared to suggest that, like the rest of us, Jesus woke up in the morning with an erection. It outraged people! And yet I went on to stress that if he hadn't, he wouldn't have been fully male.'

Perhaps not surprisingly, Dave Tomlinson had also been embarrassed by evangelical reaction to Scorsese's film: 'Imagination is treated with profound suspicion by many evangelicals, and *The Last Temptation* is an imaginative construction.' He then went on to make an intriguing point about the work of Frank Peretti, whose graphic novels of demonic warfare in small-town America have been a massive hit with the more charismatically minded: 'Peretti's books are equally fantastic and unfactual, but people often seem to take them quite literally. No doubt it's because Peretti doesn't threaten them, because he confirms their worldview, whereas Scorsese challenges that worldview very deeply.'

Personal reflections

My own view is that *The Last Temptation of Christ* was probably a bad target to pick. I doubt whether it would convert anyone, but that in itself is not a reason to ban it. The fact that so many of those who complained about it had obviously not seen it hardly strengthens the evangelical case. I realise that you do not have to put your hand in the fire to know it will burn you, but Scorsese's film is a good deal more complex and subtle than fire. Those who would seriously criticise it need to watch it. My exposition of it may be unduly generous, but I have offered it here as one example of how evangelicals might deal with a postmodern artwork.

I do recognise, of course, that other artistic treatments of Christian subjects may have less to commend them. I have argued that *The Last Temptation* is neither pornographic nor blasphemous, but this is not to deny that other so-called art may come much closer to porn and blasphemy.

The Need for an Informed Ethic

In November 1996, the European Court of Human Rights refused to overturn the decision of the British Board of Film Censors to withhold a certificate from Nigel Wingrove's short film *Visions of Ecstasy*. Wingrove shows St Teresa of Avila acting out a series of sensual visions, in which she embraces, kisses and licks the wounds of the crucified Christ. The circumstances of the ban mean that I have only seen parts and stills of the film, but even these suggest that Wingrove has considerably sexualised the (admittedly ecstatic) visions of the real St Teresa. Unlike Scorsese, he appears to have 'ironed out' complexities of his source material, recasting Teresa's medieval spirituality as late-twentieth-century eroticism, and filming it accordingly (orgasmic close-ups and back-lit clinches included). It certainly appears clichéd and crude in the manner of much contemporary pornography. Its depiction of Christ is hardly rounded in the way Scorsese's is – the figure on the cross may be human, but he functions as little more than an blank object of desire.

Martyn Eden, the Public Affairs Director of the Evangelical Alliance, thinks the BBFC and European Court were right to acknowledge that blasphemy still has a legal dimension. Shortly after the case he wrote:

Freedom of speech is an important element of democracy, which we should treasure. Our own freedom to evangelise depends on it. Every restriction on it has to be justified. Even so, we do set restrictions against slander, libel and racism, and rightly so. For similar reasons we need a blasphemy law. The law makes it an offence to revile Jesus Christ or treat him contemptuously. This is not to protect God so much as ourselves. Jesus is not just an idea for artists to manipulate for their own ends, He is a living person around whom Christian lives are centred. The law protects believers from a deeply hurtful violation.[29]

This argument has an internal logic, but I cannot help thinking that in the postmodern world evangelicals will need as much to develop a coherent aesthetic as to hope that the courts will protect them from 'hurtful violation'. For every banned film like *Visions of Ecstacy*, there will be others passed which could do as much to dishonour God, and we must get ourselves equipped to put informed but robust arguments against them *once they are in the public domain*. The period 1996–7 alone saw certificates granted to David Cronenberg's *Crash*, which implies that car accidents could enhance sexual pleasure, and *Kids*, which depicts an endless cycle of juvenile intercourse. Much as our first instinct might be to get such things outlawed, it is at least as important that we offer persuasive critiques of them when they go on display. If it *had* been released, Wingrove's obscure little film would probably have sunk without trace, or else been written off as plain bad moviemaking. Developing and articulating a robust theology of the arts might help us more in the long term than cheering from the sidelines when the odd ban goes our way.

But what I am suggesting has a positive, as well as a negative, side to it. Postmodernity may at times exalt the wanton, the superficial and the banal, but this need not always be the case. Sometimes, the postmodern divergence from literal representation, linear plotting and documentary storytelling can open up new perspectives on Christian themes. If we do not realise this, we may miss the profound theological depth of better films than *The Last Temptation* – of Krystov Kieslowski's *Dekalog*, for instance, or Lars von Trier's *Breaking the Waves*. We must not mistake the blasphemous for the unconventional. That, after all, is the error the Pharisees made with Jesus.

Evangelicals and the 'New Morality'

Another good reason for developing an informed rather

than a merely censorious outlook is that the tide may be turning in our favour. Even as channels of communication are liberalised and deregulated, society at large seems to be recovering a desire for moral values and standards. In recent times, the senseless murder of Jamie Bulger, the massacre of sixteen children and their teacher at Dunblane, and the case of the stabbed headmaster Philip Lawrence seem to have galvanised British people into a new yearning for decency and restraint. No longer is it just feisty evangelicals like Mary Whitehouse who are saying that things have gone too far. Links between screen sex and violence and real immorality continue to be debated, but Bulger's young killers at least watched horror videos rated way above their age group.

Even those with a vested interest are questioning what is shown and permitted. Bruce Gyngell, Managing Director of Yorkshire–Tyne Tees Television, told an audience of media executives in June 1996 that some of ITV's late-night programming would previously have been allowed only in Soho clip joints, while even peak-time dramas subjected viewers to an unremitting diet of violence. 'In the past five years,' he said, 'there has been a steady corrosion of values. A medium that once celebrated all that was positive and good in our culture is now beginning to denigrate [it].'[30] Gyngell's views echoed a similar debate in the USA, which had been boosted by the film critic Michael Medved's bestselling book *Hollywood and America*, a savage critique of the film industry's attachment to sex and violence.

These may turn out to be little more than 'straws in the wind', but there are more general signs of a new moral mood. In the Labour landslide election of May 1997, the veteran BBC war reporter Martin Bell stood as an 'anti-sleaze' Independent and overturned a massive Conservative majority in Tatton, Cheshire. He had run against the sitting MP, Neil Hamilton. Hamilton had been charged with serious corruption, including receipt of cash for asking questions in the House of Commons – an allegation which had been made against several other politicians in the preceding months.

Throughout 1996–7 the press, radio and TV were full of discussion about ethics, and the incoming Labour government included a Christian Socialist bloc larger and more active than at any time in living memory.

Apart from laws to ban handguns and combat knives and a curb on the distribution of violent videos to the young, very little of this 'new morality' has been enshrined in the statute book. It is out of keeping with postmodernity to legislate for ethics from the centre. And yet in the postmodern marketplace of ideas, it does seem that recognisably Christian values have come back to prominence. Whether or not this trend continues, evangelicals find themselves with an opportunity to make more of an impact on the conscience of the nation than for some considerable time.

Given such an opportunity, it will be crucial to present morality as something which is more than simply private. Neither can we be content with the odd gagging order on a film or video, or even with our continuing (and quite proper) fight against abortion. I have already mentioned the resurgence of evangelical social concern in the last twenty years. But for all its achievements, this has tended to be pragmatically focused on specific needs and issues. Now, the new climate presents evangelicals with the chance to develop a more coherent social ethic – one which may be received more sympathetically than for many years.

New Models of Social Action

Towards an evangelical social strategy

The changing moral mood is very apparent to Fran Beckett. She is the Chief Executive Officer of the Shaftesbury Society. The Society is named after the great Victorian evangelical reformer Lord Shaftesbury, and continues his work of support for the disabled, the disadvantaged and the poor. Although not all the Society's staff are Christians, Beckett herself serves on the Executive Committee of the Evangelical Alliance and helps lead an Ichthus congregation in South London. As we talked in her office, she told me:

> It's fair to say that we don't do a lot of talking about social action here; we do it. In fact, hitherto we've never done much coherent thinking on social policy issues. But now we're setting up a public policy working group within the organisation, so that we can develop a shared understanding of key political decisions and how they impact what we're trying to achieve. We're still very activist, but we're becoming more strategic.

Without doubt, the Shaftesbury Society has seen the need to address what Beckett described to me as 'the causes, rather than just the consequences, of social change'. Specifically, she singled out one 'cause' above all others which needs to be taken up by evangelicals as a matter of urgency: 'I long for evangelicals to develop models in response to the progressive dismantling of the welfare state. Evangelicals are really not grappling with this. We seem simply to be acquiescing to it. We have been remarkably quiet, for example, about recent housing legislation.'

As she has begun to think more strategically on these issues, Beckett has seen clear connections with the shift from a modern to a postmodern world: 'From my perspective, postmodernity is manifested as the increasing fragmentation of society. It means more competition for resources in the care and social work sectors. It also means having to "tout for business" as social services are privatised.' As Beckett sees it, many of the people with which Shaftesbury deals have their roots in another key facet of postmodern life: 'The growth of individualism and social mobility has affected us very directly. The mushrooming need for care provision among older people is a good example. It is now the exception rather than the rule that older people are supported by the family within home or the community.'

If postmodern trends have affected those areas of the community in which the Shaftesbury Society works, they are also impinging on the organisation of the Society itself – as well as on other Christian care agencies. Whereas church bodies have long relied on volunteer labour drawn mainly from housewives and the retired, the competitive culture of postmodern care has brought increasing 'professionalisation' to the sector. Shaftesbury's payroll has grown to 1,700 while the relative proportion of voluntary workers is quite low. Beckett sees this shift reflected more widely:

> It has created a very live tension in the whole social action arena. Local authorities want higher quality work, and that means a more professional emphasis. But they want that work at an ever lower cost, which is where the volunteers come in. We at Shaftesbury are committed to excellence, but we're also committed to forming appropriate partnerships with local churches, and working with the volunteers they've got on the ground.

In Chapter 3 we saw how Holme United Reformed Church has managed to integrate professional community care with its ongoing congregational life. Although Alan Evans is a deeply pastoral man who puts the Bradford church's worship and prayer at the centre of everything else that is done, he is also something of a power-broker. As well as helping to attract a grant of £37 million to the area from the City Challenge initiative, Evans has learned how to network: 'One of the advantages of being in post a long time is that you get asked to do things you wouldn't otherwise get asked to do. For the last six years, I have chaired the Executive of the Estate, which is an elected body of twelve people. I also head up the community council, which is a gathering of key professionals.'

Evans's social pragmatism has roots which go back not least to Shaftesbury himself. In more recent times, however, his style of community work has tended to characterise liberal churches more than evangelical ones. As he put it: 'When I started out here, I was heavily criticised by evangelicals who said that I was going off the rails. But then, there have been those from the opposite side who've said, "Isn't it a pity he spoils everything with his evangelicalism?"'

In a postmodern context, the polarity described by Evans is likely to become ever more meaningless. In a culture where 'the state' can be relied on less and less to handle 'social work' while the Church gets on with 'saving souls', Holme's blend of social engagement and evangelical faith provides a model for the way ahead. As Stanley Grenz has put it, 'The Church is far more than a collection of saved individuals who band together for the task of winning the lost, for the programme of God moves beyond the salvation of the isolated individual. The divine programme overflows the individual to encompass social interaction. And it moves beyond the isolated human realm to encompass all creation.'[31]

Much as evangelical clergy and congregations might resist the idea, postmodernity will force them increasingly to become what Rob Frost calls 'missionary entrepreneurs' – combining visionary outreach programmes with well-managed professional care projects.[32] As the resources of the historic denominations dwindle and the welfare state becomes relatively less dominant whichever party is in power, it will be less possible for churches to rely on institutional safety nets – whether ecclesiastical or governmental. While avoiding ungodly competition with other churches, they will have seriously to engage the 'social care market' if they wish to develop a holistic mission for the twenty-first century.

A new kind of evangelical education?

On Well's Way in London's Camberwell stands the Ichthus primary school. A small establishment with just ninety pupils, it takes children from reception to year Six. The maximum class size is seventeen. Although the majority of its intake is local and drawn from unchurched backgrounds, it is one of a growing number of independent evangelical schools which have either 'opted out' of the state's system of 'common schools'[33] or applied for special grant-maintained status from the government.[34] These strategies could well be seen as examples of evangelicals embracing postmodern pluralism. Indeed, evangelical educationalists routinely refer to the latter approach as the 'structural pluralist model'.[35] Trevor Cooling has traced the philosophy behind such approaches as follows:

> Educationalists have, in the past, rested the case for the common school on one main foundation, namely the Enlightenment idea that human beings share common knowledge which is independent of disputed beliefs. Knowledge is considered to have universal authority, whereas belief is a matter of personal choice . . . The Enlightenment foundation, however, has been eroded by developments in the theory of knowledge. Many educationalists would now agree with the statement that 'culture is a window, not a cell', meaning that we learn through our beliefs rather than independently of them . . . Some Christians are therefore arguing, rightly in my opinion, that all knowledge is religious in the sense that we cannot know anything without holding fundamental beliefs about the nature of reality.[36]

This, of course, is one aspect of postmodern perspectivism which may redound to evangelicals' benefit. Cooling continues:

> Some commentators are now saying that the common school is a redundant concept, because it is parasitic on the Enlightenment model of knowledge and the idea that schools can be neutral. They argue that some

framework of beliefs has to be assumed if we are going to be able to teach anything. The key question in a plural society is 'Whose?' The major objection to common schools in the current context is that it is the beliefs of humanistic liberalism that are being imposed on everyone else. Evangelical Christians find this objectionable and protest against it as an infringement of religious liberty. Non-Christians, in turn, find any attempt to reinstate Christianity as the assumed belief system objectionable. It seems that whatever beliefs are assumed, imposition is inevitable . . . The only way forward for common schools which does not entail imposition may seem to be to find some minimal set of beliefs upon which it is in fact possible to obtain agreement. A major criticism of these 'low doctrine' schools, however, is that they provide a low-value education. Education should offer youngsters a vision for life. Common schools deprive everyone equally of a high set of binding beliefs and values on which to base their lives.[37]

The Ichthus school largely bears out the arguments summarised by Cooling – although not every concept was defined when it began. Roger Forster told me: 'We set it up as a response to a need, rather than as an embodiment of a definite philosophy. As so often with evangelicals, we're activists. We do it, and then we start to work out our theology!'

Ichthus had seen inner-London state schools failing local children, and had taken advantage of recent moves towards autonomy and devolved power in education to strike out on their own. Forster continued: 'The first big state education project took place in Nazi Germany, and it was a very serious and dangerous thing. If there's not a way of challenging the monopoly, that danger can re-surface.' He warmed to his theme: 'I don't believe it's right for the state to take our children away from us and – let me be provocative – make their lives thoroughly miserable. I've never gone along with the line that we stand by and let any government offer as much bad education as they can! It is our responsibility to educate – a responsibility given by God to parents and spiritual leaders within the community.'

Despite all this, Forster challenges the idea that the Ichthus school is a 'sell out' to postmodernity – a compromise pact with the moral relativism of society at large:

> We didn't base our school on postmodern plurality as such. We didn't set it up on the basis that we, like everyone else, had a right to do what we liked. We based it on the belief that God is Father, creates family, creates relationships and the responsibilities which go with them. This is, of course, a view which postmodernists don't like. We do stop our kids misbehaving because we've got a clear *mandate* to do so. We are reflecting God's desire to bring order and authority into children's lives.

One feature of the school which mitigates accusations of sectarianism is its generous acceptance of children from non-Christian homes. Forster was keen to stress this: 'Non-Ichthus parents are absolutely thrilled that their kids can get this kind of education,' he told me. Nor is it only Ichthus who have experienced such a reaction. Many more traditional, state-funded church schools are inundated with applications from parents who have lost faith in the 'common' system, and there is growing concern about those who register on parish rolls, have their children baptised, or start attending church purely in order to secure a place at a local Christian school.

Even when they encourage mixed intakes, however, one cannot help wondering at the longer-term implications of projects like the Ichthus school for postmodern evangelical witness. Having considered the arguments for independence, Cooling suggests four main reasons why they may not be so attractive. First, he argues that while they may make an impact on small numbers of children in a few areas, independent Christian schools are unlikely to have a major effect on society at large, where the vast majority of children still attend common schools. Only in common schools, he contends, can Christians realistically promote 'co-operation and harmony between people of different communities'. He adds soberingly: 'We should never assume that a Bosnia could not develop in Britain.'[38] While such a scenario may seem very distant, Lesslie Newbigin raised a parallel which is much closer to home: 'Even certain Muslims I know do not want to go down the independent road for fear of reproducing the Northern Ireland situation, where segregation in schools has contributed to the mutual incomprehension of Catholic and Protestant.'

The second argument for common schools promoted by Cooling is that they offer a context in which Christians can be 'active in promoting the good of other people as part of their evangelistic concern to incarnate the gospel'. Although it is easy to see how this view could be criticised as a 'low doctrine' descent into works-righteousness, it is one with which certain other evangelicals agree. Rob Frost told me that although he understood the move towards evangelical schools, 'I have a deep unease that it's not enough about salt and light, that it's not sufficiently "in the world".' Nick Mercer concurred: 'What would happen to society if all Christian parents took their children out of state schools, and all Christian teachers left the state sector to teach them? When I was a teacher, it was a great privilege to stand in front of hundreds of non-Christian pupils week by week.'

Third, Cooling contends that common schools allow the gospel story to be told 'to children of many different communities in a way that would not be possible in a system where schools are exclusively based on a variety of primary cultures.' But there are big questions to be asked about the *context* in which the story is related. Some evangelicals would no doubt claim that if it is simply compared to other religious stories by an uncommitted teacher with an

Enlightenment view of 'objectivity', very little of substance is likely to be achieved.

Finally, Cooling supports common schools against independent Christian ones on the basis that they 'offer a context in which Christians can seek to shape public life by involvement in a sphere of activity which impacts on the lives of most citizens'. This underlines Frost's point about 'salt and light', but I cannot help wondering at its appeal to the average evangelical parent. As Fran Beckett confirmed from the care sector, most evangelicals are not driven by a grand, integrated social policy. We respond on a pragmatic, local, *ad hoc* basis. This is how the Ichthus school emerged, and we have seen Roger Forster confirm that those who established it did not trace through all the consequences for national education.

In this respect, most evangelicals are no different from other people: they think first about what is best for their particular child. A few may get involved in local education as governors, but I doubt whether even those who believe in the comprehensive system have much of a national agenda for Christian education. While postmodernity encourages such parochialism, it presents evangelicals with a dilemma: it may allow us to change the lives of a few, but what about the rest? What about those whose secular schooling makes them so much more resistant to the gospel in adulthood?

I am sure that Ichthus feels it is doing what it can on its own patch – and independent Christian education is hardly a novel idea. Furthermore, while the quality of state education continues to vary as wildly as it does from area to area, the 'evangelical school' may turn out to be a genuine boon for those who find themselves living with failing education authorities. My own is one of the worst – Islington – and my concerns for my own young children are acute.

More generally, though, evangelicals must beware of letting the state system 'go to the devil'. Postmodern culture may allow greater independence, but state schools will continue to dominate for the foreseeable future, and we cannot afford to regard them as beyond our influence or our mission. Because of the local variations I have mentioned, this matter will need to be tackled co-operatively, and at a national level. As with the care agenda, postmodernity may force us to be more strategic and 'political' than we have been before.[39]

A new approach to politics

Evangelicals have fallen into two errors with regard to politics. On the one hand, some have taken the view that we can't do anything. They've supposed that the world is big, bad and ugly and that we ought to come out from it and be holy. At the opposite pole are the religious right, who believe that we can do *everything*. They reckon that if they get a good enough database, and deploy all the best *Reader's Digest* techniques, they can form the world in their own image.

Graham Dale was reflecting on church action in a pluralist culture. As Project Consultant of the EA's recently formed Whitefield Associates, he is trying to chart a course between these two extremes.

A canny but passionate Scot, Dale combines great commitment to his work with a heavy dose of realism. He told me:

It is a mark of political maturity to realise that we live in a world whose values we mostly don't share. Given this, we have to find common ground with people who don't recognise Jesus Christ as Lord. For Christians as much as for others, politics is the art of the possible. Too often as evangelicals, we've made it seem like the art of the *im*possible.

If some would see this as unduly pessimistic, Dale was

quick to argue that his kind of engagement requires more commitment, rather than less: 'I think we need to give genuine thought to a fifteen-year programme of political education for evangelicals. A lot of evangelicals simply haven't come to terms with political realities. It took Karl Marx thirty years to do so! This would be a good way of developing a systematic analysis of society from a biblical perspective.'

The formation of Whitefield Associates is one sign that evangelicals in Britain are becoming more engaged with the political process. It is part of a trend which takes in the related monitoring service Westminster Watch, the rise of the Movement for Christian Democracy, the increasing work of CARE and the Jubilee Centre and a number of less direct and more specific lobbying initiatives.[40] It provides a corrective to the 'ambush' mentality of much evangelicalism, which assumes that believers can 'take this nation for God' if only they say it loud and often enough.

There is little doubt that in the moral, cultural and political world of postmodernity, evangelicals have acquired a 'place at the table'. The extent to which we go on from this to influence the menu will depend on how fully we recover the social idealism and strategic thinking which distinguished the great evangelical reformers of the past. But it will also depend on a *realpolitik* which proves us, yet again, to be not only 'innocent as doves', but 'wise as serpents' to boot (Matt. 10:16).

13

BIBLE REFLECTION: ROMANS 14:14–18

As one who is in the Lord Jesus, I am fully convinced that no food is unclean in itself. But if anyone regards something as unclean, then for him it is unclean. If your brother is distressed because of what you eat, you are no longer acting in love. Do not by your eating destroy your brother for whom Christ died. Do not allow what you consider good to be spoken of as evil. For the kingdom of God is not a matter of eating and drinking, but of righteousness, peace and joy in the Holy Spirit, because anyone who serves Christ in this way is pleasing to God and approved by men.

In the late 1970s, the Monty Python comedy team made a film called *The Life of Brian*. Like *The Last Temptation of Christ*, it aroused a fair deal of evangelical protest. Although the film is careful to point out that the Brian of the title is not the real Jesus, his adventures are a comic mirror-image of those we read about in the gospels. Through mistaken identity, mass gullibility and a series of accidents, he gets hailed as the Messiah, and although he denies it, he ends up on a cross, where he sings the incongruous and now famous song, 'Always Look on the Bright Side of Life'. The Pythons were careful to make it clear that they were satirising institutional religion and authority rather than Jesus himself, and some scenes are frankly hilarious (those in the know will remember the People's Front of Judaea, Romans Go

Home and Lisping Pilate). Then again, even for open-minded evangelicals, there are awkward moments: that crucifixion scene, and a recurring hint that miracles are basically in the mind, to name but two.

When we spoke together, Rob Frost recalled having been asked to review *The Life of Brian* when it first came out. He told me:

> I wrote in the local newspaper that it wasn't blasphem-ous, and that it was very funny. But on the other side of the page was an article by an evangelical vicar condemning it. The editor put a cartoon between the two columns showing the local Odeon, with a queue of clergy waiting to see the film. In the caption, one was saying, 'If Rob Frost has seen it, so can I!'

This may be a fairly lighthearted example, but it does under-line that evangelicals who want to relate to contemporary culture face a dilemma. To get a properly informed view of that culture, they need to immerse themselves in it. And yet, even if some can cope with the experience, they may be wary about suggesting that others do the same, for fear that such people may be compromised or upset. No doubt there are those who take offence too easily. No doubt God will survive without our having to protect him from every slight. None-theless, Scripture suggests that we should be careful about putting our own cultural liberty before others' feelings.

In this passage, Paul addresses two distinct groups within the church at Rome. First, there are the indigenous Romans, converted from a pagan lifestyle marked by the worship of many gods. Then there are the Jews, with their heritage of belief in one true God and their hatred of idolatry. Here, Paul addresses the vexed question of pagan food which under Jewish law would have been considered 'unclean'. In a related passage in 1 Corinthians chapter 8, he focuses specifically on food sacrificed to idols. Obviously, this is in many ways a very distinct historical issue. But it suggests important bases for the triangular relationship between our-selves as Christians, the secular world in which we live, and the sensibilities of others.

It is clear from verse 13 that there has been a dispute between Jews and Gentiles in the church about what should and should not be consumed. The Jews have been hurt by Gentiles continuing to eat things which the Law condemns. The former pagans do not see why they, who look to Jesus rather than the dietary codes of the Old Testament, should be bound by ancient Hebrew custom.

First and foremost, Paul appeals equally to both sides. He asks them to stop judging *one another*. Later, he implores them to be tolerant, and to keep their feelings on this matter between themselves and God (v. 22). He thus accepts a degree of moral ambiguity and appeals not to an absolute ethical standard for eating, as such, but to individual con-science (cf. 1 Cor. 8:7ff.). He gives the Christians in Rome a free vote, rather than a three-line whip.

Paul himself is 'fully convinced' that 'no food is unclean in itself' (v. 14). He accepts that diet is one of a number of lifestyle issues over which God allows us a fair amount of leeway. He knows that Jesus had made it clear when teaching on Jewish food laws that 'Nothing outside a man can make him "unclean" by going into him. Rather, it is what comes out of a man that makes him "unclean"' (Mark 7:15). He suggests that much of what we find in 'secular' culture is neither inherently good nor inherently bad: it is morally neutral, and it is only our own ignorance, weakness and sin which might make it perilous to us (cf. 1 Cor. 8:1ff.). The same basic precept applies to money (1 Tim. 6:10).

One can, I think, extrapolate from this and say that much of what we do, wear, read, watch and listen to today would fall into a similar category. There is no rigid Christian dress-code, no official reading list of novels, plays and poems, no blanket prescription for what films, videos and TV programmes we should view. Some, no doubt, would find it easier if there were, but this is the way of the sect and the cult rather than the mature Church. There are certainly guidelines (e.g. Matt. 6:22; 1 Tim. 2:9), but when Paul attempts to define a rule of behaviour elsewhere, he ends up with a broad commendation of 'whatever is true, noble, right, pure, lovely, admirable, excellent or praiseworthy' (Phil. 4:8–9). Beyond what Jesus himself specified and what is laid down by apostolic authority, we must apply our God-given reason and conscience to determine which things do and do not fit these adjectives.

But then it all gets more complicated. Having established that no food is immoral in itself, Paul goes on to argue that, despite this, the sensitivities of others should come before our own ethical liberty. In 1 Corinthians 8, he says that those of more robust conscience should defer to the 'weaker brother' – the one for whom 'unclean' food is still a source of offence. Here (v. 15) he claims that to do this is to go beyond both legalism and self-assertion to the highest rule of all – the rule of love.

As we have seen, postmodernity places great stress on individual autonomy and personal choice. Insofar as it has a defining ethic, it is the ethic of self-determination. Paul allows this up to a point, but ultimately, the needs of our neighbour must come first. As he writes to the Philippians, 'in humility consider others better than yourselves. Each of you should look not only to your own interests, but also to the interests of others'(Phil. 2:3–4). There is no place in this scheme for the continual postmodern clash of rights – no room for forcing single issues at the expense of the greater good of the community.

In terms of 'private' morality, the mutual submission called for by Paul makes it difficult to predict for sure whether, say, body-piercing will be right or wrong in a particular circumstance. If a Christian has it done knowing it will offend the vast majority of his or her fellowship, it could well be mistaken, even though the fellowship's reasons for objecting may be questionable. Then again, those who would object have at least as much obligation to understand why someone might want to wear a ring or a stud in their nose, and not to ostracise them for it without discussing the matter respectfully first.

A more traditional example of the ethic of mutual submission might be drinking, which is not in itself condemned by Scripture, and which may at times be quite acceptable, but which is hardly to be advised in the presence of an alcoholic. Similarly, while my own tolerance for more difficult or disturbing art may be relatively high, there are cases when I would refrain from commending it to my congregation, for fear that some may find it unhelpful or confusing.

When we met, Brian Draper had just seen three films in a week. Working as he does for a Christian cultural magazine, he has to keep up. The three films in question were *Seven*, *Strange Days* and *Trainspotting*. All '18' certificates. All violent, full of expletives and harrowing. *Seven* is about the hunt for a serial killer whose murders reflect each one of the deadly sins. *Strange Days* depicts a virtual-reality world in which ever more extreme physical and sexual experiences are engineered and sold for kicks to passive consumers. *Trainspotting* follows the lives of a group of Scottish heroin addicts.

None of these films is a cheap exploitation flick. They all have serious points to make. *Seven* is an intense study of the nature of morality and the ethics of revenge. *Strange Days* explores the implications of cyberspace for human behaviour. *Trainspotting* offers an amoral but instructive view of the drug culture. Having said this, I am not recommending that you see them. Neither is Brian Draper: 'It was too much for me, watching them so close together,' he told me. Indeed, my guess is that many evangelicals would find them so shocking and repulsive that their gut instinct might be to call for the censor. This, however, would be to risk the kind of error made by the Jews in Rome – namely to assume that what *they* considered thoroughly 'unclean' could have no possible value whatever to anybody else, and thus to forbid its consumption by all.

On the other hand, this passage does show us one wise and informed expert offering a moral prescription to the whole community. Like a regulator, he sets limits which he trusts will serve the greater good. As things stand, Paul strongly implies a norm for all of abstinence from 'unclean' foods, and all are expected to comply. It is a norm derived not from the 'inherent' moral quality of pagan food as such, but from the universal principle of love for the weaker brother. This is not to say that love is the only law, however, and Paul has already made it clear that activities such as homosexual practice cannot be justified by it (Rom. 1:26–7). Nonetheless, it does suggest the need to create a consensual 'moral climate' within the community before individual rights can be pressed. For this reason, the food issue is as much a matter of social policy as individual conscience.

For Jews and Gentiles to co-operate in Rome or Corinth was at least as much of a challenge as evangelicals and Roman Catholics co-operating today on issues like abortion, homelessness, poverty and the future of Northern Ireland. One might even go so far as to say that it is more comparable to evangelicals working with non-Christians and secular agencies to further their concerns within Parliament, the law and society in general. No doubt, out of respect for the conscience of fellow evangelicals, it may be necessary to think hard before forging such alliances. Then again, those who are more separatist in their approach will in their turn need to concede that the plural culture of postmodernity will sometimes make it necessary to draw on 'unclean' sources to further the Kingdom of God.

This ethic of mutual submission is one of the most distinctive things which Christianity has to offer the postmodern moral marketplace. In a nation which, against the odds, seems to be searching for something more than a merely rights-based morality, evangelicals have a genuine opportunity, as they work with other Christians, to take it from their churches into the public square.

14

THEOLOGY AND DOCTRINE

But as surely as God is faithful, our message to you is not 'Yes' and 'No'. For the Son of God, Jesus Christ, who was preached among you by me and Silas and Timothy, was not 'Yes' and 'No', but in him it has always been 'Yes'. For no matter how many promises God has made, they are 'Yes' in Christ. And so through him the 'Amen' is spoken by us to the glory of God. Now it is God who makes both us and you stand firm in Christ. He anointed us, set his seal of ownership on us, and put his Spirit in our hearts as a deposit, guaranteeing what is to come. (2 Cor. 1:18–22)

Until now, I have examined the relationship between evangelicalism and postmodernity, and have then reflected on it biblically. In this chapter, I want to integrate cultural analysis more closely with scriptural exegesis. There are two reasons for this. First, we have reached the point where we need to consider the implications of postmodernity for systematic theology, which is a fusion and culmination of biblical, sociological and philosophical study. Second, the passage from 2 Corinthians quoted above suggests so many themes relevant to our subject that there is hardly a better point around which to gather the threads we have been tracing.

Changing Views of Truth

Kevin Ford tells how he once tried to share his faith with a student named Paul: 'He had a lot of questions about the reliability of the Bible, and I thought we were having a very good dialogue,' Ford recalls. He goes on: 'I had just finished my postgraduate course at that time, so I was armed with dozens of sound arguments that he could not refute. He should have been completely convinced. I had clearly "won" on debating points. But the conversation ended with Paul saying "So what?", and walking away.'[1]

Like many evangelicals schooled in modernist apologetics, Ford had assumed that his subject would either reject the gospel for lack of proof, or accept it through sheer weight of conviction. But he did neither. Instead of responding with a clear 'Yes' or 'No', he displayed postmodern ambivalence. He typified not only the relativism, but also the indifference, of our age.

Throughout this book, we have seen how even in the Church postmodernity has led to a qualification of absolute answers, grand narratives and big pictures with more local episodes, experiences and sensations. We have seen Moderators rallying people to question marks, post-evangelicals veering between a journey and a wander, evangelicals 'going for it' rather than defining 'it', alternative worshippers abandoning sermons for ambient atmospheres, neo-catholics picking and mixing liturgies, Torontoites letting manifestations speak for themselves, evangelists conflating conversion and discipleship and historic denominations blurring sexual boundaries. Some of these moves have been exhilarating and some more dubious, but all have raised serious questions about the Church's understanding and presentation of truth.

In the world at large, even if the idea of truth is maintained, it has often become a hazy, mysterious, almost Gnostic thing. *The X Files* is not only an immensely successful TV show – it has become an icon of postmodern popular culture. In it, there are truths to be discovered, but they are hidden away and kept secret by the government. They are not *revealed* truths. They are placed under lock and key because they concern phenomena which, by definition, are 'unexplained' – from UFOs to alien abductions, from extrasensory perception to occult wisdom. The *X Files* may acknowledge some kind of truth, but it is not a truth which has been disclosed; it is not accessible to ordinary people. The now famous slogan of the programme declares that 'THE TRUTH IS OUT THERE', but as far as Joe and Josie public are concerned it is a very tentative and unresolved kind of truth. It is truth followed by a question mark.

And the answer to the question is left open. It might be 'Yes', but then again it might be 'No'. The ambiguity of *The X Files* is embodied in the two FBI agents who are its lead characters. Scully is a sceptic. She wants hard, rational verification before she will say 'Yes' to anything supernatural. Muldur, on the other hand, is a 'Believer' (yes – this is the word which is used). He is convinced that his sister was stolen away by extraterrestrials when she was young, and he is driven by his faith in that truth which is 'out there'.

The makers of *The X Files* never entirely come down on one side or the other. They may lean towards the Believers, but they never totally vindicate them. The casebook is never quite closed. Everything is partial and provisional. The attitude of the show may not exactly be 'So what?', but there is a distinct feel of 'Maybe – maybe not'. When watching *The X Files* we must live as Zygmunt Bauman said we should live – with ambivalence, in contingency, devoid of anything certain.

Paul and Propositional Truth

I often wonder what Bauman and postmodernists like him would make of St Paul. Perhaps they might excuse him for being the product of a more naive and more confident time. Whatever, we can be much clearer about how they would regard those of *us* who still take Paul's letters to be the Word of God at the turn of the twenty-first century. They would probably think we were deluded 'crusaders' intent on denying an ambivalence that is staring us in the face.

We shall see that there are some aspects of 2 Corinthians 1:18–22 which fit rather well with a postmodern worldview. Even so, the overriding impression created by this passage is surely one of certain faith in a certain truth, of absolute belief in an absolute Lord, and exclusive commitment to the one true God. Where postmodernism is ambivalent, Paul is convinced. Where postmodernists say 'Yes' and 'No', he says 'Yes' – 'Yes' to Jesus Christ.

What is more, Paul does not keep his convictions to himself! He is not content with privatised religion. He will not keep his 'preferred form of life' in the closet. On the contrary, Paul is an evangelist. He is one of those 'cultural crusaders' Bauman warns us about. He wants everyone *else* to say 'Yes' to Jesus, too – even if they already worship some other god, or profess some other creed. Indeed, the historical context of this passage is one of Paul's main evangelistic journeys.

Some time before he wrote these words, Paul had evangelised the bustling Greek port city of Corinth. Many Corinthians had turned from paganism to Christianity, but there had been a lot of teething troubles in the congregation. Different factions had been vying for leadership. Someone had been sleeping with his stepmother. Someone else was suing a fellow-member. Worship had become cacophonous and disordered.

Paul addressed these problems in the letter we now know as 1 Corinthians – and he may be thinking of that epistle when he writes in chapter 2 of *this* letter about having sent a 'painful letter' to the Corinthians. After a while, he had discovered that that letter had done a lot of good (2 Cor. 7:15–16), but here he makes it clear that the difficulties

are not over yet. Although most seem to have responded
to Paul's stern words, one group in the church has deeply
resented them. That group appears to have been a party
of 'Judaisers'. These Judaisers are not the same as the
Judaisers of Galatians or Colossians. They have not been
insisting on Gentile circumcision (cf. Gal. 6:12–13) or strict
observance of the Hebrew calendar (cf. Col. 2:16). But they
do seem to have a problem with Paul's claim to be an apostle
(11:7–11; 12:11–15) – and they are looking for an excuse to
undermine him. And reading this passage, it is clear that Paul
has given them just such an excuse. It is flimsy, insubstantial
and unwarranted, but it is an excuse nonetheless.

But what is Paul's great crime? What has he done
which is so dreadful? He has changed his travel plans!
He has switched route and left Corinth out of his itinerary.
Originally, he had told the Corinthians that he would pay
them a personal visit on his way from Ephesus to Macedonia,
and then again on his way back from Macedonia to Judaea.
The precise details are more complex, but that is the gist of
things. Furthermore, because Paul's companion Titus has
gone missing (2:13), Paul has had to go direct to Macedonia
to find him, and has missed visiting the Corinthians as a
result. Obviously word has reached Paul that the Judaisers
are using this against him. They have been saying that he
is double-minded; that he cannot stick to his decisions; that
he is not a man of his word. Now in chapter 2 verse 1 Paul
admits that his diversion spared him a 'sorrowful' time in
Corinth, but here he is adamant that he was not shirking
his responsibilities. He would have come if he could, but
he had to find Titus first. His original intentions were
godly but, as it happened, God led him elsewhere. What
looks like indecision was in fact decisive submission to the
Father. Indeed, at the end of verse 17 – two thousand years
before postmodernism – Paul implies that ambivalence is
a 'worldly' thing. It is unworthy of the gospel to say in
the same breath 'Yes, Yes' and 'No, No'. Postmodern
ambivalence may be more acute and more thoroughgoing

than ancient near-Eastern ambivalence, but it is clear from Paul's words that ambivalence has always been around, and that it is not usually compatible with the Church's faith and mission.

Well, this is the context of the passage. This is the background and the intention of the author. As all evangelical exegetes are supposed to, I have sketched out the social and historical setting of the text. But as Kevin Ford's friend might say, 'So what?' What has this antiquarian record of an obscure dispute about travel plans got to do with God and the postmodern world? So Paul said he was not being ambivalent – fine – but what is the big deal?

The big deal is what Paul writes next. The big deal is that Paul does something which I was told never to do when I was training for the ministry. He theologises his personal experience. He relates his own character to the character of God. He says that it is important that he should not be accused of ambivalence because he is God's apostle – and when all is said and done, God is not ambivalent. In verse 18, Paul begins to make this link explicit. 'As surely as God is faithful,' he says, 'our message to you is not "Yes" and "No".'

What Paul is stressing here is the doctrine of Numbers 23:19 and Psalm 110:4. He is saying that 'God is not a man, that he should change his mind.' When Paul says 'God is faithful,' he means that God is *true* – true in both a moral and a philosophical sense. He means that God is true to his Word, but he also means that in and of himself, God is Truth – the source of all meaning and purpose in the cosmos. He is what Paul elsewhere described him to be: 'The One in whom we live and move and have our being' (Acts 17:28).

Now if Paul had left things here, we should have inherited a forceful assertion of absolutes. God is consistent, not ambivalent. He is Truth. In him there is no ambiguity. And no doubt this aspect of Paul's message really does stand *over against* the postmodern ethos. All the same, I cannot see how, on its own, it readily *engages* the postmodern ethos. I can still hear Kevin Ford's friend saying, 'So what?' I can still see him shrugging his shoulders and walking away. 'So you believe God is true,' he might add. 'That's nice for you. I guess a lot of Muslims believe the same kind of thing – and those Orthodox Jews at the Wailing Wall. It's old-fashioned, but I'm not going to condemn you for it. Just realise that some of us think you have to live with more uncertainty than that. And don't offend us by trying to convince us otherwise.'

If Paul *had* stopped here, we should have been left with no more than a bare philosophy of theism – a set of propositions asserting the existence of God in a fairly rationalistic, abstract way.

But Paul does not stop here. He is not content with mere assertions and propositions. He moves on from defining the character of God in philosophical terms to telling a story – the story of his encounter with God in the living person of Jesus Christ, and in the living community of the Church.

Alternative Models of Truth

Personal truth

We saw in Chapter 5 how, during the Enlightenment, evangelicals began to ape scientists in the way they framed their doctrine. Paul may affirm the certainty and consistency of God to the Corinthians, but consider this, from the Westminster Confession of 1647:

There is but one only living and true God, who is infinite in being and perfection, a most pure spirit, invisible, without body, parts, or passions, immutable, immense, eternal, incomprehensible, almighty, most wise, most holy, most free, most absolute, working all things according to the counsel of his own immutable and most righteous will, for his own glory.[2]

It reads rather like a geometrical formula, or an architectural specification. Even though it stresses that God is 'incomprehensible', it still feels compelled to define him in minute detail, and goes on doing so at considerable length beyond the extract quoted! I am not saying for one moment that this kind of propositional theology is wrong. It has its place – and we have already seen it at work in verse 18 of our text: 'God is faithful,' says Paul, 'he does not lie.' But this is not the *only* way to speak about God. Doctrinal propositions are important, but they do not tell the whole story, because the whole story of the Christian gospel includes the story of how God deals with *people* – how he relates to them, and how they relate to him both personally and collectively, both as individuals and as the Church. And this is the point at which it might be possible for Christians to dialogue more constructively with postmodern culture.

We cannot afford to be ambivalent about God, but we can afford to admit that our certainty rests on more than a series of dogmatic assertions about his being and nature. This is borne out precisely by what Paul goes on to say in verses 19 to 22. In verse 19 the apostle moves on from talking purely about God the unchanging, immutable creator to talking about the One who came from God's heart as a child in a manger; the One who walked through Palestine and spoke words of eternal life; the One who washed his disciples' feet and dignified the worst of sinners. He reminds the Corinthians that God is not distant or disinterested, as so many of their pagan deities had been. He confirms that God is more than the sum of our propositions about him. He emphasises that God has got involved with the world in a personal, intimate way, and that there is a real, human story to be told about that involvement. That story is the story of Jesus: 'For the Son of God, Jesus Christ, who was preached among you by me and Silas and Timothy, was not

"Yes" and "No", but in him it has always been "Yes". For no matter how many promises God has made, they are "Yes" in Christ.'

This, in turn, suggests another crucial aspect of truth.

Covenantal truth

From the time of Noah onwards, the Bible shows that God has revealed himself *covenantally*. He has made solemn agreements with his people, and these agreements have been the primary means through which God has decided to reveal his will and purpose to the world.

Now the covenants of God contain many truths, and in several cases those truths are absolute, universal and eternal. But the covenants of God are more than just a set of propositions. The truth they mediate is more than merely *factual* truth. The central truths of God's covenants are conveyed as *promises*. Promises are different from sheer propositions because *by their very nature* they involve a human response. Promises are made *to someone*; they are not just statements *about something*.

One of the reasons Kevin Ford's student companion said 'So what?' and walked away was because, by his own admission, Ford had set out to win an argument *about* something – the authority of Scripture – without engaging the student with the promises God had made to him *through* Scripture. Clearly, debates on biblical authority have their place, just as doctrinal statements have their place. But the language of doctrinal assertion and doctrinal argument is different from the language of divine promise, and as Tony Thiselton has demonstrated powerfully, it is the promissory aspect of divine communication which stands to offer the more fruitful apologetic in a postmodern context.[3]

Doctrinal statements largely stand on their own, as self-contained 'atoms' of truth. Covenant truths, on the other hand, far more directly implicate others. They draw us into communion with God. They challenge people to commit their whole lives to him; they do not simply try to convince them intellectually that some aspect of religion is 'true'.

When God promises the land of Canaan to Abraham in Genesis 17, he tells Abraham that Abraham also has a promise to keep. His side of the covenant is to get circumcised, and to circumcise all eight-day-old males in his family. This is a crucial element in the covenant promise – the promise of God to bless Abraham's descendants and give them a land for their possession.

In much the same way, when God makes a *legal* covenant with Israel on Mount Sinai in Exodus 19, he promises the people that they will be his 'chosen race', but he also implicates them in that promise. He does not just state the truth – he involves them in the fulfilment of that truth. He says: 'If you obey me fully and keep my covenant, then out of all nations you will be my treasured possession' (Exod. 19:5). Covenants have human conditions because they are promises which arise from God's interaction with human beings.

This human, relational quality is intensified much later, in the promise made by God to Israel and Judah in Jeremiah 31:31:

'The time is coming', declares the LORD,
'when I will make a new covenant
with the House of Israel
and with the house of Judah.
It will not be like the covenant
I made with their forefathers
when I took them by the hand
to lead them out of Egypt,
because they broke my covenant,
though I was a husband to them,' declares the LORD.
'This is the covenant that I will make
with the house of Israel
after that time,' declares the LORD.

'I will put my law in their minds
and write it on their hearts.
I will be their God,
and they will be my people.'

Maybe Kevin Ford's friend said, 'So what?' and walked
away because Kevin Ford had tried to relate God's law to
his mind, but had forgotten also to relate it to his heart. The
covenant promises of God are promises which engage the
whole person. They are more than rational proofs of God's
existence.

One of the complaints many postmoderns make about
evangelicals is that we are too attached to a 'law court'
model of God. We can see here that such a model is hardly
adequate. Indeed, if we want to be true biblicists going into
the next century, we shall need to recover and re-emphasise
the relational truth of God's covenant promises. For us as
Christians, of course, this means re-emphasising what Paul
so powerfully emphasises in verse 20: 'For no matter how
many promises God has made, they are "Yes" in Christ.'

When all is said and done, God's covenant promises
encounter us not as a code of law, nor as a stack of propositions, nor as a set of conditions. They come to us in a
person. They are embodied and fulfilled in Jesus.

When God came to dwell with us on earth, he did not
come as a book of doctrines or statutes. He came to us
as one of us. Jesus was fully God but also fully human,
and in his life and work he made it clear that if we really
wanted to know the truth, we would have to get to know
him personally. Jesus said, 'I AM the truth', but he also
said, 'I AM the way' and 'the life'. This was of a piece
with his call that we should follow him. In Jesus, God
delivered on the promises of his covenants, and in Jesus
the conditions of the covenants were fully met. Jesus knew
the truths of the Law backwards: he knew all the logical
proofs for God's existence, and he had an extremely high
view of the authority of scripture. Yet to those Pharisees

who searched the pages of scripture for propositional truths
about God, he said, 'You have never heard his voice nor seen
his form, nor does he dwell in you, for you do not believe the
one he sent' (John 5:37–8).

Relational truth

It is hugely significant for evangelicals living in postmodernity that Paul chooses to call Jesus the great 'Yes' of
God. 'Yes', too, is a relational word. Almost always, if you
say 'Yes', you say it directly *to* someone. You use it as part
of a dialogue. It is an affirmation of what someone else has
said, or a positive answer to someone else's question. More
specifically, though, the word 'Yes' can seal a promise:
'Yes, I will do that'; 'Yes, I accept your offer.' And
again, saying 'Yes' to a person or to people entails much
more than assenting to a proposition. It implies more than
acknowledging something to be true; it means participating
in that truth, and living it out in relationship. Saying 'Yes'
to someone in this case implies dedication, faithfulness and
respect.

When I said 'Yes' to my wife Mia at our wedding,
I committed myself to much more than the doctrine of
marriage. I committed myself to *her*. What is more, I did
so as part of a community, in the presence of my church
and family, within a network of relationships formed and
blessed by God. In the light of all this, it comes as no
surprise that metaphors of marriage are used elsewhere
in the New Testament to convey the kind of relationship
which exists between Jesus and his people (cf. Eph. 5:32;
Rev. 21:2ff.).

Eschatological truth

To respond to God's 'Yes' in Jesus by in turn saying 'Yes'

to Jesus is in a very real sense to leave ambivalence behind. It is an act which embraces absolute truth and absolute justice, absolute right and absolute love. Even so, we need to realise that such absolutes will not be fully or immediately present to us. Because they are embodied in a person, and because it takes time to understand people, it may be some while before we can take in the immense glory of Christ. I may have said 'Yes' to Mia nine years ago, but I am still discovering new things about her. I said 'Yes' to Jesus eighteen years ago, but I am still discovering new things about him. The truth of Christ is absolute, but it is not absolutely apparent all at once. It is what theologians call eschatological truth: it is both 'now' and 'not yet'. As C. K. Barrett says in his commentary on this text, 'God has not yet finished his work [even though] what he still has to do will be done though Jesus.'[4] Or as Paul himself puts it: 'Now we see through a glass darkly; then we shall see face to face. Now I know in part; then I shall know fully, even as I am fully known' (1 Cor. 13:12).

Another point about saying 'Yes' to a person rather than a proposition is that people can be paradoxical and elliptical in a way propositions tend not to be. My wife and I may be in a covenant relationship with one another. The 'Yes' I said to her in 1988 may be absolute and binding. But that does not mean that I comprehend why she cannot back into tight parking spaces, or why she does not like cheese. And at the risk of sounding irreverent, I have to confess that there are things about Jesus which I struggle to grasp. He may have been without sin, but that does not mean that he made everything perfectly clear. He may have been God's 'Yes' to the world, but even so, he was the one who said that he did not know when he would come again (Mark 13:32). It was Jesus who said, 'Give to Caesar what is Caesar's' (Matt. 22:21), and thereby set a puzzle for Christian economists to ponder down the centuries.

These and other areas of the gospel may be perplexing, but they need not in any way undermine the Christian claim to truth. When we respond to God's 'Yes' with our own 'Yes', it does not make us omniscient. We do not suddenly gain access to every truth there is to know. We commit ourselves absolutely to the absolute truth embodied in Jesus, but that does not mean that we have to gain immediate knowledge of absolutely everything. Christian truth is found in a promise which is fulfilled over the whole course of our lives – a promise which is worked out as we 'work out' our salvation 'with fear and trembling' (Phil. 2:12).

Paul brings all this to life in verses 21 and 22 when he writes, 'It is God who makes both us and you stand firm in Christ. He anointed us, set his seal of ownership on us, and put his Spirit in our hearts as a deposit, guaranteeing what is to come.'

In Paul's day, kings and priests were anointed for a particular task. The anointing did not fulfil that task, but it gave them the power and the authority to fulfil it in due course. A seal on a letter was also a mark of authority. It confirmed the status of the sender and the importance of the message, but the letter still had to be opened, and acted upon. In the same way, a 'deposit' was not a full payment, but rather something which secured property – a guarantee of something yet to come.

As Christians, we do not know everything here and now, but the clear message of this text is that we can know enough. If we commit ourselves now to the One who said, 'I AM the truth,' he will give us the seal and guarantee of the Holy Spirit, and we can be confident in the hope that this same Spirit will lead us 'into all truth' (John 16:13). This is a far cry from the postmodern ambivalence of Zygmunt Bauman, who has written that to live authentically as a postmodern person, 'one needs to learn to live without the hope that [supplies] . . . meaning . . . to life'.[5] It also contrasts starkly with Bauman's later remark that postmodern existence means 'living without a guarantee, with just a provisional, pragmatic . . . certainty'.[6] Evangelicals may well be pragmatists, but our pragmatism can only afford

to be exercised in the service of the purposed ends of God.
It can never be an end in itself.

Trinitarian truth

For Paul, the truth of the gospel is not simply relational,
it is *trinitarian*. In this text, God the Father makes faithful
promises, and consummates them in God the Son. These
promises then become real for us as God the Holy Spirit
secures them in our hearts and leads us towards the full
measure of divine truth.

A number of theologians from various traditions are
beginning to realise that the model of God as Trinity provides Christians with a powerful response to the postmodern
challenge.[7] It affirms the diversity, difference and mystery typically exalted by postmodernists, and yet maintains
the order, unity and finality so often denied by them. It
emphasises the importance of personhood and relationship,
yet still stands as an objective, transcendent reality – a
divine 'other'.

Ecclesial truth

For Paul, the truth of the gospel is also *ecclesial*. It is
truth which comes not just through community in general,
but through the church community in particular. Verses 19
and 20 have a strongly liturgical ring about them. First,
Paul talks about God's 'Yes' in relation to preaching and
proclamation. He says that the Son of God was 'preached'
(or 'proclaimed') among the Corinthians by Silas, Timothy
and himself (v.19). Then, in verse 20, he evokes the pattern
of communal worship in the early Church when he writes,
'And so through Christ the "Amen" is spoken by us to the
glory of God.'

Then, as now, the congregation would join in saying

'Amen' after the prayers of a church service, and by seeing divine truth as something mediated through worship, preaching and communion, Paul invites another profound distinction between purely propositional truth and the holistic truth of the full gospel. One of the great watchwords of the early Church was *lex orandi lex credendi* – the 'rule' of worship precedes the 'rule' of doctrine. Good theology springs from the true worship of God, rather than worship being parasitic upon our doctrinal formulations. After all, the first Christians worshipped well before they wrote down creeds.

There is, of course, a great danger in relying too heavily on 'spiritual experience' – and we have examined the ways in which postmodernity might entice evangelicals down this path. Nonetheless, I think it is fair to say that, overall, evangelicals have had the opposite problem. We have been so concerned to reason out every last detail of our dogma that we have neglected the beauty, movement, colour and communality of worship. We have exalted the sermon and the preacher, but we have mistaken sound exposition for profound worship. Too often, we have turned *lex orandi lex credendi* on its head. We have assumed that if only we can convince people of the reasonableness and logicality of our faith, they will surely turn to Christ. We have reckoned that if only we rehearse all our arguments well enough, we shall win the great debate of ideas and evangelise the world.

Kevin Ford thought all this, but like countless other postmoderns, his friend said, 'So what?' and walked away. The truth of the Christian faith is often rational; it can often be asserted propositionally. But this passage shows that the Christian faith is true in other ways – ways which might just have more appeal to our postmodern culture.

I must stress that the alternative models of truth suggested by 2 Corinthians 1 are not *replacements* for the propositional approach; they are, rather, *complements* to it. What is more, they are still a long, long way from thoroughgoing postmodern ambivalence. In fact, in the biblical context, they stand as a clear challenge to such ambivalence – and thank God for that. Nonetheless, for the growing numbers in the postmodern West who are responding to propositionally driven evangelicalism by saying 'So what?' and walking away, they might just prove to be a seed of joy, a ground of blessing and a source of hope.

15

SUMMARY: AGENDA FOR POSTMODERN EVANGELICALISM

As we have seen, one of the more dubious features of postmodern culture is its tendency to reduce complex issues to soundbites and slogans. For this reason, I am wary of summarising the main points of this book in a few short points. Then again, I am enough of an evangelical pragmatist to know that this approach can be a boon to discussion-group leaders, busy ministers and those who, like Billy Crystal's character in the film *When Harry Met Sally*, always read the end of a book first! In any case, I have been referring throughout to 'postmodern evangelicalism', and this gives me the opportunity to define it more sharply.

1 Postmodern evangelicals will acknowledge that the shift from modernity to postmodernity represents a major transition in philosophy and culture, and that this transition has crucial implications for Christian faith and practice.

2 Postmodern evangelicals will make an active distinction between evangelical belief and evangelical sub-culture, and will sustain a vigilant and critical view of the latter. However, unlike post-evangelicals, they will develop their critique from *within* the evangelical community.

3 Postmodern evangelicals will demonstrate a genuine

pastoral concern for those who leave the evangelical fold – not least for those who fail to find a home elsewhere in the Christian Church. Where appropriate, they will honestly re-evaluate their own ministry in the light of criticisms made by those who leave.

4 Postmodern evangelicals will demonstrably prioritise theology, and will not allow pragmatism to sideline serious theological reflection. They will be culturally adaptable, but they will not subordinate good doctrine to church growth strategies, management techniques and profit.

5 Postmodern evangelicals will entertain models of truth other than correspondence and propositionalist models. They will be especially open to personal, covenantal, promissory, relational, communitarian, discoursal, dialogical, narrative, analogical, paradoxical and eschatological models of truth, and will find clear warrant for these in Scripture. At the same time, however, they will resist thoroughgoing relativism and ambivalence, and will hold a *teleological* view of even the most mystical truths: i.e. where a given truth is not immediately available, they will still expect it to be made known by God at some future point.

6 Postmodern evangelicals will pay particular attention to trinitarian theology, seeing it as a valuable way in to the rest of theology, and to modelling community both within and beyond the Church.

7 Postmodern evangelicals will seek to develop a more thoroughgoing ecclesiology or doctrine of the Church. This will celebrate the diversity of evangelicalism, but will regard evangelical unity as something which must be practical and visible rather than merely 'spiritual'. Furthermore, it will emphasise that God's Church

extends beyond the evangelical churches. While remaining critical of much in institutional ecumenism, it will not automatically damn ecumenical ventures, and will endorse them where the cause of the gospel is served.

8 Postmodern evangelicals will cultivate a mature understanding of church history. They will readily accept that three-quarters of the Church's life has been non-Protestant, and nineteen-twentieths of it non-Pentecostal. They will cherish the work of God in other Christian traditions, even where those traditions have in other ways fallen into error. They will also be honest about the blots on the evangelical record.

9 Postmodern evangelicals will be open to a critical dialogue with postliberals.

10 While acknowledging a link between biblical form and biblical function, postmodern evangelicals will be less concerned with the formal inerrancy of Scripture than with its functional authority. In the same vein, they will see the hermeneutical task as central and not incidental to the maintenance of evangelical biblicism.

11 Postmodern evangelicals will characteristically accept that God can act in a supernatural way today. They will thus be open to the full range of charismata and to deliverance ministry where appropriate. They will not, however, define themselves by these convictions, because they will want to move beyond the old charismatic–conservative dualism towards a more holistic and socially oriented identity.

12 Postmodern evangelicals will re-explore the contemplative life. While doing so through study of past evangelical spiritualities, they will not be afraid to investigate

non-evangelical paths in the Celtic, Roman Catholic, Eastern Orthodox and other traditions. They will resist the idea that one necessarily acquires 'guilt by association' with these traditions.

13 Postmodern evangelicals will accept journey and pilgrimage as metaphors for spiritual development, but will still insist on a specific direction and destination in Jesus Christ.

14 Postmodern evangelicals will demonstrate a clear ecological awareness in their theology, spirituality and social action. They will not instantly dismiss the green agenda as 'New Age', but will instead work towards a genuinely evangelical response to it.

15 Postmodern evangelicals will value lay participation in worship. They will also value non-verbal modes of praise and prayer alongside verbal ones. In order to realise this, they may well look beyond evangelicalism to more obviously liturgical traditions.

16 Postmodern evangelicals will typically have an eclectic approach to the church service. They will adhere neither to a rigidly 'high' nor a rigidly 'low' worship culture. They will be neither uniformly 'ancient' nor uniformly 'contemporary' in style. Musical genres will be blended, as will forms of prayer and response.

17 Postmodern evangelicals will strive for a greater balance between Word and sacraments, and will tend to make more of the Lord's Supper, regarding it neither simply as a memorial nor as a mere appendix to preaching.

18 Postmodern evangelicals will be instinctively open to 'alternative worship', but will be wary of allowing it to become more of a performance than a communal act.

They will also seek to integrate innovations from youth-oriented services into standard congregational worship.

19 Postmodern evangelicals will have a flexible and adaptable view of preaching. They will value the classic expository model, but will not treat it as a badge of evangelical orthodoxy. In particular, they will develop narrative, dialogical and multi-media approaches to the sermon.

20 Postmodern evangelicals will value non-verbal expressions of truth and, while accepting the dangers of idolatry, will not be kneejerk iconoclasts. Indeed, they will be alert to the dangers of *linguistic* idolatry. They will readily see the Holy Spirit at work in painting, music, dance, drama and other artforms – even those produced by non-Christians.

21 Postmodern evangelicals will see conversion and discipleship as intimately linked, and will develop programmes of outreach and nurture accordingly. Although they will continue to see Christian commitment depending on decisive rejection of an 'old' life in favour of 'new' life in Christ, they will not insist that this decision be linked to a specific 'crisis' or date.

22 Postmodern evangelicals will tend to favour 'inductive' over 'deductive' modes of evangelism. They will continue to value 'set piece' campaigns and crusades, but plan their outreach on the basis that most people come to faith relationally – i.e. through the witness of Christian friends or personal contact with church leaders.

23 Postmodern evangelicals will readily use TV and radio to promote the gospel, but will seek to retain a 'broadcasting' rather than a 'narrowcasting' ethos. They will strive for the highest possible production values and

maintain good journalistic standards. They will readily embrace computer technology and the Internet, but will be alive to the drawbacks of replacing actual churches with 'virtual' ones.

24 Postmodern evangelicals will maintain evangelism among people of other faiths, but in an increasingly multi-cultural society will accept that much of this evangelism must take place through dialogue. Having said this, they will expect such dialogue to be robust, and will approach it with clear convictions and an honest conversionist agenda.

25 Postmodern evangelicals will be careful to distinguish moral absolutes from cultural conventions. Even so, they will not relativise ethics where there is no biblical mandate to do so – e.g. on sex outside marriage or homosexual activity. Having said this, they will seek to temper past stridency with humility and compassion.

26 Postmodern evangelicals will cherish the right of free speech as something which enables them to witness and publish their views. Even when they are personally offended by material, they will think very hard before calling for blanket censorship. Rather, they will develop a refined critical sensibility so that they can put the evangelical perspective in open debate.

27 Postmodern evangelicals will cherish religious freedom, not only for themselves but for other faiths, too. They will not confuse the theological errors of such faiths with their right to exist and practise what they believe. They will recognise the inadequacy of current blasphemy law and will rather support its extension to other religions than see it disappear altogether.

28 Postmodern evangelicals will not expect secular laws

to correspond exactly with their own codes of church discipline. They will not be Reconstructionists.[1] Rather, they will campaign selectively, on issues of particular concern (e.g. abortion, the availability of violent videos to youngsters, etc.).

29 Even while recognising the need to pick and choose their targets, postmodern evangelicals will nonetheless seek to develop a more coherent social policy.

30 In their social and political campaigning, postmodern evangelicals will be ready, where appropriate, to make common cause with both non-evangelical Christians and non-Christians.

31 Postmodern evangelicals will take the opportunity to develop independent evangelical schools where there is a clear need. Otherwise, they will seek to maintain an influence in state education.

32 Postmodern evangelicals will be able to laugh at themselves from time to time, and will cope with a degree of humour at their own expense.

Of course, this is not a comprehensive statement of faith. It takes for granted many of the convictions around which evangelicals have gathered down the years. Indeed, there is no reason why postmodern evangelicals should not be considered as authentically evangelical as, say, Victorian evangelicals. What I have done in this summary, as in this book as a whole, is to highlight those areas in which we shall need seriously to review, or change, our approach as we head into the twenty-first century.

As we have seen, evangelicals tend to be an adaptable lot, and I remain hopeful that we can meet the challenges of postmodernity without diverting into the vagaries of post-evangelicalism. Even so, we must not be complacent. If this book helps to keep us on our toes, it will have served its purpose.

NOTES

Chapter 1   Postmodernism in Evangelical Perspective

1 C. Jencks, *The Language of Post-Modern Architecture* (Rizzoli, 1984), Part One, 'The Death of Modern Architecture', pp. 9–10.
2 ibid.
3 ibid.
4 W. Truett Anderson (ed.), *The Fontana Postmodernism Reader* (Fontana, 1996).
5 C. Jencks, *The Language of Postmodern Architecture*, p. 3.
6 U. Eco, '"I Love You Madly", He Said Self-Consciously', in W. Truett Anderson (ed.) *The Fontana Postmodernism Reader*, p. 31.
7 *Independent*, 24th December 1987. Cit. M. Featherstone, *Consumer Culture and Postmodernism* (Sage, 1991), p. 1.
8 D. Bebbington, *Evangelicalism in Modern Britain* (Routledge, 1989), pp. 10–12, 65–6.
9 A. E. McGrath, *Evangelicalism and the Future of Christianity* (Hodder and Stoughton, 1994), pp. 51, 67–73.
10 O. Guinness, *Fit Bodies, Fat Minds: Why Evangelicals Don't Think and What to Do About It* (Hodder and Stoughton, 1995), p. 61.
11 D. Tomlinson, *The Post-Evangelical* (Triangle, 1995).
12 ibid., p. 8.
13 For a report of this debate see *Christian Impact Newsletter*, Autumn 1996, pp. 4–5.
14 Cit. *Alpha*, September 1996, p.32.
15 See, for example, the debate between Tomlinson and Alister McGrath in the leading Christian monthly *Alpha*, August 1996, pp. 28–30; September 1996, pp. 32–4.

16 As part of a presentation entitled 'Where are we going?' produced by the London Bible College and since issued as a video and booklet (*The Hero*, London Bible College/Evangelical Alliance, 1997), Brian Draper, whom I interviewed for this book, identified himself thus: 'Here, I'm an evangelical; at Holy Joe's [Dave Tomlinson's alternative 'church in a pub' in Clapham, which is discussed in Chapter 7], I'm a post-evangelical.'

17 D. Lyon, *Postmodernity* (Open University, 1994), pp. 37–53.

18 D. Bell, *The Coming of Post-Industrial Society* (Basic Books, 1973).

19 U. Eco, '"I Love You Madly", He Said Self-Consciously', p. 31.

20 For an account of this transition see A. Walker, *Telling the Story: Gospel, Mission and Culture* (SPCK, 1996), pp. 184–6.

21 Central Statistical Office, *Social Trends 26* (HMSO, 1996), p. 119.

22 ibid., p. 75.

23 ibid., p. 57.

24 D. Coupland, *Generation X: Tales for an Accelerated Culture*, (Abacus, 1991).

25 See, for example, C. Brown *Christianity and Western Thought* (Intervarsity Press, 1991), pp. 173ff.; D. Allen, *Philosophy for Understanding Theology* (SCM/John Knox Press, 1985), pp. 171ff.; D. Harvey, *The Condition of Postmodernity* (Blackwell, 1990); L. E. Cahoone (ed.) *From Modernism to Postmodernism* (Blackwell, 1996).

26 R. Descartes, *Regulae Ad Directionem Ingeneii*, cit. A. Flew (ed.) *A Dictionary of Philosophy* (Pan, 1979), p. 89.

27 A point reinforced by F. Kerr, *Theology after Wittgenstein* (Blackwell, 1986), p. 3.

28 I. Kant, *Critique of Pure Reason*, trans. N. K. Smith (Macmillan [1781] 1933); *Religion Within the Limits of Reason Alone*, trans. T. M. Greene and H. H. Hudson (Harper and Row [1793] 1960).

29 G. Veith, *Guide to Contemporary Culture* (Crossway, 1994), pp. 32–5; D. Cook, *Blind Alley Beliefs*, (IVP [1979], 1996), pp. 97–122.

30 T. C. Oden 'The Death of Modernity and Postmodern Evan-

gelical Spirituality' in D. Dockery (ed.) *The Challenge of Postmodernism: An Evangelical Engagement* (Bridgepoint, 1995), pp. 20, 23ff.

31 ibid., p. 24.

32 T. Garton Ash, *We the People: The Revolution of '89* (Granta, 1990).

33 J. R. Middleton and B. J. Walsh *Truth is Stranger than It Used to Be* (SPCK, 1995), p. 12.

34 ibid., p. 10.

35 ibid., p. 11.

36 ibid., p. 13.

37 J. Drane, *Evangelism for a New Age* (Marshall Pickering, 1994), pp. 1–57.

38 Terry Eagleton, for instance, charts its rise from the ashes of orthodox Left politics which were scattered after the failed Paris uprising of May 1968 (*Literary Theory*, Blackwell, 1983, p. 148). James M. Houston, however, implies that it cannot be said to have emerged coherently until the 1980s: 'Spiritual Life for Today' in M. Eden and D. F. Wells (eds), *The Gospel in the Modern World* (IVP, 1991), p. 185).

39 For example, I. Hasan 'POSTmodernISM: A Paracritical Bibliography', in *Paracriticisms: Seven Speculations of the Times* (University of Illinois Press, 1975), pp. 39–59, reprinted in L. Cahoone (ed.), *From Modernism to Postmodernism: An Anthology* (Blackwell, 1996), pp. 382–400. F. Jameson, *Postmodernism, or, The Cultural Logic of Late Capitalism* (Duke University Press, 1991); A. E. McGrath, *A Passion for Truth* (IVP, 1996), pp. 163–200.

40 A. Toynbee, *A Study of History*, (Oxford University Press, 1939), vol. V, pp.43ff.

41 D. Lyon, 'What's in the post?', *Third Way*, April 1996, p. 20.

42 I. Hasan 'POSTmodernISM: A Paracritical Bibliography', especially pp. 391–5.

43 C. Jencks 'What is Post-Modernism?' in L. Cahoone, (ed.) From *Modernism to Postmodernism: An Anthology* p. 474.

44 L. Cahoone, 'Introduction', in L. Cahoone (ed.) *From Modernism to Postmodernism: An Anthology*, p. 11.

45 G. Veith, *Guide to Contemporary Culture*, pp. 24, 210.

Chapter 2 Postmodern Themes and Christian Consequences

1 For a passing and incidental use of this metaphor to describe the relation of Christians to postmodern culture, see G. Veith, *A Guide to Contemporary Culture*, pp. 72–3.

2 For example, I. Hasan, 'The culture of postmodernism', *Theory, Culture and Society*, 2 (3), pp. 123–4; S. Kvale, 'Themes of postmodernity', in W. Truett Anderson (ed.), *The Fontana Postmodernism Reader*, pp. 18–25; A. E. McGrath, *A Passion for Truth*, p. 185.

3 D. H. Hilton, *To follow truth and thus . . .*, the Moderator's Address to Assembly, 5th July 1993 (United Reformed Church, 1993).

4 ibid., p. 11.

5 ibid., p. 12.

6 ibid., p. 8.

7 Z. Bauman, 'Postmodernity, or Living with Ambivalence', in *Modernity and Ambivalence* (Cornell University Press/ Blackwell, 1991). Reprinted in J. Natoli and L. Hutcheon (eds), *A Postmodern Reader* (State University of New York Press, 1993), pp. 9–24.

8 J. F. Lyotard, *The Postmodern Condition: A Report on Knowledge*, trans. G. Bennington and B. Massumi (Manchester [1979], 1984), p. xxiv.

9 Steinar Kvale, 'Themes of Postmodernity' in W. Truett Anderson (ed.), *The Fontana Postmodernism Reader*, p. 21.

10 A. E. McGrath, *A Passion for Truth*, p. 154.

11 S. Grenz, *A Primer on Postmodernism* (Eerdmans, 1996), p. 41.

12 C. F. H. Henry, *God, Revelation and Authority* (Word Books, 1976); F. Schaeffer, *Trilogy* (*The God Who is There; Escape from Reason; He is There and He is Not Silent*) (IVP, 1990); cf. S. Grenz, *Revisioning Evangelical Theology* (Intervarsity Press, 1993), pp. 69–72.

13 Y. Bar-Hillel, 'Indexical Expressions', *Mind*, 63, pp. 359–79. For more on correspondence v. coherence, see S. Blackburn, *Spreading the Word: Groundings in the Philosophy of*

Language (Oxford University Press, 1984), pp. 224–60.

14 I. Berlin, 'The idea of pluralism', in W. Truett Anderson (ed.) *The Fontana Postmodernism Reader*, p. 45.

15 R. Schweder, 'Santa Claus on the Cross', in W. Truett Anderson (ed.), *The Fontana Postmodernism Reader*, p. 69.

16 T. C. Oden *Two Worlds: Notes on the Death of Modernity in America and Russia* (Intervarsity Press, 1992), p. 54.

17 J. Derrida, 'Signature Event Context' in *Glyph 1*, Johns Hopkins Textual Studies (Johns Hopkins, 1977), pp. 172–97; *Of Grammatology* (Johns Hopkins [1967], 1976), p. 158.

18 W. Truett Anderson, *Reality isn't What it Used to be*, p. 75, cit. J. R. Middleton and B. J. Walsh, *Truth is Stranger than It Used to be*, p. 31.

19 On Nietzsche, Christianity and postmodern perspectivism see R. Lundin, *The Culture of Interpretation* (Eerdmans, 1993), pp. 37–8.

20 Tania Guha, 'God', *Time Out*, 16–23 April 1997, p. 45.

21 R. Ridley, 'All About Eve', *Independent*, 'Tabloid' section, 3rd February 1997, pp. 12–13.

22 See W. Truett Anderson's book of the same name.

23 See, for example, *The Other Side of 1984* (World Council of Churches, 1983); *Foolishness to the Greeks* (SPCK, 1986); *The Gospel in a Pluralist Society* (SPCK, 1989).

24 For a survey of current views see M. J. Wilkins and J. P. Moreland (eds), *Jesus Under Fire* (Paternoster Press, 1996).

25 G. Steiner, *Real Presences* (Faber and Faber, 1989).

26 J. Baudrillard, 'The procession of simulacra', in *Simulations*, trans. P. Foss, P. Patton and P. Beitchmann (Semiotext(e), 1983), pp. 1–75, reprinted in J. Natoli and L. Hutcheon (eds), *A Postmodern Reader*, pp. 342–75.

27 J. Derrida, 'Signature Event Context' in *Glyph I*, Johns Hopkins Textual Studies (John Hopkins, 1977), pp. 172–97; *Of Grammatology* (Johns Hopkins [1967], 1976), p. 158.

28 J. Baudrillard, 'The procession of simulacra' in J. Natoli and L. Hutcheon (eds), *A Postmodern Reader*, pp. 342–75.

29 R. Barthes, *Image, Music, Text* (Fontana, 1977), p. 147.

30 D. Coupland, *Life After God* (Touchstone, 1994), p. 273.

31 R. Barthes, *The Pleasure of the Text*, trans. R. Howard (Jonathan Cape, 1976).

32 D. Harvey, *The Condition of Postmodernity* (Blackwell, 1990), pp. 141ff. G. Cray, *From Here to Where? The Culture of the Nineties*, Board of Mission Occasional Paper No. 3 (n.d.), p. 11.

33 See, for example, J. McGregor, 'Madonna: Icon of Postmodernity', L'Abri lecture, cit. D. Cook, *Blind Alley Beliefs* (IVP, 1996), pp. 15–16.; G. Cray, *From Here to Where? The Culture of the Nineties* p. 11.

34 G. Cray, *From Here to Where?*, p. 11.

35 K. Richardson, 'Disorientations in Christian belief: The problem of de-traditionalization in the postmodern context' in D. S. Dockery (ed.) *The Challenge of Postmodernism: An Evangelical Response*, pp. 53–66.

36 D. Coupland, *Generation X: Tales for an Accelerated Culture* (Abacus, 1991).

37 M. Lawson, 'Welcome to a Land Without Heroes', *Guardian*, 23rd March 1997.

38 W. Truett Anderson, 'Introduction: what's going on here?' in W. Truett Anderson (ed.), p. 11.

39 P. Lee Tan, *Encyclopedia of 7700 Illustrations: Signs of the Times* (Assurance, 1979), pp. 1538–9, 1632–8.

40 For an accessible account of these differences see B. Magee (in dialogue with S. Morgenbesser), *The Great Philosophers* (Oxford University Press, 1987), pp. 280–97.

41 C. S. Peirce, 'How to Make Our Ideas Clear', in L. Cahoone (ed.), *From Modernism to Postmodernism*, p. 149.

42 Cit. A. Flew (ed.) *A Dictionary of Philosophy* (Pan, 1979), p.284.

43 R. Rorty, *Objectivity, Relativism and Truth* (Cambridge University Press, 1991), pp. 21ff.; S. Fish, *Is There a Text in This Class?* (Harvard University Press, 1980), pp. 97–111.

Chapter 3   Cases in Point: Three Stories

1 D. A. McGavran, 'Church Growth Movement', in W. A. Elwell (ed.), *Evangelical Dictionary of Theology* (Baker Books/Paternoster, 1984), pp. 241–3.

2 E. Gellner, *Postmodernism, Reason and Religion* (Routledge, 1992), p. 52. As a distinctive school of philosophy, American Pragmatism, which originated in the work of Charles Sanders

Peirce, William James and John Dewey at the turn of this century, offers a greatly refined version of the more instinctive pragmatism of the eighteenth-century British evangelicals. So, also, the 'Neo-Pragmatism' of Richard Rorty and Stanley Fish tends to be more radical than its predecessor in tracing the consequences of a purely functional and transactional view of truth. For an account of these finer distinctions see B. Magee (ed.), *The Great Philosophers*, pp. 278–97, and R. Rorty, *The Mirror of Nature* (Princeton, 1979).

3 D. Lyon, *Postmodernity*, pp. 56–69.

4 D. Tomlinson, *The Post-Evangelical*, pp. 6–7.

5 G. Veith, *Guide to Contemporary Culture*, p. 70.

6 N. Postman, *Technopoly: The Surrender of Culture to Technology* (Vintage Books, 1993), p. 58.

7 cf. O. Guinness, *Fit Bodies, Fat Minds: Why Evangelicals Don't Think and What to Do About It*, pp. 57–61.

8 M. Glodo, 'The Bible in Stereo: New Opportunities for Biblical Interpretation in an A-Rational Age' in D. Dockery (ed.), *The Challenge of Postmodernism*, pp. 148–72.

9 For a representative argument and bibliography based on this premise see S. Jebb, *No Laughing Matter* (Day One, 1995).

10 I. Hasan, 'The culture of postmodernism', pp. 123–4.

11 D. Tomlinson, *The Post-Evangelical*, p. 140.

12 Y. Craig, 'What in the World is Happening?', in Board of Education of the General Synod of the Church of England, *Tomorrow is Another Country: Education in a Postmodern World* (Central Board of Finance of the Church of England, 1996), p. 11.

13 C. Jencks, 'What is Postmodernism?', in W. Truett Anderson (ed.), *The Fontana Postmodernism Reader*, p. 27.

14 W. James and B. Russell, 'How has Post-Modernism Changed Education?', in Board of Education of the General Synod of the Church of England, *Tomorrow is Another Country: Education in a Postmodern World* (Central Board of Finance of the Church of England, 1996), p. 29.

15 ibid.

16 S. Kvale, 'Themes of Postmodernity', in W. Truett Anderson (ed.), *The Fontana Postmodernism Reader*, p. 23.

17 S. Grenz, *Revisioning Evangelical Theology* (IVP, 1993). p. 79.

Chapter 4 Bible Reflection: Ecclesiastes 3:5

1 J. L. Crenshaw, *Ecclesiastes: A Commentary* (SCM Press, 1988), p. 95.
2 R. N. Whybray, *Ecclesiastes: New Bible Commentary* (Eerdmans/Marshall, Morgan and Scott, 1989), p. 71.
3 ibid.
4 G. Veith, *Guide to Contemporary Culture*, pp. 39–40.
5 A. E. McGrath, *A Passion for Truth*, p. 171.

Chapter 5 Evangelicalism, Modernity and Postmodernity

1 London Bible College, *The Hero* (London Bible College/Evangelical Alliance, 1997). Video and booklet written and edited by John Ranson.
2 A. E. McGrath, *Evangelicalism and the Future of Christianity*, p. 12; D. Tidball, *Who are the Evangelicals?* (Harper Collins, 1994), p. 11.
3 For an accessible account of Luther's life and work see R. H. Benthon, *Here I Stand: A Life of Martin Luther* (Abingdon–Cokesbury, 1950).
4 A. E. McGrath, *Evangelicalism and the Future of Christianity*, p. 15.
5 For more detail on this see W. Fred Graham, 'Government, Civil', in D. McKim and D. F. Wright (eds), *Encyclopedia of Reformed Faith* (Westminster/John Knox Press, 1992), pp. 158–60.
6 For more on this movement see W. R. Ward, 'German Pietism, 1670–1750', *Journal of Ecclesiastical History* 44 (1993), pp. 476–504, and, in shorter form, M. A. Noll, 'Pietism' in W. A. Elwell (ed.), *Evangelical Dictionary of Theology* (Baker Book House/Paternoster Press, 1984), pp. 855–8.
7 C. Idle, *The Journal of John Wesley* (Lion, 1986), p. 46.
8 D. Bebbington, *Evangelicalism in Modern Britain*, p. 21.
9 ibid.
10 ibid.

11 ibid., pp. 57–60.
12 Cit. W. J. Turrell, *John Wesley: Physician and Electrotherapist* (Oxford, 1938), pp. 18–34.
13 J. H. Pratt (ed.), *The Thought of Evangelical Leaders: Notes on the Discussions of the Eclectic Society, London, During the Years 1798–1814* (Edinburgh, 1978). See also H. Frei, *The Eclipse of Biblical Narrative* (Yale University Press, 1977), p. 9.
14 D. Bebbington, *Evangelicalism in Modern Britain*, pp. 57–8.
15 A. C. Chitnis, *The Scottish Enlightenment and Early Victorian English Society* (London, 1986); D. Bebbington, 'Evangelicalism: Britain', in A. E. McGrath (ed.), *The Blackwell Encyclopedia of Modern Christian Thought* (Blackwell, 1993), pp. 184–7.
16 D. Bebbington, *Evangelicalism in Modern Britain*, pp. 59–60.
17 ibid, p. 59.
18 Alister McGrath, *A Passion for Truth*, pp. 166–79.
19 D. Bebbington, *Evangelicalism in Modern Britain*, p. 227. For a helpful summary of the contrasts between evangelicalism and fundamentalism see J. R. W. Stott, 'Response to Chapter 2', in D. L. Edwards, *Essentials*, (Hodder and Stoughton, 1988), pp. 90–1.
20 B. Reardon, 'Romanticism', in A. E. McGrath (ed.), *The Blackwell Encyclopedia of Modern Christian Thought* (Blackwell, 1993), p. 573.
21 D. Bebbington, *Evangelicalism in Modern Britain*, p. 68.
22 E. Irving, *For the Oracles of God: Four Orations for Judgment to Come: An Argument in Nine Parts* (London, 1823), p. 104.
23 D. Bebbington, *Evangelicalism in Modern Britain*, pp. 151–80.
24 ibid., p. 168.
25 ibid.
26 R. Appignanesi and C. Garratt, *Postmodernism for Beginners* (Icon, 1995), p. 173.
27 C. Peter Wagner, 'Exploring the Supernatural Dimensions of Church Growth', in *Global Church Growth* (Oct–Dec 1988), p. 3.
28 For an excellent account of the development of such churches see A. Walker, *Restoring the Kingdom* (Hodder & Stoughton, [1985], 1988).
29 P. S. Fiddes, 'The Theology of the Charismatic Movement' in

D. Martin and P. Mullen (eds), *Strange Gifts? A Guide to Charismatic Renewal* (Basil Blackwell, 1984), pp. 19–40.

30 J. Edwards, 'The Evangelical Alliance: A National Phenomenon' in S. Brady and H. Rowdon (eds), *For Such a Time As This: Perspectives on Evangelicalism, Past, Present and Future* (Evangelical Alliance, 1996), p. 51.

31 P. Lewis, 'Renewal, Recovery and Growth' in S. Brady and H. Rowdon (eds), *For Such A Time As This*, p. 186.

32 J. Edwards, 'The Evangelical Alliance: A National Phenomenon' in S. Brady and H. Rowdon (eds), *For Such a Time As This*, p. 50.

33 D. Bebbington, *Evangelicalism in Modern Britain*, p. 66.

34 ibid., p. 12.

35 D. Bebbington, 'The Decline and Resurgence of Evangelical Social Concern, 1918–1980' in J. Wolffe (ed.), *Evangelical Faith and Public Zeal* (SPCK, 1995), pp. 175–97.

36 C. Calver, 'Afterword: Hope for the Future?', in J. Wolffe (ed.), *Evangelical Faith and Public Zeal*, p. 209.

37 R. Forster and C. Dye, 'Growing a church' in S. Brady and H. Rowdon (eds), *For Such a Time As This*, pp. 229–44. See also M. Green, 'Preface' in E. Gibbs, *I Believe in Church Growth* (Hodder and Stoughton, 1981), pp. 11–12.

38 J. D. Hunter, *American Evangelicalism: Conservative Religion and the Quandary of Modernity* (Rutgers University Press, 1983); *Evangelicalism: The Coming Generation*, (Chicago University Press, 1987).

39 D. Harvey, *The Condition of Postmodernity*, p. 41; C. Norris, *Reclaiming Truth*, (Lawrence and Wishart, 1996), pp. 31ff.; R. Rorty *Consequences of Pragmatism: Essays 1972–1980* (Minneapolis, 1982).

40 C. Calver, 'Together for Truth' in C. Calver and R. Warner, *Together We Stand: Evangelical Convictions, Unity and Vision* (Hodder and Stoughton, 1996), pp. 128–30.

Chapter 7 Evangelicals, Post-Evangelicals and Postmodernity

1 D. Tomlinson, *The Post-Evangelical*, pp. 11–13. For an account of Tomlinson's former career and its relation to the New Church movement see A. Walker, *Restoring the*

Kingdom: The Radical Christianity of the House Church Movement (Hodder and Stoughton, 1988, second edition).
2 D. Tomlinson, *The Post-Evangelical*, p. 12.
3 ibid.
4 ibid., p. 13.
5 D. Tomlinson, 'Heralds of Hope?', *Alpha*, September 1996, p. 33.
6 D. Tomlinson, *The Post-Evangelical*, pp. 4, 9–10.
7 ibid., p. 10.
8 ibid., p. 76.
9 ibid., p. 7.
10 ibid., p. 7.
11 ibid., pp. 67–8.
12 ibid., p. 3.
13 ibid., pp. 47ff.
14 ibid., p. 4.
15 ibid., pp. 60–1, 70.
16 ibid., p. 8.
17 ibid., p. 72.
18 ibid., p. 73.
19 ibid., p. 8.
20 ibid., pp. 140–1.
21 ibid., p. 55.
22 ibid., pp. 69, 84–103.
23 ibid., p. 69.
24 ibid. p. 87.
25 ibid., pp. 93ff.
26 ibid., pp. 114–6.
27 ibid., p. 95.
28 ibid., pp. 75ff.
29 ibid., pp. 84ff.
30 ibid., p. 101.
31 ibid., p. 41.
32 ibid., p. 35.
33 ibid., p. 37.
34 ibid., p. 39.
35 ibid., p. 10.
36 ibid., pp. 4–5, 83.
37 ibid., pp. 80–1.
38 ibid., p. 75.

39 ibid., p. 7.
40 ibid., pp. 6–7.
41 ibid., p. 14.
42 ibid.
43 ibid., p. 18.
44 ibid., p. 15.
45 ibid., p. 2.
46 ibid., p. 25.
47 ibid., p. 26.
48 ibid.
49 A. E. McGrath, 'Prophets of Doubt', *Alpha*, August 1996, pp. 28–30.
50 ibid., p. 28.
51 ibid., p. 29.
52 Review in *Church Times*, nd.
53 This comment is quoted on the back-cover publicity for the book.
54 But for more general pointers see J. Fanstone, *The Sheep that Got Away* (Monarch, 1993); W. D. Hendricks, *Exit Interviews* (Moody Press, 1993).
55 P. Brierley, *'Christian' England* (Marc Europe, 1991), p. 161.
56 In particular see Mercer's superb contribution to London Bible College's *The Hero*.
57 A. E. McGrath, 'Prophets of Doubt', p. 29.
58 J. R. Middleton and B. J. Walsh, *Truth is Stranger than It Used to be* (SPCK, 1995), p. 11.
59 ibid., p. 174.
60 ibid., p. 176.
61 D. Tomlinson, *The Post-Evangelical*, pp. 83–103.
62 ibid., pp. 92–3.
63 ibid., pp. 95–7.
64 S. Grenz, *Revisioning Evangelical Theology* (Intervarsity Press, 1993); *Theology for the Community of God* (Paternoster Press, 1994); 'Star Trek and the Next Generation: Postmodernism and the Future of Evangelical Christianity' in D. Dockery (ed.), *The Challenge of Postmodernism: An Evangelical Engagement*, pp. 89–103.
65 S. Grenz, *Revisioning Evangelical Theology*, p. 13.
66 ibid., p. 14.

67 ibid., p. 15.
68 ibid., p. 17. Also see *Theology for the Community of God*, pp. 601–742.
69 D. Tomlinson, *The Post-Evangelical*, p. 120.
70 S. Grenz, *Revisioning Evangelical Theology*, p. 17.
71 ibid., p. 53.
72 ibid., pp. 110ff.; cf. D. Tomlinson, *The Post-Evangelical*, pp. 105–9.
73 D. Tomlinson, *The Post-Evangelical*, p. 121.
74 S. Grenz, *Revisioning Evangelical Theology*, p. 111.
75 C. H. Pinnock, *The Scripture Principle* (Hodder & Stoughton, 1985).
76 ibid., pp. 222–6.
77 D. Tomlinson, *The Post-Evangelical*, pp. 99–100.
78 C. H. Pinnock and R. C. Brow, *Unbounded Love* (Paternoster Press, 1994); C. H. Pinnock, *The Openness of God* (Paternoster Press, 1994), p. 119.
79 D. Tomlinson, *The Post-Evangelical*, pp. 99–100.
80 G. A. Lindbeck, *The Nature of Doctrine: Religion and Theology in a Postliberal Age* (Westminster Press, 1984).
81 H. W. Frei, *The Eclipse of Biblical Narrative* (Yale University Press, 1974); S. Hauerwas, *Community of Character: Toward a Constructive Christian Social Ethics* (University of Notre Dame Press, 1981); R. E. Thiemann, *Revelation and Theology: The Gospel as Narrated Promise* (University of Notre Dame Press, 1985); G. Hunsinger, 'Truth as Self-Involving: Barth and Lindbeck on the Cognitive and Performative Aspects of Truth in Theological Discourse', *Journal of the American Academy of Religion*, LXI (1), 1993, 23–40; W. C. Placher, *Unapologetic Theology: Christian Voice in a Pluralistic Conversation* (Westminster/John Knox Press, 1989). For a useful summary of postliberalism see S. G. Davaney and D. Brown, 'Postliberalism', in A. E. McGrath (ed.), *The Blackwell Encyclopedia of Modern Christian Thought* pp. 453–6.
82 D. Tomlinson, *The Post-Evangelical*, pp. 98–9.
83 T. R. Phillips and D. L. Okholm (eds), *The Nature of Confession: Evangelicals and Postliberals in Conversation* (Intervarsity Press, 1996).
84 ibid., p. 8.
85 ibid.

86 R. Lundin, *The Culture of Interpretation: Christian Faith and the Postmodern World.*

87 M. A. Noll, *The Scandal of the Evangelical Mind* (IVP, 1994).

88 T. R. Phillips and D. L. Okholm (eds) *Christian Apologetics in the Postmodern World* (Intervarsity Press, 1995).

89 D. Dockery (ed.), *The Challenge of Postmodernism: An Evangelical Engagement.*

90 N. T. Wright, *The New Testament and the People of God* (SPCK, 1992).

91 A. C. Thiselton, *Interpreting God and the Postmodern Self* (T. and T. Clark, 1995).

92 D. Tomlinson, 'Heralds of Hope?', *Alpha*, September 1996, p. 32.

93 ibid.

94 J. A. T. Robinson, *Honest to God* (SCM, 1963).

95 Cit. P. Sampson, 'Consumer Rights and Wrongs', *Third Way*, March 1977, p. 23.

96 Z. Bauman, *Postmodernity and its Discontents* (Polity Press, 1997).

97 D. Tomlinson, *The Post-Evangelical*, pp. 79–80.

98 ibid., p. 80.

99 ibid., p. 140.

100 ibid., p. 13.

101 L. Osborn, review of *Natural Grace: Dialogues on Science and Spirituality* by R. Sheldrake and M. Fox, *Third Way*, September 1996, p. 28.

102 ibid., p. 141.

103 ibid., p. 13.

103 Rather surprised by this remark, I checked with John Drane that this had in fact happened, and he confirmed it.

105 D. Tomlinson, *The Post-Evangelical*, pp. 80–1.

106 ibid., pp. 135–6.

107 ibid., pp. 60–74.

108 P. Brierley, *'Christian' England*, pp. 162–7.

109 D. Tomlinson, *The Post-Evangelical*, p. 72; L. Houlden, 'Liberalism: Britain' in A. E. McGrath (ed.), *The Blackwell Encyclopedia of Modern Christian Thought*, pp. 323–4.

110 D. Tomlinson, *The Post-Evangelical*, p. 71.

111 L. Houlden, 'Liberalism: Britain', p. 324.

112 A. Walker, *Restoring the Kingdom* pp. 111–12.

113 D. Tomlinson, *The Post-Evangelical*, p. 136.

114 ibid., pp. 136ff.

115 K. W. Clements (ed.), *Friedrich Schleiermacher: Pioneer of Modern Theology (Selected Writings)* (Collins, 1987), pp. 66–107.

116 D. Tomlinson, *The Post-Evangelical*, pp. 140–4.

117 L. Houlden, 'Liberalism: Britain', p. 323.

118 D. Tomlinson, *The Post-Evangelical*, p. 142.

119 J. Richmond, 'Liberal Protestantism', in A. Richardson and J. Bowden (eds), *A New Dictionary of Christian Theology* (SCM, 1983), pp. 325–8.

120 D. Tracy, *The Analogical Imagination: Christian Theology and the Culture of Pluralism* (SCM, 1981); *Plurality and Ambiguity: Hermeneutics, Religion, Hope* (SCM, 1987).

121 D. Tomlinson, *The Post-Evangelical*, p. 9.

122 P. Brierley, *'Christian' England*, pp. 131–3.

123 D. Tomlinson, *The Post-Evangelical*, p. 145.

Chapter 8: Worship and Preaching

1 R. Howard, *The Rise and Fall of the Nine O'Clock Service*, (Mowbray, 1996), p. 128.

2 Cit. ibid., p. 133

3 P. Ward, 'The Tribes of Evangelicalism' (MS) in *The Post-Evangelical Debate* (SPCK, forthcoming). Kindly supplied by the author.

4 R. Howard, *The Rise and Fall of the Nine O' Clock Service*, pp. 25–6.

5 ibid., p. 26.

6 ibid., p. 27.

7 G. Cray, *From Here to Where?*, p.19.

8 D. Gay, 'York II and Fox' in *Gospel and Culture*, November 1996, pp. 2–3.

9 See V. Coren, 'Getting Hip to Jesus in the Chill-Out Zone', *Evening Standard*, 18th September 1996, p. 30.

10 S. Kvale, 'Themes of Postmodernity' in W. Truett Anderson (ed.), *The Fontana Postmodernism Reader*, p. 23.

11 M. Starkey, 'Swinging High and Low', *New Christian Herald*, 9th November 1996, pp. 10–11.

12 O. Guinness, 'The Word in the Age of the Image: The Challenge to Evangelicals' in M. Tinker (ed.), *The Anglican Evangelical Crisis* (Christian Focus, 1995), pp. 156–71

13 ibid., p. 161.

14 ibid., p. 163.

15 ibid., pp. 166–70.

16 ibid., p. 163.

17 For more detail on Ward's thinking about contemporary music see his *Growing Up Evangelical: The Making of a Subculture* (SPCK, 1996), pp. 107–42 (pp. 133ff. on Kendrick).

18 M. Starkey, 'When Cool Becomes Chilling', *Church Times*, 8th September 1995.

19 P. Richter, 'Charismatic Mysticism: A Sociological Analysis of the Toronto Blessing' in S. Porter (ed.), *The Nature of Religious Language* (Sheffield Academic Press, 1996), pp. 103–6.

20 See, for example, G. Chevereau, *Catch the Fire: The Toronto Blessing – An Experience of Renewal and Revival* (Marshall Pickering, 1994), pp. 28, 42, 212.

21 P. Richter, 'Charismatic Mysticism: A Sociological Analysis of the Toronto Blessing' in S. Porter (ed.), *The Nature of Religious Language*, p. 126.

22 ibid.

23 R. Forster, 'Ichthus Christian Fellowship', in R. Forster (ed.), *Ten New Churches*, (Marc Europe, 1986), pp. 65–9.

24 H. O. Old, *Guides to the Reformed Tradition: Worship* (John Knox Press, 1984), pp. 57–85; J. Hastings Nichols, *Corporate Worship in the Reformed Tradition* (Westminster Press, 1968), pp. 71–89.

25 For more on Reformation preaching see H. O. Old, *Guides to the Reformed Tradition: Worship*, pp. 68–85; J. Hastings Nichols, *Corporate Worship in the Reformed Tradition*, pp. 71–89.

26 B. D. Spinks, *From the Lord and the Best Reformed Churches: A Study of the Eucharistic Liturgy in the English Puritan and Separatist Traditions* (CLV, 1984), pp. 45ff.; H. Davies, *The Worship of the English Puritans* (Dacre Press, 1948), pp. 35ff.; D. Hilborn, 'The Pragmatics of Liturgical Discourse; (unpublished Ph.D. Dissertation, University of Nottingham), 1994, pp. 453ff. Partly summarised as 'From performativity

to pedagogy: Jean Ladrière and the language of English Reformed worship', in S. Porter (ed.), *The Nature of Religious Language*, pp. 170–200.

27 J. Hastings Nichols, *Corporate Worship in the Reformed Tradition*, p. 96.

28 D. Hilborn, 'From Performativity to Pedagogy', pp. 180–5.

29 H. Davies, *The Worship of the English Puritans* (Dacre Press, 1948), pp. 67–9.

30 J. Hastings Nichols, *Corporate Worship in the Reformed Tradition*, p. 93.

31 H. Davies, *The Worship of the English Puritans*, p. 126.

32 N. Wolterstorff, 'The Reformed Liturgy', in D. K. McKim (ed.), *Major Themes in the Reformed Tradition* (Eerdmans, 1992), p. 297.

33 D. Hilborn, 'The Pragmatics of Liturgical Discourse'.

34 H. O. Old, 'Preaching: History of' in D. K. McKim and D. F. Wright (eds), *Encyclopedia of the Reformed Faith*, (John Knox/Westminster Press, 1992), p. 288.

35 For example, D. A. Carson, 'Accept No Substitutes: 6 Reasons Not to Abandon Expository Preaching', *Leadership*, Summer 1996, pp. 87–8; M. Lloyd Jones, *Preaching and Preachers* (Hodder & Stoughton, 1971), pp. 64ff.

36 W. Hollenweger 'Pentecostal Worship' in J. G. Davies (ed.), *A New Dictionary of Liturgy and Worship* (SCM Press, 1986), p. 431.

37 See, for example, C. J. Cocksworth, *Evangelical Eucharistic Thought in the Church of England* (Cambridge University Press, 1993); P. Southwell, 'Evangelicalism and the Sacraments' in R. T. France and A. E. McGrath (eds), *Evangelical Anglicans: Their Role and Influence in the Church* (SPCK, 1993), pp. 71–80.

38 D. C. Norrington, *To Preach or Not to Preach? The Church's Urgent Question* (Paternoster, 1996), p. 9; J. Drane, *Faith in a Changing Culture: Creating Churches for the Next Century* (Marshall Pickering, 1997), p. 134.

39 D. C. Norrington, *To Preach or Not to Preach?*, p. 7.

40 ibid., pp. 8–12; A. Richardson, 'Preach; Teach' in A. Richardson (ed.), *A Theological Word Book of the Bible* (SCM Press, 1950), pp. 171–2.

41 J. Habermas, 'An Alternative Way Out of the Philosophy of the

Subject: Communicative versus Subject-Centred Reason'
in *The Philosophical Discourse of Modernity*, trans. F.
Lawrence (MIT Press, 1987), pp. 294–326.

42 D. Coupland, *Generation X: Tales for an Accelerated Culture*,
Life After God.

43 See, for instance, H. Frei, *The Eclipse of Biblical Narrative*,
(Yale University Press, 1974); S. Hauerwas and L. G. Jones,
Why Narrative? (Eerdmans, 1989); D. Tracy, *Plurality and
Ambiguity: Hermeneutics, Religion, Hope*, (SCM Press,
1987); A. Walker, *Telling the Story* (SPCK, 1996).

44 R. Gosnell, 'Proclamation and the Postmodernist', in D. S.
Dockery (ed.), *The Challenge of Postmodernity: An Evangelical Engagement* pp. 385–6; R. L. Lewis, 'Proclaiming
the Gospel Inductively', *Review and Expositor*, 84 (1987),
52. More generally, see A. C. Thiselton, *New Horizons
in Hermeneutics* (Harper Collins, 1992), pp. 566–75;
A. E. McGrath, *A Passion for Truth* pp. 105–116; E. R.
Clendenen, 'Postholes, Postmodernism, and the Prophets:
Towards a Textlinguistic Paradigm' in D. Dockery (ed.),
The Challenge of Postmodernism, pp. 132–47. Also see my
own work on worship as communication: D. Hilborn, 'The
Pragmatics of Liturgical Discourse' and 'From Performativity
to Pedagogy'.

45 See D. Norrington, *To Preach or Not to Preach?*, pp. 5–7.

46 A view which originated with the work of A. Julicher, and
which is perpetuated, for example, by S. J. Kistemaker,
'Parables of Jesus' in W. A. Elwell (ed.), *Evangelical
Dictionary of Theology* (Baker Books/Paternoster, 1984),
pp. 824–6.

47 S. Kvale, 'Themes of Postmodernity', in W. Truett Anderson
(ed.), *The Fontana Postmodernism Reader*, p. 21.

48 R. Gosnell, 'Proclamation and the Postmodernist' in
D. Dockery (ed.) *The Challenge of Postmodernism*,
pp. 378–80.

Chapter 9   Bible Reflection: 2 Timothy 2:1–13

1 D. Jackman, 'Preparing the Preacher', in C. Green and D.
Jackman (eds), *When God's Voice is Heard: Essays on
Preaching Presented to Dick Lucas* (IVP, 1995), p. 180.

2 See D. C. Norrington, *To Preach or Not to Preach?*, p. 4 and references.

3 ibid., p. 11.

4 S. Sumithra, 'Syncretism, Secularization and Renewal' in D. A. Carson (ed.), *The Church in the Bible and the World* (Paternoster Press, 1987), pp. 261–8.

5 N. Wolterstorff, 'The Reformed Liturgy', in D. K. McKim (ed.) *Major Themes in the Reformed Tradition* (Eerdmans, 1992), pp. 273–304; D. Hilborn, 'From Performativity to Pedagogy' pp. 178ff.

6 D. C. Norrington, *To Preach or Not To Preach?*, p. 24.

7 J. Calvin, *Institutes of the Christian Religion* (Westminster Press [1559] 1960), IV, pp. xvii, 43.

10 Witness and Discipleship

1 J. Emery White, 'Evangelism in a Postmodern World' in D. Dockery (ed.), *The Challenge of Postmodernism: An Evangelical Engagement*, pp. 359–73.

2 J. Drane, *Faith in a Changing Culture*, p.41.

3 K. Ford, *Jesus for a New Generation* (Hodder & Stoughton, 1996), p. 196.

4 J. Emery White, 'Evangelism in a Postmodern World' in D. Dockery (ed.), *The Challenge of Postmodernism: An Evangelical Engagement*, p. 368.

5 J. Drane, *Faith in a Changing Culture*, pp. 85, 89–90.; C. Hudson, 'Commentary: Romans 8:15f', *Third Way*, March 1997, p. 18.

6 C. Hudson, 'Commentary: Romans 8:18f', p. 18.

7 ibid.

8 J. Finney, *Finding Faith Today: How Does It Happen?* (Bible Society, 1992).

9 ibid., p. 24.

10 ibid., pp. 26–35.

11 J. Saxbee, *Liberal Evangelism: A Flexible Response to the Decade* (SPCK, 1984).

12 D. Tomlinson, *The Post-Evangelical*, p. 143.

13 W. Bruggemann, *Texts Under Negotiation: The Bible and Postmodern Imagination* (Fortress Press, 1993), pp. 1–25.

14 G. Veith, *Guide to Contemporary Culture*, p. 212.

15 J. Emery White, 'Evangelism in a Postmodern World', p. 369.

16 L. Ford, *The Power of Story* (NavPress, 1994).

17 K. Ford, *Jesus for a New Generation*, p. 235.

18 For a succinct summary of the Bible's major narrative threads see A. Walker, *Telling the Story* (SPCK, 1996), pp. 13–14.

19 J. Finney, *Finding Faith Today*, p. 36.

20 J. Emery White, 'Evangelism in a Postmodern World', p.179.

21 K. Ford, *Jesus for a New Generation*, p. 179

22 S. Grenz, *Theology for the Community of God* (Paternoster Press, 1994), p. 655.

23 S. Kvale, 'Themes of Postmodernity', in W. Truett Anderson (ed.), *The Faber Postmodernism Reader*, p. 23.

24 R. Bellah *et al. Habits of the Heart: Individualism and Commitment in American Life* (University of California Press, 1985); A. MacIntyre, *After Virtue* (University of Notre Dame Press, 1984, second edition); D. Shelbourne, *The Principle of Duty* (Sinclair Stevenson, 1994).

25 S. J. Grenz, *A Primer on Postmodernism* (Eerdmans, 1996), p. 168.

26 Cit. J. Emery White, 'Evangelism in a Postmodern World', pp. 368–9.

27 For a review of evangelical attitudes to ecumenism see D. J. Tidball, *Who are the Evangelicals?* (Marshall Pickering, 1994), pp. 170–6.

28 P. Lewis, 'Renewal, Recovery and Growth', in S. Brady and H. Rowdon (eds), *For Such a Time As This*, p. 189.

29 See P. Brierley, *'Christian' England* pp. 107–26.

30 See J. Drane, *Faith in a Changing Culture*, p. 5.

31 For a statistical and philosophical defence of such effective diversity see R. Gill, *Competing Convictions* (SCM Press, 1989).

32 Source: *UK Christian Handbook 1996/7 Edition* (Christian Research/Evangelical Alliance/National Bible Society of Scotland, 1995), p. 12, 431–500.

33 D. Bebbington, *Evangelicalism in Modern Britain*, pp. 264–5.

34 On 'narrowcasting' in religious media see D. P. Davies, 'Hymns and Arias' in C. Arthur (ed.) *Religion and the Media* (University of Wales Press, 1993), pp. 235–45.

35 On this tendency see D. Lyon, *Postmodernity*, p. 49.
36 Central Statistical Office, *Social Trends 26* (HMSO, 1996), p. 217.
37 For example, 25 hours a week or 3.5 a day – 'Poll Watch', *The Week*, 4th January 1997, p. 11.; 4.5 hours a day – A. Walker, *Enemy Territory* (Hodder & Stoughton, 1987), pp. 142–4 (source not quoted).
38 M. McLuhan, *The Medium is the Message (Penguin, 1967)*.
39 J. Baudrillard, *Simulations*.
40 Cit. R. Appignanesi and C. Garratt, *Postmodernism for Beginners*, p. 134.
41 S. Grenz, *A Primer on Postmodernism*, p. 35.
42 For a summary of Ark2's early history, see J. Sheppard, 'Will Ark2 Weather the Storm?', *Baptist Times*, 21st November 1996, p. 9.
43 D. Tomlinson, *The Post-Evangelical*, p. 144.
44 Cit. *Sunday*, Radio 4, 16th March 1997.
45 D. Tomlinson, *The Post-Evangelical*, p. 12.
46 J. Drane, *Faith in a Changing Culture*, pp. 91–104.
47 Despite efforts to do so, I have not been able to find statistics on the precise extent of house-group growth. This is a significant area, and certainly merits empirical study if none has yet been undertaken.
48 N. Gumbel, *Telling Others: The Alpha Initiative* (Kingsway, 1994), pp. 11–13; *Alpha News*, February 1997, 12, p. 1.
49 L. G. Witlock Jnr, 'Apologetics' in W. A. Elwell (ed.), *Evangelical Dictionary of Theology* (Baker Books/Paternoster, 1984), p. 68.
50 On this connection, see Mark A. Noll, *The Scandal of the Evangelical Mind*, pp. 90–3.
51 K. Ford, *Jesus for a New Generation*, p. 179.
52 HTB Publications, *Alpha Manual* (HTB, 1995).
53 N. Gumbel, *Telling Others*, pp. 19–20.
54 ibid., p. 19.

Chapter 11   Bible Reflection: John 1:35–51

1 W. Temple, *Readings in St John's Gospel* (Macmillan, 1963), p. 28.

Chapter 12   Ethics and Social Action

1 D. Tomlinson, *The Post-Evangelical*, p. 43.
2 S. Pinker, *The Language Instinct* (Allen Lane, 1994), p. 334.
3 R. A. Hudson, *Sociolinguistics* (Cambridge University Press, 1980), p. 53.
4 D. Tomlinson, *The Post-Evangelical*, pp. 41–4.
5 ibid., pp. 35–7, 39.
6 See, for instance, the extensive bibliography in T. E. Schmidt, *Straight and Narrow* (IVP, 1995), pp. 219–36.
7 D. Tomlinson, *The Post-Evangelical*, p. 39.
8 United Reformed Church, 'Church Frames Debate on Human Sexuality', Official Press Release, April 1997, p. 1.
9 United Reformed Church, *Speaking for Ourselves: Reflections by Gay and Lesbian Christians in the United Reformed Church* (United Reformed Church, 1995).
10 G. Veith, *Guide to Contemporary Culture*, p. 82–3.
11 D. Coupland, *Generation X*, p. 83.
12 K. Ford, *Jesus for a New Generation*.
13 See, for instance, E. Stuart, 'Pulling Down the Idol' in S. Durber (ed.), *As Man and Woman Made* (United Reformed Church, 1994), pp. 35–41; M. Vasey, *Strangers and Friends: A New Exploration of Homosexuals and the Bible* (Hodder & Stoughton, 1995), pp. 80–2.
14 United Reformed Church, *Speaking for Ourselves*, p. 17.
15 *Independent*, 14th March 1995.
16 S. Thistlethwaite (ed.), *A Just Peace Church* (United Church Press, 1986), p. 139.
17 Cit. United Reformed Church, *Speaking for Ourselves*, pp. 13–14.
18 M. MacDonald, 'Natural Rights', in J. Waldron (ed.), *Theories of Rights* (Oxford University Press, 1984), pp. 21–40.
19 I. Brownlie (ed.), *Basic Documents on Human Rights* (Oxford University Press, 1992, third edition), pp. 21, 326–7.

20 See R. Wintemute, 'Sexual Orientation Discrimination', in C. McCrudden and G. Chambers (eds), *Individual Rights and the Law in Britain* (Oxford University Press, 1993), pp. 491–534.

21 See, for example, M. Macourt, 'Introduction', in M. Macourt (ed.), *Towards a Theology of Gay Liberation* (SCM, 1977), p. 3.; M. Vasey, *Evangelical Christians and Gay Rights* (Grove Ethical Study No. 80, Grove Books, 1991), and *Strangers and Friends*, pp. 179–81.

22 I. Brownlie, *Basic Documents on Human Rights*, p. 112.

23 ibid., p. 330.

24 S. Poulter, 'Minority Rights', in C. McCrudden and G. Chambers (eds), *Individual Rights and the Law in Britain* pp. 472–4.

25 Law Commission, *Offences Against Religion*, 18, cit. S. Poulter, 'Minority Rights', in C. McCrudden and G. Chambers (eds), *Individual Rights and the Law in Britain*, p. 473, n. 104.

26 ibid., p. 472, 474.

27 C. Ben Mitchell, 'Is That All There is?' in D. Dockery (ed.), *The Challenge of Postmodernism*, p. 270.

28 I am grateful to the ITC for furnishing me with a copy of their report on this episode, from which my data is drawn. Evangelical involvement in protests against the TV broadcast was confirmed in my interviews with Graham Dale, Roger Forster and Gerald Coates.

29 M. Eden, 'Roll the Credits', *Idea*, April–May 1997.

30 Cit. A. Cuff, 'Television is sinking into sleaze', *Guardian*, 20th June 1996, p. 4.

31 S. J. Grenz, *Revisioning Evangelical Theology*, pp. 184–5.

32 R. Frost, *Which Way for the Church?* (Kingsway, 1997, ms copy).

33 For more detail on these schools and the arguments for them, see R. Deakin, *Christian Schools: The Case for Public Funding* (Regius, 1989).

34 J. Carvel, 'Go-ahead for Sect School', *Guardian*, 19th October 1996, p. 1.

35 For an exposition and defence of this model, see R. M. McCarthy, D. Oppewal, W. Peterson and G. Spykman, *Society, State and Schools: A Case for Structural and Confessional Pluralism* (Eerdmans, 1981). For an evangelical

critique of it, see T. Cooling, 'In Defence of the Common School', in J. Shortt and T. Cooling (eds), *Agenda for Educational Change* (Apollos, 1997), pp. 76–86.

36 T. Cooling, 'In Defence of the Common School', p. 77.

37 ibid., pp. 77–8.

38 ibid., p. 82.

39 Trevor Cooling's own Association of Christian Teachers and Stapleford House Education Centre are pointers in this direction: their work deserves to be taken up more vigorously in the evangelical community, and I would warmly recommend the fruits of it which are gathered in Cooling and John Shortt's *Agenda for Educational Change*.

40 For a summary of these, see C. Calver, 'Afterword: Hope for the Future?', in J. Wolffe (ed.), *Evangelical Faith and Public Zeal*, pp. 198–210.

Chapter 14 Theology and Doctrine

1 K. Ford, *Jesus for a New Generation*, pp. 115–16.

2 *Westminster Confession of Faith* (Free Presbyterian Publications [1647] 1985), II.1, p. 25.

3 A. C. Thiselton, *Interpreting God and the Postmodern Self: On Meaning, Manipulation and Promise* (T. and T. Clark, 1995).

4 C. K. Barrett, *The Second Epistle to the Corinthians* (A. and C. Black, 1973), p. 77.

5 Z. Bauman, 'Postmodernity, or Living with Ambivalence', p. 12.

6 ibid., p. 15.

7 For example, C. E. Gunton, *The Promise of Trinitarian Theology* (T. and T. Clark, 1991); L. Boff, *Trinity and Society* (Orbis, 1988); J. Moltmann, *The Spirit of Life: A Universal Affirmation* (SCM Press, 1992); W. Pannenberg, *Systematic Theology* (2 vols, T. and T. Clark, 1991).

Chapter 15 Summary: Agenda for Postmodern Evangelicalism

1 Reconstruction, also known as Dominion theology and Theonomy, is defined by David L. Smith as a movement

which holds that 'the civil laws of Old Testament Israelite society are normative in all societies for all time'. Its chief proponents are R. J. Rushdoony, Greg Bahnsen and Gary North. For further detail and bibliography see D. L. Smith, *A Handbook of Contemporary Theology* (Bridgepoint, 1992), pp. 259–72.

Additional Permissions

Quotations from songs by U2: 'Gloria', 'With a Shout' and 'Tomorrow', from the album *October*, lyrics by U2, copyright Blue Mountain Music, 1981; 'Sunday, Bloody Sunday', from the album *War*, lyrics by U2, copyright Blue Mountain Music, 1983; 'I Still Haven't Found What I'm Looking For', from the album *The Joshua Tree*, lyrics by Bono, copyright Blue Mountain Music, 1987; 'MOFO', 'If God Will Send His Angels' and 'Wake Up, Dead Man', from the album *Pop*, lyrics by Bono, copyright Blue Mountain Music, 1997. Used by kind permission.

INDEX